LIBERIA

AMERICA'S AFRICAN FRIEND

LIBERIA

America's African Friend

By R. Earle Anderson

CHAPEL HILL—*The University of North Carolina Press*

MANUFACTURED IN THE UNITED STATES OF AMERICA BY
THE WILLIAM BYRD PRESS, INC.
RICHMOND, VIRGINIA

To

DR. GEORGE WAY HARLEY
AND HIS WIFE WINIFRED

whose contribution to Liberia's welfare has been beyond measure

FOREWORD

A LIFE-LONG interest in American shipping led me recently to take advantage of an opportunity to make an extended voyage along the West Coast of Africa, a trade area that has, within the last few years, developed rapidly from the standpoint of our foreign commerce, especially since the establishment of new services there by two of our major shipping companies, the Farrell and the Delta Lines.

Indeed, the whole of Africa, which some of us still think of as the Dark Continent, is figuring more and more in world strategy and as an important area commercially and politically. It is no longer either dark or remote. The spot where Stanley met the lost Dr. Livingston is now reached by air from New York in a matter of hours.

I was able, as an incident of this voyage, to spend some time in Liberia, that vaguely known and often misunderstood Negro Republic on the African West Coast, that grew out of the efforts of the American Colonization Society, a century or more ago, to solve some of the problems of slavery in our Southern States.

I visited the great Firestone Rubber Plantation, was the guest in Monrovia of the chief engineer of the mining company that was opening up a new source of high-grade iron ore, and went deep into the interior to meet the noted medical missionary, Dr. George W. Harley and to get through him a glimpse of Liberia's tribal people, aborigines whom civilization has barely touched.

At Monrovia, Liberia's capital, the artificial harbor, built with

Lend-Lease funds, was nearing completion. Roberts Field, an American World War II air base, was being refurbished, and Pan American World Airways would soon be making it a regular landing point on its through service to the Belgian Congo and to South Africa. Mr. Stettinius had just announced elaborate plans for the development of Liberia's natural resources. There was a feeling of expectancy in the air, a feeling that Liberia was on the threshold of a new era.

What I saw and heard was intriguing. On my return to the United States I began to read all that I could find about Liberia. There was an abundance of material, but most of it was of a ponderous scientific nature, or obviously biased, or badly out of date. But while there were one or two good recent books, there was little that seemed to me to give a satisfactory picture of Liberia as it is today.

So I decided to try to redraw the picture, in the hope that there might result something that would lead to a better understanding of our Liberian friends. Such a picture would need to be drawn against an historical and ethnological background; it would have both high-lights and shadows; it must be impartial.

I continued my study, sought out everyone who could give me help, and in 1950 returned to Liberia for an extended stay. This book is the result.

The information I was able to collect came from a great variety of sources. Three Presidents of the Republic, whose terms of office span nearly a third of a century, contributed to it; Mr. William V. S. Tubman, who has just been re-elected, Mr. Edwin J. Barclay, who preceded him and who has now retired from public life after twelve years in the Presidency; and Mr. Charles D. B. King, Liberia's elder statesman, President from 1920 to 1930 and now his country's first Ambassador to the United States.

Colonel Harry A. McBride, an American diplomat whose impact on Liberian history has been personal and far-reaching, gave me first-hand factual material. He read and constructively criticized the book in manuscript. Mr. Sidney de la Rue, who spent many years in Liberia, gave me valuable help. Mr. B. H. Larabee, Executive Vice President of the Firestone Plantations Company, also read the manuscript and gave me his suggestions; he arranged for my stay on the Plantation, where Mr. Fred Helm acted as my host and mentor.

Mrs. Maud A. Morris, who is sometimes referred to as the Dean of Liberian women, helped me greatly with respect to the Liberian viewpoint. To Mr. John A. Dunaway, long-time Financial Advisor to the Liberian Government, I am indebted for much of my financial information. Dr. Thomas P. Thayer of the U. S. Geological Survey read in manuscript the chapter on the Bomi Hills and gave me an authentic description of the geology of the iron ore deposit there.

Mr. James A. Farrell, Jr., President of Farrell Lines, Inc., Mr. R. S. Hecht, Chairman, and Mr. Theodore Brent, President of the Mississippi Shipping Company, and Mr. Lansdell K. Christie, President of the Liberia Mining Company did much to facilitate my trips to Liberia and my stay there. Mr. Harold Sims, Mr. Oscar Meier and Mr. K. H. Meeker of the U.S. Department of State; Dr. Kent Greenfield, Chief Historian, U.S. Army Special Staff, and Dr. Albert F. Simpson, Historian, Army Air Force, all made available to me source material from official records relating to Liberia, the Port of Monrovia, and Roberts Field.

Mr. J. O. Brew, Director of the Peabody Museum of Archaeology and Ethnology gave me permission to use material published by that organization, while consent to quote from Dr. Huberich's important book, *The Political and Legislative History of Liberia*, was kindly granted by Miss Ruth Kelton, owner of the copyright.

Above all others, I owe a debt of gratitude to Dr. and Mrs. George W. Harley. Without their generous help this book could not have been written. They made me welcome in their home at the Ganta Mission, submitted to my endless questioning, and, to the extent that I was able to absorb it, shared with me their intimate knowledge and deep understanding of Liberia and its people.

* * * * * * * *

A word about the map of Liberia that appears as the endpapers of this book. No really satisfactory map of the country exists. This is partly because of the boundary disputes and the understandable unwillingness of the Liberian Government to commit itself to demarcations that it may later call into question, and partly because of a lack of actual surveys. To a large extent the boundaries, as presently set by various treaties, are referred to certain rivers. But many of these streams, deep in the interior, follow courses that have not been explored. Even an astronomical fix, made by a French engineer in an attempt to mark part of the boundary, proved to have been miles in error.

A photographic survey of Liberia is being made, but it will be some years before it is finished. The aerial survey of the coast line is available and this I have used. For the rest, including boundaries, town locations, etc., I have tried to weigh, as best I could, the reliability of the various maps that I was able to find. The facilities of the American Geographical Society in New York supplied considerable material of British, French, and American origin. Especial weight was given to the maps prepared by the U.S. War Department, which, in turn, were based to a large extent on the map made many years ago by Dr. George W. Harley, and which he himself, quite properly, insists is a "sketch map." The present map must likewise be interpreted as a sketch map, but it will, I hope, facilitate the reading of this book. Where native geographical names appear, I have, in general, followed Dr. Harley's map, although in some cases there was evidence of a different official spelling which I have accordingly used. Naturally these native names are spelled more or less phonetically.

R. Earle Anderson

Chatham, New Jersey
January, 1952

CONTENTS

ILLUSTRATIONS

FACING PAGE

Photographs by the author

MAPS AND CHARTS

LIBERIA

AMERICA'S AFRICAN FRIEND

• *Chapter One* •

THIS IS LIBERIA

JUST around the bulge of the West Coast of Africa lies the independent Republic of Liberia. It is a very small bit of a very big continent. But it played an important part in the Second World War, is strategically located with respect to any future major conflict, and is beginning to have an influence on American commerce with West and South Africa quite out of proportion to its size.

Liberia has an area about equal to that of Louisiana or Ohio. It is typically tropical, lying just a few degrees north of the equator, its southern tip at latitude 4°-13′, its northern at 8°-35′. The climate is not oppressive. It is hot, but the temperature seldom rises much above 80 degrees. Nights are cool and refreshing. There is the usual alternation of wet and dry seasons, the rains starting about the first of May. Rainfall on the coast may be as much as eighteen or twenty feet annually; less in the higher land of the interior.

Topographically, there are three distinct belts, differentiated mainly by elevation and rainfall. The coastal belt, where the principal settlements are, including Monrovia, the capital city, is about forty miles in width and extends along the three hundred and fifty miles of the seaboard, low-lying, with few hills and many mangrove swamps, shallow lagoons, and sandy beaches.

Back of the coastal fringe is the great belt of high forest, from twenty to sixty miles in width, the land rising abruptly in elevation to form, almost, an escarpment. Much of this belt is unexplored, most of it uninhabited. Even wild game is scarce. The density of the forest has discouraged the clearings needed for native farming. Rainfall is heavy, though somewhat less than on the coast.

Inland is the plateau of the Liberian hinterland, with an elevation of a thousand feet or more. The forest is less dense, rainfall less. It is a country that lends itself to the native farming, and there are many mud-hut villages and towns. Foot-trails are numerous and here and there a bit of road has been built by an ambitious Chief or District Commissioner.

Politically Liberia is unique. It is the only African republic governed by the Negro race. And it is the only instance in modern history of a nation deliberately founded without the support of a mother country.

It is peopled by two entirely distinct groups—the aboriginal tribes, natives just emerging from savagery, and the highly cultured Americo-Liberians, the so-called "ruling class," descendants mainly of American Negroes who had been manumitted or had otherwise gained their freedom, and who had been induced by philanthropic organizations in the United States, the Colonization Societies, to leave America and establish themselves on the African coast in an attempt to solve the racial problem which, even in the early 1800's was causing serious concern.

The aboriginal tribes number perhaps a million and a half, perhaps two million—estimates differ. Some fifty thousand or so of them are partly civilized, mainly those who live on or near the coast. Of the descendants of the American settlers there are about fifteen thousand. It is important to distinguish clearly between the Americo-Liberians and the tribal people. For the purposes of this study they will be referred to respectively as "Liberians" and as "natives," except where there is need to be more specific. But it is to be borne in mind that the line of demarcation is becoming less and less distinct. Education, intermarriage, a changing political status, are having a noteworthy effect. To an increasing degree all are being regarded as Liberians.

When the movement to colonize free American Negroes in their native Africa began, manumitted slaves did not readily become enthusiastic about leaving. But there were a few who were willing to undertake the adventure. They gained a foothold on the African shore, fought disease and savage tribes, nearly succumbed to both foes. They brought with them the culture of the American Southern States. But they had to stand on their own feet, fight their own battles. For upwards of two decades they led a precarious existence both physically and politically. Then in 1847 they adopted a constitution, declared themselves a free and independent nation, and began the great experiment of self-government.

To the European powers whose colonies surrounded Liberia the existence of a republic in the midst of their colonial empire, especially a republic under Negro rule, was a sore trial. Constantly they bullied the Liberians, first refusing to recognize them politically, then ruthlessly robbing them of territory, while they minutely scrutinized the relations between the ruling class and the tribal people, magnified and publicized every fault without first pulling the beams out of their own eyes, and finally, during the period between the two world wars, attempting, through the League of Nations, to bring about the downfall of the Republic. That the Liberians succeeded not only in establishing their independence but in maintaining it against almost overwhelming odds is little short of astonishing.

Economically Liberia must be classed among the underdeveloped areas of the world, although this condition seems to be on the verge of change at an increasing tempo. The period since the adoption of the constitution has been dominated by constant struggle for mere existence. The Liberians have never been able to accumulate the capital needed for the development of their natural resources. All about them the African colonies of the European powers were being developed by their parent countries. A stream of outside capital flowed into them. Private interests, such as the great British Unilever organization, were undertaking constructive projects. Some of the colonies were growing rich, or at least were enriching their overlords. Bauxite, manganese, chromium, diamonds, and gold were being mined. Palm oil and palm kernels were being produced on a vast scale. A great cocoa industry, supplying half the world, was being built up in near-by Gold Coast and Nigeria. Railroads were being constructed, motor roads built, schools and hospitals established. Thriving cities with modern public utilities were growing up. African trade was booming. Only Liberia stood still.

America's interest in Liberia had been confined largely to the activities of the missionary societies. The very nature and extent of the country's natural wealth remained in the realm of mystery. American capital was busy elsewhere.

But in 1924 there occurred an event that was to revolutionize the economic relations between Liberia and America. It was then that President Charles D. B. King concluded with the Firestone interests the agreement that made possible the establishment of the great rubber plantation, the story of which is told in some detail in a later chapter of this book. It is sufficient here to note that the signing of that agreement broke down the barriers that had kept foreign capital out of Liberia. With the coming of Firestone, and the start of what was to become the largest single rubber plantation in the world, the economy of the country began to undergo a basic change. Actual money wages, first a trickle, then an increasing stream, found their way into the hands of native labor, recruited largely from the interior. A mere subsistence economy began to give way to a wage economy.

The Second World War accelerated the change. The United States urgently needed an air base on the African coast. The Liberians were willing to cooperate, at considerable political risk to themselves. The result was the creation of Roberts Field, followed by the opening up of much-needed roads and by the construction, with American Lend-Lease funds, of a modern port at Monrovia, undertakings the effect of which has been cumulative.

Liberia's mineral resources are beginning to emerge from the haze of myth into reality. The utilization of the country's remarkably rich iron ore has been made possible by the construction of the port. The possibility of developing the agricultural products is appealing to the imagination: not only rubber, the growing of which has proved so profitable, but coffee, cocoa (cacao), bananas, palm oil and kernels, piassava. Liberia can grow the most delicious pineapples! There is alluvial gold in Liberia, how much and whether it can profitably be worked are not known. There are probably diamonds, too, but these also are a mystery.

Because so much relating to Liberia's resources has been left to the imagination, there has been some tendency to paint the picture of natural wealth and of opportunity in too glowing colors.

The fact is that the possibilities cannot as yet be accurately measured. Yet it seems clear that there is a real field for the bold and the resourceful. Liberia is welcoming American capital and skill. Those who accept the invitation will find many problems to be solved. Some of the going will be hard. Patience will be needed. There will be risks to be run, lessons to be learned the hard way. But the problems are intriguing, the possibilities tempting.

• *Chapter Two* •

THE TRIBAL PEOPLE

FOR every member of the ruling class in Liberia there are a hundred or more tribal people. They are the country's greatest problem. They are also its greatest asset, an undeveloped natural resource of far more potential value than its forests or its minerals. Those who would come to Liberia with a serious intention of helping in the development of the country will do well to learn all they can, from every available source, of the mental and social habits of the aborigines, for it is on them that they must build their hopes and plans. For this reason the following pages are devoted to an outline (it can be only an outline) of the native manner of life.

Here in Liberia, as though spread out on a single page, is the whole story of a race in the process of advancing from savagery to civilization. Here some erudite ethnologist, were he keen enough in his perceptions, thorough enough in his investigations, deeply enough read in the history of the human race, could make a first-hand study of the beginnings of intelligence, of mental growth, of changing habits, a study that would cover the ages of man from the naked savage who has never seen a white man to the chief justice, a civilized tribesman, who presides with dignity and ability over the nation's Supreme Court.

But the ethnologist will need to hurry if the lower end of the spectrum is to be still within the range of his vision. He can now step back, within a distance of a mile or less, out of the twentieth century into the early ages; but he will not long be able to do so. Already cannibalism has vanished. No longer is there ritualistic killing, no longer human sacrifice. The generation that knew these things is passing. Another decade or so, and the wild savagery of the older tribal life will be only a legend. The upward path ahead of the indigenous people is a long one, the climb steep. But the "closed door" that once effectively barred the Liberian native from admission to the ruling class is now an open door, has been so for nearly a generation. On the fringe of contact between the civilized areas and the deep interior the once immutable rule of tribal custom is giving way to change.

Although Liberia is small in area, it is peopled by more than twenty separate tribes, each with its own language.[1] These tribes did not originate in Liberia. They settled there many centuries ago as a result of migrations from the north and east, bringing with them remnants of the ancient culture of Egypt and Arabia, such as the spinning of cotton, weaving of cloth, and smelting of iron.

There is evidence of a still earlier people: bits of earthenware found on the hilltops. Who these earlier people were, what age they belonged to, why they disappeared, will probably never be known. Except for the few fragments that have been found nothing is known about them. They, and not the present natives, were the real indigines of Liberia; that is, unless they themselves were immigrants.

Language similarities lead scientists to divide the Liberian tribes into four main groups, Mande-tan, Mande-fu, West Atlantic, and Kru; and these probably correspond roughly to the directions from which the various tribes came into the country. Thus the Vai people, of the Mande-tan group, although they came like the rest from the northeast, circled around through the area now known as Sierra Leone and entered Liberia from the west. They are an intelligent people, physically well proportioned, in color light brown to dark. They are one of the most progressive groups in Liberia's native population. Over a century ago they invented a syllabic script, using about 160 signs, the authorship attributed to one Momolu Doalu Bukere. The Vai take readily to education when it is offered to them by the various missions working in their area, and they are capable of being trained to hold clerical positions, perhaps finally to go much further. But living in the low coastal strip where farming by the crude native methods is more difficult than it is farther inland, they do not take so well to agriculture. Their number may be roughly estimated as a hundred thousand. (See map of Native Tribes on page 13.)

Upland from the Vai country are the Gola and Kisi tribes, an older West Atlantic group, lighter complexioned, slender of figure, warlike, proud, and stubborn. They are skillful farmers, within the limits of their knowledge and tribal customs, and produce a superabundance of rice, much of which goes to waste each year because of lack of transportation, while their neighbors, the Vai, produce less than their own subsistence requires. There are, within the boundaries of Liberia, perhaps fifty thousand of the Gola, maybe more, and about the same number of the Kisi tribe.

The central part of Liberia's interior is peopled by a group of tribes classified, from their language similarities, as Mande-fu, with a total of about four hundred thousand. They probably entered Liberia more or less directly from the northeast, after skirting the great desert and crossing the Mandingo plateau in what is now French Guinea. They seem to have been a hill people, tending, in their migrations, to follow the ridges between river valleys. The streams of the country they occupied gave them water but not transportation, possibly because many of the watercourses were not readily usable by canoes, but more likely because these tribes had no background of experience of travel by water.

There are no less than ten distinct tribes in this Mande-fu group: the Mende (who lap over into the territory, once Liberian, that is now part of Sierra Leone), the Gbande, Gbunde, Belle, Buzi or Loma, Kpelle, Mano, Geh, Gio, and Kra. Some of these tribes extend into that part of French Guinea that was lost to Liberia in 1910, when the French claimed it by asserting a right of discovery and exploration; some extend into the Ivory Coast.

While these tribes are grouped together by scientists because of language similarities, there are distinct differences in their physical characteristics. Two basic types are to be distinguished, one short and stocky, very dark of skin and with pronounced negroid features; the other taller, lighter in color and with finer features. The short, pure negroid type are believed by some to be of aboriginal stock, in the stricter sense of the term. The taller, lighter people may reflect traits of a more northerly Sudanic origin. The Gbunde and Loma tribes, which probably have a common ancestry, were, in the past, especially warlike. Today they are relied on to furnish some of the best soldiers of the Liberian Frontier Force.

By far the largest group of Liberian tribes is that classified as Kru, the name of its most important member. There are nine separate tribes in this category. Their total number it is impossible to estimate, for they are found, especially the Kru, not only in Liberia but in every port, from Sierra Leone to the Gold Coast and beyond. The tribes, in the order, roughly, of their importance, are the Kru, Bassa, Grebo, Padebo or Half-Grebo, Sikon or Bush Bassa, Sapa, Tchien, Pudu, and Teni.

The Bassa, Kru and Grebo tribes constitute the bulk of this group. They live along the coast, which they occupy from Monrovia to Cape Palmas. Probably they entered the part of Liberia where they now live by way of the sea. Some may have come down the Cavalla River in canoes. Legend has it that as some of the migrants reached the sea their canoes capsized, and these, because they had shown themselves incapable of handling their small craft in rough water, were sent inland, for how could they survive in the heavy surf of the coast? Perhaps that accounts for the small tribes of this group that now, sparsely, live in the interior.

The Kru tribe proper are seafarers and quite fearless. They are of typical Negro type, rather short and sturdy, dark-skinned, good-natured, and always ready for a hearty laugh. They are of good intellect, industrious, and thrifty. In the old days of slave trading, they acted as middlemen, but were themselves never sold into slavery. From earliest boyhood they take to the water, spending the days of their youth in canoes, sometimes under the tutelage of their elders, sometimes alone, learning to shoot the heavy surf as it rolls over the sand bars at the river mouths. Thus they prepare for their later life afloat, for it is the Krus who build and man the heavy surf boats that ply up and down the coast not only of Liberia but of Sierra Leone, Ivory Coast, and beyond, and that transfer cargo from ship to shore at Liberia's "surf ports."

Of all the Liberian tribes the Krus have had the closest contact with the outside world, and they have been the most independent. Living on the coast, it was they with whom the early traders dealt in the first instance, as they bartered trade goods for country products. Since the advent of steam, it has been the practice for vessels operating along the coast to take aboard a gang of Kru boys to do the stevedoring as the ship calls at port after port all along the African West Coast. They come aboard at Freetown (for they are found far outside Liberia), or at Monrovia, perhaps as many as seventy, working under a Kru head-man. On the ship they live under a canvas tent erected over one of the hatches, cook their own meals on a stove furnished by the ship and installed on deck, sleep sometimes on the bare hatch cover, more often on canvas cots which they bring with them. They spend a month, perhaps two months, afloat, depending on how long it takes the vessel to handle its business on the coast. Finally they are landed at the port of their embarkation. Their forty cents a day grosses them about twelve dollars for a month's work. Out of that come fees to their hiring agent ashore and to their head-man afloat, and whatever taxes may be assessed by the Government. Aboard ship, they will have been furnished a stipulated ration of rice.

The Kru boys, until a couple of decades ago, were also recruited for contract labor service on the Spanish cocoa farms on the Island of Fernando Po, in the Bight of Biafra, a practice that led to bitter political attacks on the Liberians by the British, who were developing their own cocoa industry in Gold Coast and Nigeria and who were jealous of the labor furnished to their nearest competitor.[2]

Largely because of their contact with the outside world, the Kru tribe proved the least tractable of the Liberian natives. For many years there were occasional conflicts between the Krus and the Government forces, often taking on the fierceness of tribal warfare. It was a full decade after control of the interior tribes was accomplished before the Kru coast ceased to be more or less belligerent. But not since the early 1930's has there been conflict, and today the Krus have accepted the Government of the Republic, the last of the native tribes to do so.

The Krus consider Liberia their home, not only now, but in the sense that they are original inhabitants, an idea that is not shared by ethnologists. An interesting custom indicating that these people came to Liberia from the sea is that of giving burial to important

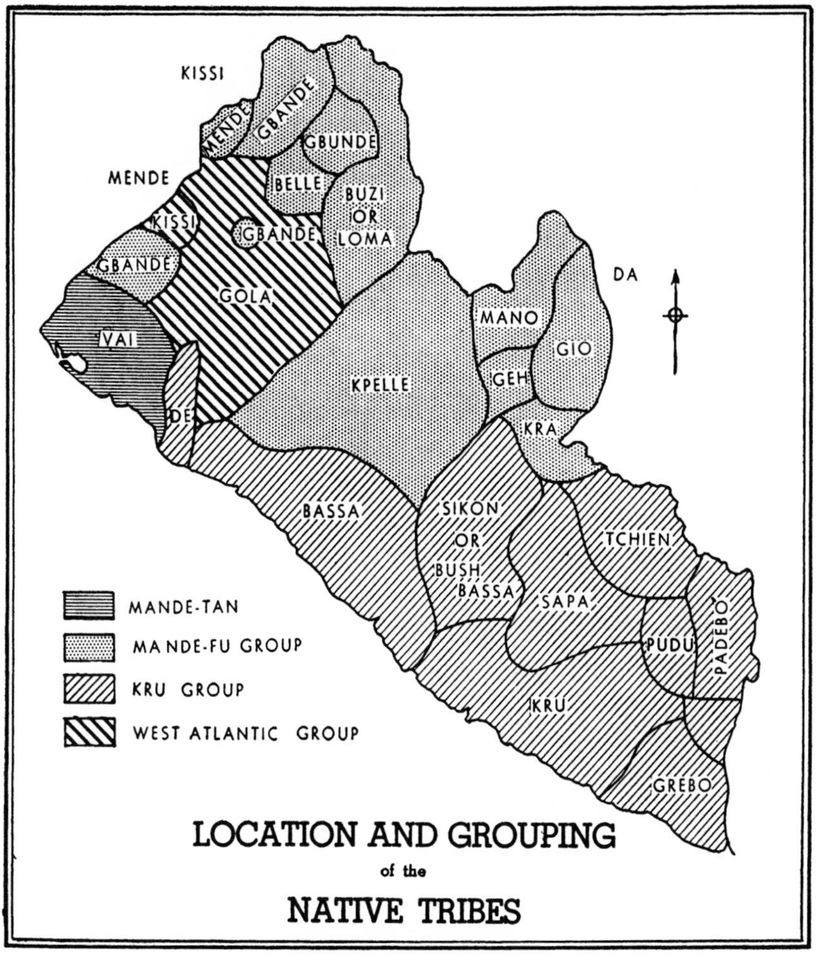

Based on map contained in Charles Schwab's *Tribes of the Liberian Hinterland*

members of their tribe by placing their bodies on the ocean-washed rocks of the coast.

Two of the tribes, not strictly Liberian, require mention, the Mandingo and the Fanti. The Mandingos are Mohammedan nomadic traders, coming from the area to the northeast. They differ greatly from the Liberian tribes in both language and culture. Until quite recently they have been regarded as foreigners, both legally and basically, in Liberia on sufferance, paying fees to the Government for a license to trade within the country. It is they who, a generation ago, brought into the Liberian hinterland such few products of civilization as the natives were able to buy—enamelled ware, trade cloth, salt. On market days in designated towns of the interior, these Mandingos, in their long flowing robes, would be much in evidence, coming across the French border, bartering for cola nuts, palm oil, palm kernels, or whatever the natives might have for sale, or exchanging their goods for money—French or English coins, some of which were in circulation. In the coastal towns and cities, the Mandingos were always present. In recent years the restrictions on their living and doing business in Liberia have been removed. There are even Mandingo Paramount Chiefs, and Mandingo blood is beginning to mix with Liberian. But still they remain the shrewd traders, reluctant to build houses or otherwise contribute to the permanent welfare, and often the source of minor but annoying differences with the local natives.

The other foreign tribe, the Fanti, come from the Gold Coast. They are fishermen and are found all along the Liberian shore. In Monrovia there are several groups of them, living their own lives in contact with the Liberians of the city but keeping largely within their own quarter, where tier upon tier of cylindrical mud or cement stoves are built for the smoking of fish. Only the Fanti men come to Liberia. They stay for four or five years, accumulate what is to them wealth, accumulate also wives and a flock of children. The wives are temporary—native women whose lot is not enviable, for they are left behind when the Fanti fisherman leaves for home, taking his children with him.

Physically these Fanti are magnificent specimens, tall, straight, muscular, ebony-skinned. Ashore, they drape a length of cloth toga-wise over the left shoulder, concealing their cotton shorts. Sometimes it is a figured cloth; more often a deep rich blue. Mixing on Monrovia's Water Street with the vari-costumed crowd, whose apparel includes the white linen tailored suits of the Liberians, the long robes and fezzes of the Mandingos, the sometimes skimpy or wholly missing singlets of native children, these Fanti are picturesque and colorful. By daylight each morning they are at sea in their great dugout canoes, spreading their nets, encircling the schools of fish with which their craft are soon heavily loaded. By late morning or early afternoon they are on their way toward land, a crude sail of patched and dirty cloth held out to the breeze by poles and cords. The fleet of incoming Fanti canoes, spread out over the ocean as they head for the bar at the mouth of the Mesurado River, is one of the sights of Monrovia.

The craft themselves are highly decorated. Each is made from a great log, hollowed out to extreme thinness, the sides made higher by a sheer-plank that serves as a base for elaborate and often artistic decoration, weird carving set off by polychrome in bright pigments against the blackened wood.

On shore a crowd of natives, eager to buy the catch, awaits the beaching of the Fanti fleet as it skims along before the wind, or with sail doused runs the surf over the bar. If the catch is unusually good, the day's fishing may be followed by a night of celebration, with raucous shouts, the beating of drums or of kerosene cans, dancing, a general uproar stimulated by libations of palm wine or trade gin, which is slept off the next day. Perhaps the celebration will be resumed the following night.

The Liberian tribes, although they are distinct from each other ethnologically, are not to be thought of as political units. The Paramount Chief, presiding more or less definitely over a tribal area, is the creation of the Government, set up for the purpose of simplifying administration. Before the Government asserted its authority over the hinterland, tribal organization went no further than the clan. It is not even the clan, but the household, that is the real basic unit of tribal society.

This household may consist of a man, his wife, and children; it may be made up of a man and his various wives, together with all their children and perhaps other dependents. All live together, in one house or in adjoining houses, sometimes in houses within a compound. Their life is communal. All work together to furnish food and other needs of life.

A number of households related to each other constitute a family, a group that is highly organized and has for its objective security against danger, injustice, and want. Ordinarily the oldest male member is the family head. This organized family group therefore really consists of its head, his brothers, and all their children and grandchildren. The wives, however, are not identified with the family of the husband. Instead, they remain members of the family from which they came, and to it they return if wife and husband separate.

Although it is the custom that the oldest of the brothers be the family head, he is chosen as such by the elders of the family, is inducted into office by them, and remains the family head really by their sufferance, based on his bodily and mental fitness. When called upon to make important decisions he will do so only after taking counsel of the elders, for without their concurrence his position is weak. He has certain definite responsibilities, not the least of which is that of being keeper of the family medicine and seeing to it that the necessary sacrifices are made to keep the medicine in working order.

For mutual safety, a number of families might join forces to form a town, each family grouping its huts in one quarter. As a town grew, a household or family might move away and found a new town, perhaps the better to work the near-by land. When this happened, the family head naturally became the town chief and thereafter the succession was ordinarily hereditary. But if two or more families joined to form a new town, they might agree to some form of rotation in the chieftaincy among the family heads.

The town chief has a responsible job. He must care for the town property, see that the laws are carried out, take proper steps for providing food and shelter for strangers passing through. He must care for the town medicines. Like the family heads, he must take counsel of the elders of the town, for on their support rests his strength. In fact, except for his positive duties, he is little more than an executive head.

A number of towns made up of families who all claim a common ancestry constitute a clan. It is in the clan that the ties of kinship have a focus. The clan, made up of family units, is the real political entity in the Liberian hinterland. It is to the level of the clan that the native organization extends, not beyond it. The various towns of the clan have been founded by families or households that at some time in the past have come from an original settlement. Kinship is thus the basis of the clan. Outsiders may be permitted to move into a town and perhaps, after a generation or two, will be accepted as belonging there, but they will never be regarded as actual members of the clan because of their alien ancestry.

At the head of each clan is the Clan Chief, and his town, usually the oldest and the place where the clan's earliest ancestors settled, is the chief town. Succession to the chieftaincy varies among the tribes and clans. The office may pass to a deceased chief's oldest brother. Or it may devolve upon the chief's oldest son, or upon his sister's son. When there is no legitimate successor, the town chiefs may be called upon to make selection among the several aspirants.

Theoretically, the Clan Chief has supreme authority. He is the father of the clan and in legal matters is the court of last resort, except for the overriding power of the Poro, to be described later. When disputes arise that cannot be settled by palaver at his own town, the Chief may journey, with all his retinue, to the town concerned. Such a visitation may be an impressive event and costly to the town that has to act as host. Despite all this, the Clan Chief, like the town chiefs and family head-men, exercises limited power. If he disregards the counsel of the elders of the clan, his chieftaincy will be cut short. He also is really an executive. The power behind him is that of public opinion exercised and expressed by the old men of the clan, the men of experience and judgment. As will be seen later when we come to a discussion of the Poro Society, there are other forces that serve to limit the power of the Chief.

When the tribes were first brought under the control of the Liberian Government, the hinterland was divided into a number of districts, each administered by an Americo-Liberian District Commissioner. Each district would cover territory occupied by several tribes and many clans. The problem was a complicated one, made more so by language differences. So within each district certain Clan Chiefs, one for each tribe, were designated as Paramount Chiefs. In theory, if not in actual fact, these Paramount Chiefs derived their authority from the Government at Monrovia. To some extent they were elected by their tribal constituents. But any departure from the established tribal customs in the selection of chiefs was apt to cause trouble, as the Government discovered in various instances. The designation of Paramount Chiefs worked out most satisfactorily when it followed natural tribal lines. The Paramount Chiefs not only became the points of contact between the clans and the Government; they also act somewhat as a superior court, above the clan-chief level.

A Chief, whether clan or paramount, has quite a staff of functionaries. There is, for example, a sort of prime minister, sometimes called the "speaker." At the court of a Paramount Chief the speaker will himself be a Clan Chief, generally one of considerable standing. He acts more or less as a deputy of the Paramount Chief, handling many of the current affairs. In important palavers he may lead the discussion, gather the evidence, and pass it on to the Paramount Chief, who will remain silent until the time comes for him to render decision. Thus the speaker acts somewhat like a referee in one of our courts.

Since English is the official language of the country, the Chief must have an interpreter. Even when the Chief understands and speaks English the interpreter is employed, both for reasons of tribal pride and also in order that all may understand the proceedings. The Chief also has a "singer," who is an expert in the history and traditions of the clan and who may also serve as entertainer.

Besides these, there is a sort of town crier, who makes announcements and may also act as the Chief's messenger. Finally there are "palaver men," skilled in argument and oratory and able to make "strong palaver." The Chief's decisions are arrived at only after lengthy discussions, during which everyone is heard, for while the Chief has authority to decide, he is very sensitive to public opinion. In a community where there is no written law and where custom rules, the system has many advantages, and it is closely followed even by the President of the Republic, when, as sometimes happens, he goes into the interior to hold palaver in important cases.

A town that is the headquarters of a Paramount Chief may have as many as five or six hundred huts, with perhaps 2500 to 3000 inhabitants. But towns of this size are the exception. Except for Monrovia, and a few organized settlements on the coastal fringe, Liberia is a country of small towns and villages, unevenly distributed through the primeval forest and typically of from 30 to 100 huts, with from 150 to 500 inhabitants. Some villages may have only three or four shelters. Some are sequestered, to escape the advance of a culture alien to their customs and desires, or to avoid discovery by the ubiquitous tax collector. Some are hidden away in the forest out of the way of passers-by who would have to be given shelter and sustenance.

Before the Liberian Government established itself in the interior, travel was practically nonexistent, and the duty of providing for the occasional wayfarer was not onerous. A stranger was always welcome, for he would bring news from the outside. Providing him with entertainment was a matter of village pride, and when he left he would give a suitable present or "dash" to his host.

But with the advent of Government control, traffic rapidly increased. District Commissioners and their retinues, soldiers, others bent on Government business, came in a stream over the trails, all of them expecting free entertainment and native hospitality, until well-meaning town chiefs were at times reduced to poverty. Many towns were abandoned to escape the burden, and new towns built elsewhere, away from the passing throng.

Where motor roads have been opened up and the entire conditions of travel have changed as a consequence, with trading posts appearing in the larger towns, the people who fled from the advance of civilization are now coming back, reversing the trend away from the arteries of traffic.

The most favored locations for towns were on high land near a stream, sometimes on a hilltop. A site immediately on a stream was not favored, but a near-by water supply is important, and this, together with a sufficiency of easily accessible land suitable for farming, was a determining factor.

There is no "city planning," no laying out of streets. Huts are frequently so crowded together that scant room is left for passage between them. Usually the towns are treeless, but some will have a sacred tree in a clear space within the town, and it is believed that the town will prosper only so long as the tree lives and thrives. There is little room for grass or weeds to grow. Space between huts that might, with some stretch of imagination, be called a street, is bare clay. But the towns are clean. Refuse is removed daily and added to the compost heap outside the town. Cleanliness is noteworthy inside the huts as well as outside. Houses turned over to guests for overnight or longer use are freshly swept before occupancy and must be kept clean by the guests and left so on departure.

The fact that most towns are occupied by several families results in a division into more or less distinct sections or quarters. There may be nothing to indicate where one section ends and another begins, but frequently each family will have its own compound, enclosed with a fence. Inside this compound will be the huts wherein the family head, his wives, children, and dependents live. Here will be his guest huts, his family medicine hut, his private sacrifice place. Within the enclosure will also be the dye-pots, fowl baskets, and such other household paraphernalia as are not kept within the huts. Either just inside the compound or close to its entrance will be the bathing place, a circular enclosure of raffia, surrounding a flat rock, providing for the daily hot bath that is *de rigueur* among the natives of Liberia.

There was a time when a chief, together with all his wives and all the men to whom they had been loaned, might be found living under one roof to reduce taxes, which were assessed as a "hut tax." But a law was passed requiring a separate hut for each wife, a sort of tax-begotten slum clearance law.

In the middle of the town, and usually in each quarter, is a "palaver house." Around it the life of the village revolves. Here the chief and his elders meet to discuss the affairs of the village and clan. Here cases are tried, sentences pronounced. It is the spot for the midday siesta, and here the chief, his older sons, his friends, and sometimes one or two of his wives eat their meals together. The space before it on moonlight nights is filled with dancers, while the drums beat out the rhythm.

Typically, the palaver house is like the other huts of the village, except that it has no enclosing walls, just a floor and thatched roof, perhaps a low parapet. Sometimes raffia strips provide an enclosure; sometimes the eaves of the thatched roof extend to the ground. Headroom may be very low, as little as five feet, restricted by the loft overhead. Ordinarily there is no furniture; men going to the palaver house will bring their own seats, perhaps some low native chairs, a mat, an animal skin. But sometimes there will be a table and a bench or two. In some sections of the country the palaver house is rectangular, in others circular. There are areas where it has almost the status of a temple, and from its medicines, buried in its floor or stored in its loft, the influences radiate that guard the town from evil or insure its well-being.

The huts in which the natives live glisten white in the sun. Usually they are circular, topped by a high conical thatched roof, with wide overhanging eaves that shade a sort of portico around the outside of the structure. The material is mud, finished with a coat of kaolin, the white clay that abounds in Liberia and is used by the women in place of rouge. Incidentally, it is an excellent material for use in fine pottery, but the Liberians have never developed the potter's art beyond crude earthenware vessels.

To build one of these circular mud huts, a pole is driven into the ground and from it a circle is marked out. Uprights of rough sharpened sticks are then driven into the ground around this circle and tied together by heavy vines, laced in and out horizontally. On top of this a ceiling is framed, also of poles made from saplings, and other poles are erected as rafters for the conical roof, running to a central peak and likewise bound together by horizontal rows of vine lacing. Vines and poles of side walls and roof are securely tied together, making a fairly strong and rigid skeleton. Bundles of raffia fronds, carefully selected, have been drying for use as thatch. These are tied, row upon row, to the roof framing, each row overlapping the row below, shingle-wise, the final row extending some inches vertically and bound securely with vine wrappings.

The clay floor, raised above the surrounding level and extending beyond the circular framework so as to form the outer portico, is pounded solid, leveled off, and later given a hard and waterproof finish by rubbing in with charred cow-dung or charcoal. A low doorframe has been prepared, of slabs hewn from buttress roots of forest trees. When this has been set in place, plastering begins. The fine clay obtained from the great mounds of the white ants is the preferred material, prepared by mixing with water and treading by the small boys. With this the mud wall is built up by plastering inside and out against the stick-and-vine framework, until a thickness of six inches or so is reached. As the clay dries and shrinkage cracks develop, more clay is applied, until a solid, smooth, and tight wall is obtained, ready for its final coat of white, and perhaps an outside dado of cow-dung paint for waterproofing. Often this black finish takes the form of a crude fresco, giving vent to the owner's artistic urge.

Typically, there is only one doorway and no window. Daylight enters through the doorway which, by night, is closed against the chill of the air and the inquisitiveness of wild beasts by a heavy door turning on hewn pintles. Within the hut are clay shelves, serving as beds and as platforms for water jars and perhaps for an iron or brass kettle or two. Most important of all is the hearth, around which center the household activities. The sacrificial shrine may be conspicuous, and also the personal or family medicines of the occupant. Floor, beds, walls are often covered with palm or raffia mats. In the loft, above the matting ceiling, may be a store of rice and other foods, supplementing the main store, which is in the loft of the wall-less kitchen or palaver house.

Recently, as contact with the outer world has increased, the tendency has been toward supplementing the single door of the hut by the addition of small windows. Low wooden bedsteads and sometimes iron beds are taking the place of the hard clay shelf. The picturesque circular hut is giving way to the rectangular, which lends itself more readily to subdivision into two or more rooms. In some areas the District Commissioners are insisting on "modernization" of this type, even to the extent of causing some of the circular huts to be razed and replaced by larger rectangular structures, complete with man-high doors and windows.

If a new house is to be built in a native village, the chief must be consulted as to its location. Perhaps a diviner will be called in to assist in selecting the site. At any rate the diviner's or medicine man's services will be needed to determine what sacrifices will be required, what medicines must be buried on the chosen site. When the house is finished a big feast will be prepared by the owner's wives. But not until four months later may the builder kill a fowl, lest his household be scattered as fowls scatter dust when they scratch for food.

The towns and villages of the Liberian hinterland are connected by a network of foot-trails—narrow paths in the bush and forest, shaded tunnels through the dense tropical growth. Very slowly motor roads are replacing the trails, but they still form the only arteries of travel over the larger part of the interior. These native trails have existed, most of them, for centuries. Over them the barefooted aborigines would carry on their heads all the goods that moved within the country—rice, cocoa, piassava fibre, palm kernels, cola nuts, coffee—sixty pounds or so to a head load.

Before motor roads began to give access to the interior, movement of trade goods from the coast into the Liberian hinterland was a difficult and complicated matter. Head-loading could serve for only a relatively few miles at a time. Men at the coast traded with the next group inland, and they in turn with the next, and so on. An article reaching its final buyer deep in the interior would have acquired "value" due both to cost of transportation and to a pyramiding of profits that would be expressed finally in the barter price. The barter goods, in turn, would have to find their difficult way back to the coast by similar stages, until finally they reached the hands of the trader who would ship them in export. The chain of trade seldom involved cash until the original seller on the coast at long last realized on his transaction.

It was over these same trails that travel into the interior had to be accomplished. Locally, the traveller went afoot. If it was a long journey, or if his dignity required it, he went by hammock slung from a framework that formed a canopy and enabled the carriers to support the weight on heads or shoulders. Thus travelled the missionaries on their journeys into the hinterland; thus travelled the native chiefs and their retinues and an occasional Government official. At each town where an overnight stop must be made, custom required not only that shelter be provided but also a relay of carriers for the following day's journey, a service known as *tatua.* If a town was made up of quarter-towns, each quarter chief or head-man was in turn responsible for *tatua;* but if the men of the village were away cutting farm, or travel was more than usually heavy, it might take several days before carriers could be provided. A journey by trail and hammock met with many such delays.

Some of Liberia's trails date back to a period before their use for human travel, and close observers have been able to trace something of their history. First would come the paths made by wild animals from their lairs to their watering places. Many of these wild animal trails are still in existence. Often the animal, meeting an obstacle such as a fallen log, would burrow under it rather than go around; later a crude footpath would mark the natural route of the natives, utilizing the animal trail but going around the obstacle under which the animals had burrowed. Then would follow the improved native trail, kept cleared and in repair and carrying the traffic between villages or from village to farm tract.

In general the trails ran from village to village in fairly straight lines. Grades meant little to the Liberian native, padding along with his (or more often her) head load, and so the air-line route was usually kept to, rather than one that would minimize the hills. The natives had no way of running a sight line through the bush; so they depended on sound. We may let Momolu Gray tell us how this was done. He was an experienced road builder, but even in laying out a motor road he used the methods of the native trail builders. "We do not use a surveyor," says Momolu. "We do that ourselves by means of a horn. The site is selected and I would stand at the starting point while another would locate the track into the bush. After going a certain distance he would blow the horn and I would follow out my line to get to him. Then he would proceed further; and so on."

By such means a trail connecting two villages would follow the general direction of a straight line, running to right and left of it, seldom more than a few rods straight, then correcting to get back onto the line. The trails thus went up hill and down dale regardless of obstacles. Usually they crossed the streams at right angles, sometimes by crude bridges, sometimes by the intricate suspension bridges built of interlaced vines, the construction of which was a secret art.

When a District Commissioner or a Paramount Chief undertook the building of a few miles of motor road, it tended to follow the route of the trail, which was the natural traffic route. But although some attempt would be made to rectify the zigzags of the trail, its disregard of hills would be continued; there was no competent engineering skill available for highway location work. Even so, the results were not too bad.

Each village, by long-established custom, is responsible for trail upkeep from boundary to boundary (usually a water course), between villages. If the trail gets into disrepair, so that the women who traverse it on their way to and from the rice and cassava patches complain, the village medicine man will get together a gang and clear it secretly at night. Next day the women will find the trail cleared and attribute it to the magic of the medicine man.

At the instance of the Government, markets have been set up in many of the towns of the interior, each with its own market day. To these markets on the appointed days come endless streams of natives over the trails, or, where they exist, over the motor roads. They are women, mostly, with head loads of farm produce or whatever they may have to sell. To buy from them while they are on their way to market is impossible; that would take away the excitement of the bargaining, which is the real object of their trek. To the market come also the Mandingo traders, some of them crossing the boundary from French Guinea, if the market town is near the frontier.

The opening of the market is a formal affair, presided over by the Town or Clan Chief, perhaps by a Paramount Chief. No business is transacted until the Chief, through the mouth of his "speaker," declares the market open. First, new laws are proclaimed and special announcements are made. When the speaker finally announces, "Market is open," the babel begins. It is the great social event of the week. Most of the transactions, especially if the market is at a distance from a motor road, are by barter. French and British coins formerly trickled into the hinterland across the borders or from the coast and passed as currency, but they had to be coins with which the native was familiar. Old British shillings bearing the image of Queen Victoria were questioned, for, said the natives, the "Ole Mammy" was dead; the coins must be dead too! American coins have now replaced those of France and England. Perhaps the Roosevelt dime will raise the same doubts as did the Victoria shilling. Or perhaps not—for the Liberian native is learning.

A generation ago, before the Liberian Government succeeded in establishing its authority over the native tribes, a constant state of actual or incipient warfare prevailed, now and then marked by cannibalism. War was the principal avocation of the primitive African. Yet the people of the Liberian hinterland went far toward settling down to a culture of agriculture and hunting.

Tribal warfare did not mean the arraying of warriors of one tribe against those of another in formal battle. Organized war was unknown to the tribal people of Liberia. An "army" might be a band of a hundred men, hardly more. These tribal conflicts were really raids, stealthy attacks upon a town, carried out by the fighters of another town, sometimes of another tribe. Usually the approach was by night; the favorite time for an attack was the hour just after the break of dawn.

Silently the raiders would steal through the forest or bush. When the first of the townspeople, always a woman, opened the gate of the stockade that surrounded the town and came out for water, she would be quietly seized, and the attacking party would swarm through the gate into the town, to plunder and to capture or kill the half-awake inhabitants.

It was because of the constant threat of attack that the natives lived in towns rather than in scattered homesteads near their farms. It was best to travel some distance each day by trail to do the farm work, and so enjoy the relative safety of a community. In some parts of the country the towns were protected by stockades; in others by walls five or six feet thick, built of sun-dried clay, perhaps as much as fifteen feet high. Sometimes a fence of living trees, closely planted, was used. The age, or rather the youth of some of these living fences shows that fortification against marauders was needed as late as the beginning of this century.

Lust for power or for property was one of the chief motives for these tribal raids, just as it is among "civilized" nations. Revenge for accidental or intentional killings might lead to tribal warfare. A raid might be undertaken for the liberation of captives, the repossession of runaway wives or daughters. In fact any palaver not settled peaceably might lead to hostilities. Since surprise was relied upon to insure the success of a raid, rumors of an impending attack would keep a town in a more or less constant state of suspense, so that native life was not far different from that of the hunted animals that lived in the near-by bush.

The time of full moon was a period of especial danger, and

fear of attack might lead to night-long dancing by the warriors of a town, sleeplessly guarding against possible surprise. Such moonlight dances, now that danger no longer exists, have become a custom in some areas, but for fun rather than for protection.

When a raid was at its height not many captives were spared. Those who were not slain were carried off as prisoners and generally accepted the status of slaves in their new home; some were finally assimilated by their captors. Young girls who might make desirable wives were usually carried off. So, sometimes, were the mothers of very young children. With the burning and sacking of a town and the carrying off of the captives by the raiders the "war" would be over, unless a counterattack was made from some other quarter. If the raid was not entirely successful a truce might be effected, perhaps some tribute agreed upon as the price of calling off hostilities.

To bring about the end of fighting among the savage tribes of an almost inaccessible hinterland was the task the Liberian Government had to face as it attempted to assert its right to govern the interior. At first it found the problem an impossible one. Liberia's neighbors had similar problems, but had available the needed military power that the Government at Monrovia lacked. One result was the loss of much territory that was rightfully Liberian, as will be seen later in this book.[4] Finally, in 1908, the Liberian Frontier Force was organized. Recruited of necessity largely from the tribes themselves, its early history was marked by much the same cruelty as characterized the warfare they were set to stop. But all this has changed. The Frontier Force, after some vicissitudes, has become a well disciplined and effective arm of the Government, and tribal warfare, with all its savagery, has been abolished, to the great benefit of the native people.

• *Chapter Three* •

LIFE IN THE HINTERLAND

AMONG the tribal people of Liberia, sex is about the most important thing in life, unless, perhaps, the matter of food takes precedence from sheer necessity. The attitude of the native toward sex is entirely frank. He accepts it as a matter of course, but he does not take it lightly. Quite the contrary. Its influence enters into everything he does. Inanimate objects are held to possess sex. A native's medicine must contain both male and female elements. Strength, such as exists in stones or in potent drugs, is male. Unprocessed palm oil is male; when "burned" or clarified it is female.

Because the normal native household lives all in one room, there can be no concealment. Sex matters are discussed openly and freely. Children from infancy are acquainted with what we call the facts of life. Consequently sexual relations before marriage are the rule rather than the exception, even among youths of tender age. Children born as a result of such relations carry no stigma, and there is no disgrace to the mother. She has, in fact, demonstrated that she is fruitful, and when the time comes for her to marry, her family will be entitled to set a higher figure on her dowry price. Children born out of wedlock belong to the mother's father. When the mother weds, the child may be given to her, but if it is a girl baby the mother has only a 50 per cent interest in the dowry that will be paid when the child grows up and marries; the other 50 per cent must go to the mother's parents. Children born to a woman while she is a wife belong to the husband, whether he is the actual father or not. It is often not easy to know definitely who really begat the child, and so the line of heredity is deemed stronger through the female side of the family. There is much rejoicing when a baby is born, no matter what the circumstances of its parentage.

Every detail of midwifery connected with the child's birth is governed by ritual, which is fixed by tribal custom and often very complex. In some parts of the country the midwife takes the new-born infant, sticks a finger into finely-ground capsicum pods, and rubs the inside of mouth and throat with pepper, pushing her finger far back so as to force the child to gag, after which it is made to swallow a mixture of palm oil and water. When a girl baby is three days old, or a boy baby four, it is smeared with white clay and with medicine designed to please the spirits that preside over fertility. Then there is a formal presentation of the child to the father and to the public. At the beginning of the second month, it is fed rice flour boiled with water and with palm "butter" added. Perhaps its little belly will be stuffed with unwashed soft boiled rice. An infant has something less than an even chance of survival. Children are at a premium, and whether produced in or out of wedlock are more than welcome. Because family and village life are communal, there is no question as to responsibility for the child's support and upbringing. He is a valuable asset and will be well cared for. The conditions that have imposed responsibility on parenthood in civilization simply have not existed in tribal life.

Primarily the tribal culture is monogamous. But a man may have more than one wife, may indeed have many, for monogamy in the hinterland is not a matter of morals but of economics. Marriage to the Liberian is a business affair. Wives signify wealth and prestige. A man of position will keep as many wives as possible. They may serve not only as a measure of his worldly wealth according to tribal standards, but perhaps enable him to become a head-man, a village chief or Clan Chief, even a Paramount Chief.

Men who have many wives usually reserve a number for themselves; the rest can be loaned, generally with their consent, to other men to work out in farm hamlets. Except for the heavy task of clearing or "cutting" farm, the woman is the farm worker. Wives therefore represent so many farm hands. If a man can acquire a monopoly of the desirable women in his vicinity he has quite a hold on his fellow villagers to whom the wives have been loaned. They may, in fact, become part of his personal household. It is the route to tribal prestige.

Naturally it is the few, not the many, who thus rise to eminence. The average native has one wife; some have none. Whether it is a matter of plural wives or of plural automobiles, the psychology of wealth is the same in primitive as in civilized life. That polygamy among the tribal people is not only tolerated but looked upon as an evidence of success is not to be wondered at in a country where labor in the field is largely performed by women and where infant mortality is so high.

There is a popular idea that among Liberia's aborigines wives are bought. This is a misconception. True, they are paid for, but the transaction is not a sale. The family is thought to have, as a whole, a more or less fixed value. When a daughter is taken from the family in marriage, something of value is removed. This must be made whole, the family total value restored. The dowry, therefore, the price paid by the groom, is a payment to the parents by way of filling the gap in the family wealth. If the wife leaves her husband and returns to her parents the dowry must be paid back; the gap has been filled by her return.

Before the marriage agreement is arranged, the prospective husband will have sought to win the favor of the parents by numerous gifts which are not part of the dower itself. There may be other suitors. A parent may accept gifts from several as a means of learning which is likely to be the most generous husband. The bride thus acquires a sense of her value which serves to strengthen the tie between herself and her husband. There have been instances where parents, seeking to imitate the white man, have given a daughter in marriage without exacting a dowry payment, disregarding the deep-rooted tribal principle, only to find that the woman, knowing that nothing has been given for her, knows equally well that there is nothing binding her to her spouse. Since her relatives have nothing at stake, she packs up and goes home on the slightest provocation.

How much a man must give to obtain a woman for his wife depends to a large extent upon circumstances. Nominally it is fixed by law, part of the regulations for the administration of the hinterland enacted after the Liberian Government got control. Actually, the natives prefer to disregard the Government's price-fixing and to make their own bargain, as they did in the past. A typical dowry, determined by mutual agreement, might be one or two head of cattle plus some native cloths plus some such household utensils as brass buckets or iron pots. Frequently the price exceeds what the groom can pay out of hand; it will be paid on the installment plan.

The taking of a wife, that is to say the "wedding," is, as everywhere, a festive occasion. The bride is escorted from her town with much noise-making and dancing. She will be met on the way by the groom, accompanied by his relatives and his previous wives if he has them. The combined wedding company proceeds to the groom's town and hut. After sunset a mat is laid in the husband's hut and on it the bride and groom are seated. The dowry price, or the first installment of it, is now paid over. Meanwhile preparations have been made for a big feast, accompanied by much music and dancing. The husband presses more gifts on his new relatives, which they courteously refuse, but which, before their departure, they "reluctantly" accept.

When the festivities are over, the bride, if she is her husband's first wife, takes her place as the head wife. If she is number two, she becomes a member of the household, welcomed by wife number one, many of whose duties devolve on the junior spouse. The husband is supposed to receive food twice a day from each of his wives, which, if he has many, might be a rather overwhelming diet. But whether or not he gets it is another matter.

On a journey it has been the custom for the woman to carry the burden, leaving the husband free to fight at a moment's notice if attacked. Since the abolition of tribal wars and the consequent safety of travel, it is not uncommon for a man to carry part of the load if it is too heavy for his wife. It is often considered a sign of dignity for a man travelling to have with him at least one of his wives who has nothing to carry. A big chief may have several of his favorite wives walk close behind him carrying nothing.

Household duties of course fall to the women. But farm work is divided according to its character, the men performing the heavy task of "cutting farm" or clearing the bush preparatory to planting, the women tending the growing crops and gathering the harvest.

Genuine affection between husband and wife is the rule rather than the exception, even though it is traditional among the tribal people for the men to spend much of their ingenuity in keeping the women in their place and in excluding them from the mysteries that make up a large part of the life of the native, even though the wives sometimes hold their husbands in their power through a covert threat inherent in the knowledge of poisons supposedly the possession of the women.

Liberian children, when they are well, are bright and attractive. They have an inborn power of mimicry. Whatever they see they imitate. They are taught by precept and example, rarely by the stimulus of punishment. Boys will imitate every occupation of their fathers. Little girls accompany their mothers to farm or stream, help with the household work so far as they can. They are carefree little creatures, their bodies clean and shining, happy in the evident affection of their parents.

The women are skilled cooks. Their art is a simple one, but the country abounds in wild roots, spices, and herbs which they know well how to use. The family hearth is inside the hut, and there the cooking is usually done. Rice is the staple food, together with cassava and palm oil. Meat is scarce and always at a premium. There are few domestic animals for lack of grazing land and in some areas because of the tsetse fly. Goats and chickens are everywhere, but little use is made of hen's eggs. Cow's milk is not produced, and goat's milk is not acceptable to the Liberian native. But chickens and goats are important not only for food; they are used when sacrifice is necessary.

Wild animals are in great demand but are not plentiful, and the elephant, once regarded as the only really proper food for a chief, is now nearly extinct. Small wild animals such as the squirrel help out the food supply; so do lizards and snakes, fresh-water crabs and snails. Termites, especially queen termites, are regarded as a delicacy. When the termites swarm they are collected, dried, the wings winnowed out. They may then be eaten as they are, or toasted. Or they may serve for soup stock. Bananas and plantains are used, either raw or cooked, but oranges and grapefruit, although easily grown and of excellent quality, are little used by the Liberian native.

Rice is cooked so that the grains are distinct, quite up to the standard of the best Creole cooking. The native rice has all the vitamins of its outer surface retained, being much like the so-called wild rice that brings a premium in American fancy food shops. It is upland rice, differing from the swamp rice of other lands, with which the Liberian tribes are not familiar. In eating rice the native scoops up a handful from the kettle or dish, presses it into a ball, dips it into some palm-oil gravy or whatever soup is available, then plumps it into his mouth and swallows it whole. The amount of rice that an individual can consume in this way at a single meal is almost beyond belief.

Cassava is eaten in much the same way, but its preparation is one of the most exacting of the women's household duties. The roots are first boiled, the fibers pulled out, and the residue pounded in a wooden mortar, a small quantity at a time. The mortars are made from hollowed-out logs set on end, standing perhaps two feet high and hewn down to an hourglass shape. The pestles are heavy poles, two inches or more in diameter, maybe four feet long. In every village, and even in the cities, the pounding of cassava in these mortars is constantly to be seen, the pestles sometimes moving languidly, sometimes with energetic speed, always with rhythm. When a bit of cassava has been reduced in the mortar to a heavy dough, it is pressed into a ball or flat round cake. A deep impression, made with the thumb, forms a receptacle for the palm-oil gravy, and it is then ready to be popped into the mouth and, like the ball of rice, swallowed whole.

The palm oil is made by boiling the ripe nuts in water and beating them in a wooden mortar to loosen the fleshy pericarp. Washing and heating then promote the separation of the oil from the fleshy pulp and the skimming of it off for storage in earthen pots, ready for use. The palm kernels, which contain oil of a much better variety than that from the pulp of the pericarp, are difficult to crack and so are usually discarded unless they are produced near enough to a center of trade to permit their sale.

The Liberian native has no rigidly fixed meal times. He may eat whenever food is ready. How often he eats and when is largely dependent on his food supply and the number of his wives. There may be a midday meal, but usually the main repast is at night when the day's activities are over. If he actually gets one full meal a day he may consider himself well off. The Liberian native seldom is fat; on the average his nutrition is below par.

Water is, of course, the usual drink, and while the native does not boil or otherwise purify his water supply he is careful to obtain it upstream from the town. In the use of alcohol the people as a whole are rather temperate. The drinking of palm wine, however, is widespread. It is made by tapping the young fruit cluster of the oil palm and obtaining the sap that oozes out of the bud, or by cutting down the tree itself. A felled oil palm may continue its dripping for a fortnight. To promote fermentation and make the resulting product "strong" (which it is!), small pieces of the bark of a certain tree are put into the vessel in which the sap is caught. The appearance of heavy foam indicates the readiness of the drink for use.

Imported alcoholic beverages, especially gin, are more acceptable in trade in the interior than is currency, and the continual passing of Government messengers and soldiers has tended to promote the use of hard liquor, especially by the chiefs. The opening of roads has brought beer into the interior. It has also brought Coca Cola. Wherever there is motor access today the red "Drink Coca Cola" signs appear.

Every year toward the end of the dry season the Liberian villagers "cut farm." That is, they clear a new area for planting. The farms are small clearings, usually about three to six acres, planted generally for two or three successive years, then allowed to go back to bush, so that they lie fallow for five or six years, maybe longer, until the softwood trees that spring up as soon as the field is abandoned have attained a good size. This is known as "bush farming." It is a crude form of crop rotation, common throughout aboriginal Africa.

The native's main reliance for food is on agriculture, the growing of rice principally, with some cassava, perhaps corn and plantains. So fundamentally he is an agriculturist, although his acquaintance with the principles of farming is slight. What knowledge he has of how to grow the few crops that he plants has been handed down through countless generations, unchanged by any attempt at experimentation.

Upper left, Chief Keletike (Mano tribe) in formal dress at Ganta, where he was attending market. When he found that his picture was to be taken, he rushed off to don official robes. *Upper right*, a Mandingo trader. These traders are not Liberians but come across the border on market days. They are Mohammedan and wear long robes, white or blue.

Lower left, Paramount Chief of the Kru tribe, largest and most independent of Liberian tribes. They are a sea-faring people and operate surf-boats along the coast. *Lower right*, a Town Chief from the Bassa country on the coast. A deck passenger on a small coaster, he used the length of figured cloth sometimes as a wrap or toga, sometimes as a skirt.

A foot-trail through the high forest. There are few roads in Liberia. Travel in the roadless areas is by foot or hammock over the trails that run from village to village. Often the tangle of branches and vines overhead is so thick that the sun does not penetrate and the traveller walks in deep shade. The giant trees reach an immense height.

The task of clearing a patch for planting starts with an attack by machetes on the tangle of vines, undergrowth, and shrubs. Probably a diviner has been consulted in the selection of the area to be cleared. The small slash is left to dry, hanging in drab festoons from the tree tops with which it is entangled. Then the smaller trees are cut, leaving perhaps a big one to be felled last; it will bring down with it the mass of vines, creepers and tree tops. When all has been dried out by the hot tropical sun, fire is applied. There is no danger of a resultant forest fire, such as sometimes sweeps our pine timberlands, for the tropical forest and jungle is too green to burn. After the fire has died out at the edge of the clearing, the unburned rubbish is cleared away, the small stuff burned, material useful for firewood put aside and saved. The fire has left the cleared land covered with a layer of ashes. This the native knows to be good for the soil. It has also broken up the soil itself, to some extent, by making steam out of whatever moisture was in the ground near enough to the surface to be affected by the heat. Insects, disease germs, and weeds have been killed by the fire. No plow is used. The farm is ready for the planting of rice, cassava, or other crop by the women and girls.

Every effort is made to have the farm work finished before the heavy rains come to wash away the ashes. A crop failure in such a primitive country can be a calamity. The margin between a bare sufficiency of food and insufficiency is small at best. Serious drought or deluge may mean months of scarcity. There is always the chance that crops will be bewitched, with the result that growing plants will rot or burn.

To ward off spiritual enemies proper precautions must be taken, such as sacrifices and the burying of suitable medicines as prescribed by the local *zo*, or medicine man. There are tangible enemies too: monkeys, wild hogs, antelope, a host of insect pests, and flocks of parrots and other birds. Some of the animal depredations can be kept off by noise, some by fencing, some, like the wild hogs, have to be guarded against by very special medicines and taboos.

The rice is harvested by snipping it off, stalk by stalk, with a small knife made by the local blacksmith. The patience needed to glean a field in this way is hard for anyone who has not seen it to appreciate.

The total area exposed to this type of "shifting farming" is believed to be something like ten million acres.[2] Probably as much as seven hundred thousand acres are cleared each year by the process of cutting farm and burning, and a like amount allowed to revert to bush. The fertilizing effect of the ashes and the favorable condition of "new ground" usually give fair yields. The drain on the soil by bush-farm rotation is not great, although soils under secondary bush are found to have lost about 25 per cent of their organic matter as compared with those under virgin forest.

The yield from native farming is on a subsistence level. The tribal people are not too well nourished. There are indications, however, that the standard is rising. The ability to store rice and the increased possibilities of transportation with motor road construction are said to have resulted in a doubling of the rice crop in recent years. The cost to Liberia in the destruction of virgin forest and its replacement by a second growth of soft wood is not readily calculated—depends, in fact, on whether the timber of the forest lands can be made commercially valuable.

Because meat is so scarce hunting and fishing are important. Hunting requires great patience and skill, especially where firearms are lacking or ammunition is scarce. Even fish, in the interior, are more of a delicacy than they are a staple, while on the coast deep-sea fishing is largely done by the foreign Fanti.

It is at the end of the rainy season, in the hinterland, that fish are most easily caught. It is then that, as the waters subside, the larger fish begin to go downstream and may readily be taken with scoop nets, small drag nets, or seines. Women may be seen, wherever there is a river or a small stream, carrying their conical nets fashioned out of cord made from the fiber of the oil palm and fastened to a rigid hoop of vine. Perhaps the woman will find a stony riffle through which the fish must pass. Perhaps she will build a bit of rough stone dam, or even a dam of mud, and then try to drive the fish downstream into the net that she has fixed in place. Every nook where a fish may be lurking will have to be explored, every stone upturned that might be a hiding place. She will bring home only a few small fish, unless she is very lucky. Should there be more than are needed for immediate use, they can be dried in the sun or smoked. Perhaps there will be enough for her to take to the market town. There are always a few dried fish for sale on market days.

Sometimes the men go fishing. They may use barbless hooks made by the village blacksmith, or perhaps they will have acquired a few trade hooks from the Mandingos. More likely they will use fish poison, especially if there is a good pool where fish are fairly plentiful. Leaves of the plant *pephrosia*, sasswood bark, possibly other poisons, are mixed together and beaten into a pulpy mass which is thrown into the pool where it will mix with the water before the current carries it away. The poison stupifies rather than kills the fish, so that they come to the surface, where they are dispatched by the waiting men armed with cutlasses. Usually for this kind of fishing a fairly large party is organized, for the cutlass work must be done rapidly, before the fish and the poison are carried down stream.

In hunting, bows and arrows were formerly used, also spears, but they are now virtually obsolete. The hunter with bow and arrow had his dogs. In some parts of the country long nets were set up into which the game was driven, to be killed with spears or arrows. The effort involved in making the nets was considerable.

Firearms in the hinterland are of every type, often ancient flintlocks that have been modified to take percussion caps. Breech-loading shotguns and rifles have been scarce, but are becoming less so, especially in the areas where motor roads have been opened up. In fact as one drives over such a road, natives carrying rifles are constantly met. Recently many shotguns have come into the hands of the tribal people. Shells are, of course, costly, but there is some local loading of shotgun shells. The Liberian native is not distinguished for marksmanship; yet even in this he is improving. He used to fire from the elbow, which resulted in his aim being a bit sketchy, but he is learning to shoot from the shoulder. What he lacks in accuracy of aim is compensated for in part by his keenness of vision.

Trapping is more to the taste of the Liberian native, and in this he has great skill. Pit traps, cleverly concealed, serve for a variety of small animals. Noose traps are also common. An animal that has followed the crude raffia fence leading him to a noose trap and has set off the delicate trigger device may find himself suddenly strangled or swung high in the air by the spring of a bent-over sapling.

For the leopard, which is the great prize as well as the great enemy, neither the pit trap nor the noose will serve. He can climb too easily out of the one, and the other cannot hold him. So the leopard trap has to be a rather elaborate affair. A stake-lined path will be built, into which the animal will be guided by light fences. At the end of the path, where the stake walls are made especially strong and close together, a heavy log will be suspended, supported by a sensitively adjusted system of triggers so arranged that when the leopard attempts to clear away a slight obstruction, an unobtrusive network of fiber, the log will suddenly fall and crush him. Some leopard traps are in the form of a cage, baited with a live sheep or goat. The trigger, instead of causing a crushing weight to fall, releases a heavy door that descends behind the luckless animal. Then ensues the excitement of killing the beast.

The leopard is feared and hated throughout the Liberian hinterland. By whatever means one is killed, the occasion calls for festivities and special ceremonies. The building of a leopard trap is an art reserved for one of the secret societies. Rarely is a leopard killed in the open, for while they are not known as man-eaters, a hunter has small chance of surviving an encounter with one. The technique of building these traps is handed down from generation to generation through the secret societies. Their ingenuity and the delicacy of their setting bear eloquent witness to the innate inventive genius of the Liberian native.

The tribal people take great pride in dress. This sometimes comes as a surprise to anyone who has pictured the natives in his mind as naked savages. Clothing is not needed for protection from cold in this tropical land, at least not in the daytime. Nor is it worn for modesty; the native takes the human body, both male and female, very much for granted, thinks nothing about it. Rather, clothing is a matter of pride.

It may be that fondness for dress is a fairly recent development, perhaps resulting from contact with Europeans, perhaps transmitted through the itinerant Mandingos, who themselves always appear in long gowns. Or it may be that it has come down through the ages. At least we know that the making of cloth, both from cotton and from fine raffia, is a native art that stretches back into antiquity.

A native chief regards his wardrobe of more or less elaborate gowns as of the utmost importance to the maintenance of his dignity. His long robe of striped country cloth is to him what the wig is to an English barrister. He wears it on all formal occasions. Even if he dons European clothing, as for example, if he has business in Monrovia, he will wear the gown as an outer covering.

On the Firestone Plantation, the worker, while engaged in his daily task of tapping the rubber trees, will wear whatever tattered rags may be handy. But once the day's work is over, and on Sundays, utility gives way to neatness and he appears in spotless white trousers and shirt, or perhaps in neat shorts of country cloth. Native office workers on the Plantation are noticeably careful about their apparel.

In the interior, the typical native, man or woman, makes use of a length of cloth about a yard wide and two yards or so long. By day it serves as a garment, by night as a blanket. Beneath it the women will wear some kind of loin cloth, and a bead girdle; the men a loin cloth or perhaps cotton shorts. This length of cloth the woman wraps around her body, generally at about the waistline, the ends secured by a deft hitch, leaving the upper part of the body bare. Sometimes a woman will wear the cloth above the breasts, tucking the ends in below the left armpit. Every mother, as in all Africa, carries her latest baby at her back supported by the cloth which is wrapped around mother and child, the baby's little head bobbing about above the folds. Going to and from the farms the women will be thus clothed, but in the field, or when fishing, unnecessary clothing is discarded.

Imported cotton prints are popular for these wrap-arounds, especially where motor roads have brought in a good supply of trade goods. The native women have an eye for color. Dark figured patterns, in rich reds or bright orange designs, are favored. There has been a noticeable improvement in the quality and variety of prints available in the last few years, undoubtedly because of the recovery in the textile mills of America and Europe from the effects of the war.

There is a recent tendency also for native men to wear shorts and singlets in place of the cumbersome wrap-around garment. This is especially the case in the area of the motor roads and the vicinity of the larger towns. The gradual spread into the interior of treadle-operated sewing machines is having its effect on dress, particularly that of the men. In the larger towns there are native tailor shops, each with its row of machines, mainly engaged in turning out shorts made sometimes of country cloth, more often of stout trade cloth. In the dress of both men and women there is as much variation as there is in individual fancy.

Everywhere in the interior small boys and girls go naked until they are six or eight years old. Then the boys begin to wear loin cloths, the girls amulets or beads. As boys grow older some kind of shirt may be worn, often of a sketchy nature.

Young men usually wear no head covering. Often they have had their heads shaved in fancy patterns that they do not wish to hide. Older men frequently wear second-hand felt trade hats, especially near the cities. Men of distinction, such as village headmen, elders, and chiefs, wear ornate caps, cylindrical in form and low, somewhat like a skull cap, but elaborately embroidered. The formal, decorated cap may be an important part of a chief's official costume. One chief of the older generation was the proud possessor of several rather battered "stovepipe" hats of which he was very proud. But oddities of this kind have become rare since the tribes came under Government control and the chiefs became accustomed to contact with officers of the administration, including, at times, the President.

Most Liberian natives go barefoot, even in the cities. Mandingos usually wear rawhide sandals, and so, sometimes, do native chiefs. In the rainy season wooden clogs may be used. The advent of the automobile has led many native men to use sandals made from old tires. But the tribal people do not really take to footwear of the more formal European or American type, even when otherwise they adopt the dress of civilization.

Rhythm is an integral part of the Liberian native. Whether he cuts farm with his machete or fells a tree with axe, or pulls an oar in a surf boat, he will swing to the accompaniment of a song or a drum. He will dance all night, often, in his village, even after a hard day's work. Every event of village life leads to the dance.

When the moon is full is the time of greatest rhythmic activity.

Drums give voice to the most intricate beats, some of which almost defy the notations of a civilized musician. When regular drums are not available, almost anything will do, a battered kerosene can, an overturned pot or pail. The native drums vary widely in type. Some, the great war drums of the passing era, are as much as a dozen feet in length; to beat them the drummers must stand on platforms. Then there are the "talking drums," shaped somewhat like an hourglass, laced from head to head by a cord network so arranged that the tension and hence the pitch can be varied by squeezing, as the instrument is carried under the arm. The variety of sounds that can be drawn from these talking drums is augmented by striking in different positions, sometimes in the center, sometimes near or on the edge, or by muting with the left hand. These are the drums that give rise to the almost unbelievable tales of the mysterious conveying of elaborate messages.

Sometimes drums are in sets of varying length, the percussion choir of the forest symphony. Bead rattles, a bell or two, may be added. Several horns may contribute melody to the exotic orchestra. There may even be stringed instruments, crudely fashioned from a gourd, a forked stick and some piassava fibers. When such an orchestra is in full blast its effect is indescribable.

Vocal music varies with the tribe. The Krus are rich in harmony; the Fanti and Mandingos have little feeling for music but are given more to oral noise, monotonous cries in chorus, and drum or tin-can beating with little or no rhythm. In the interior, Liberian vocal music is at its best. There is part singing, largely antiphonal, with highly developed rhythm. In some parts of the country there are troops of wandering minstrels, with orchestra and dancers, sometimes acrobats and dancers on stilts.

The old songs and choruses, the chants and harmony of the Liberian hinterland are passing. Gradually, as civilization encroaches on tribal life, something is lost, something that had a bit of savage tone in it now and then, but a deeper meaning to the heart of the aborigine. Whether as a whole it is being replaced by something better only time can tell, and that time is not yet.

· *Chapter Four* ·

MEDICINES AND DEVILS

THE Liberian native lives in a world that is full of mystery. He is surrounded by forces that he cannot understand. Deep in his inner consciousness is a belief in the inevitable connection of cause and effect. If the cause is not apparent to him he must find it in some supernatural element, in some power beyond the range of his senses which he must, if possible, find some way of controlling.[1]

So all the voids of his experience are filled, if not with something tangible, then with something spiritual. Everything about him, animate or inanimate, has for him some spiritual existence. Every tree, every stone, may be a living, a sentient thing, having an influence upon his everyday affairs. These voiceless objects that impinge upon his life may be talked to, appeased, fed.

To get the upper hand over these mysterious forces, the native creates for himself "medicines," on which he may rely to protect him from evil influences or to act favorably for his good. Many of these medicines are directed toward the prevention or cure of bodily ailments, and so the term "medicine" has common usage. But the word implies a much too limited scope. To the native it is *nye*, power. It is not the medicine itself that brings about the desired result, but the *power* that resides in it, and this power may be exerted over an unlimited range of life's problems and experiences.

Medicines take many forms, but always they are related to the object for which they were created. Thus to give courage to a warrior, in the old days of tribal raids and conflicts, the medicine to be carried into battle would if possible include some part of the body of a slain enemy. Medicine needed to give power over a personal enemy, real or imagined, might contain a bit of his hair or a fingernail paring. It was important so to dispose of such personal items that they could not be used in medicines against oneself.

The power to promote swiftness could be given to a medicine by including a leaf, blown by the wind. A stone would give endurance. Bones, claws, beaks of birds, were useful ingredients, for they do not disintegrate. Parasitic plants, whose roots tend to strangle their hosts, made good medicines for use against an enemy. Anything in fact might be used to which some special power or advantage could be attributed. Medicines are often a mass of many ingredients, made up into small packages, or perhaps stuffed into a small horn so as to be easily carried.

It is important that a medicine be strong, if it is to work beneficially for its possessor, for when two medicines come into conflict, the stronger will prevail. Obviously this matter of strength is of prime importance in medicines intended to work magic either by being definitely harmful or by overcoming the good effect of a weaker white-magic medicine. The native lives in constant fear that bad medicine, in the hands of an enemy or a witch, may be used against him.

There are town medicines, family medicines, personal medicines; medicines for every conceivable purpose. Family medicines are kept in the house of the family head. When a town is founded, the chief medicine place is made. It may be a small cylindrical clay hut erected near the entrance of the town, especially if the medicines to be kept in it are intended to ward off bad influences that might otherwise enter the town. Or the medicine may be kept within the town itself, perhaps in association with a sacred tree. Personal medicines may be kept in the owner's hut, or may accompany him wherever he goes.

Care must be taken to keep the medicine alive, and for this the responsibility rests on the family head, the town chief or, in the case of personal medicines, upon the owner himself. To keep them alive most medicines must be fed, generally at the time of the new moon, but sometimes special sacrifices and feedings are needed to strengthen a medicine so that it may have maximum potency when most needed, as when a journey is to be undertaken or some danger is imminent. The feeding may be the blood of a chicken, sacrificed for the purpose, or even some rice and palm oil.

Any native may prepare himself medicine to suit his purpose, but the matter is usually of such great importance as to call for special skill, and for this the services of a *zo* are availed of.

The *zo* may be roughly defined as a native medicine man, but the term has a broader significance. More accurately, a *zo* is someone possessing great skill. It may be in the treatment of physical ailments; it may be as a master blacksmith. There can even be women *zo's*. A *zo* may be more powerful than a chief, for he is the possessor of mystic knowledge and power.

Every *zo* has a small replica of a mask in his possession, as part of his personal medicine. It is called a *ma*, and is of such size as to be easily concealed in the hand. No one other than himself is ever supposed to see it. At the new moon it must be washed and fed. Every morning the *zo* takes out his *ma* and in secret spits on its face, rubs it against his forehead, and prays to it for good luck. He may talk to it at great length. To him it is the embodiment of the spirit of his ancestors, and through it he has communion with them.

Considerable rivalry may develop between *zo's*, for their reputation and hence their power is based on their real or supposed skill. Power among *zo's*, as among men elsewhere, is a thing to be coveted. Rivalry may go so far as to tempt one *zo* to do away with another. In the older days this was not a difficult matter. *Zo's* often ate together, and it was traditional that an invitation to such a meal was not to be refused. The jealous *zo*, in preparation for the repast to which he had invited his rival, could carefully poison one side of his knife. He had only to remember, when cutting the meat, which side of the knife was carrying the poison to insure the death of his guest.

Not all of the native medicines are hocus-pocus. Dr. George W. Harley, in his treatise on native African medicine, gives a list of ninety-eight diseases and related ills, the native treatment for which is, in sixty-five instances, rational, and in thirty-three magical. The ills for which there are rational treatments range from the common cold to smallpox; those for which the treatment is magic run from hiccough to pneumonia.

The *zo's* who practice medicine have a wide and often practical knowledge of medicinal plants, hypnotism, psychology, and, to a limited extent, anatomy. Many of the drugs used by primitive people have found their way into the pharmacopoeia of civilization and, indeed, until the advent of modern synthetic drugs and biologicals, the practice of medicine was largely a matter of experiment with the *materia medica*, whether the doctor was an M.D. from Johns Hopkins or a *zo* of the hinterland. American medical men have found much to commend in the art as practiced by the natives, even though there is often little distinction between the real and the magical. But that is true elsewhere than among the aborigines, for the breed of quacks is not entirely extinct, even in lands where there is an abundance of scientific knowledge.

The *zo*, in treating disease, makes no fuss, goes through no incantations. He even has a "bed-side manner," quiet, confident, dignified. Often he uses local heat and poultices, makes small incisions over abscesses, applies a tourniquet in cases of snake-bite, uses splints for fractures, knows how to give an enema with a long-stemmed gourd, has a limited knowledge of surgery and bone-setting. He will isolate patients suffering from smallpox, and when the disease has run its course will cause the isolation hut to be burned. Often a sick person will have a special hut enclosed within a fence and fitted with two beds, one for the patient and one for an attendant.

The medical lore of the *zo* is therefore something on which to build, rather than something to be thrown into the discard. The ailing native may not understand the hypodermic needle or realize that it is not a cure-all, but he comes to the modern clinic believing in the efficacy of medicine, whether compounded by a pharmacist or by his tribal *zo*.

When a native is attacked by some form of sickness that does not yield to the simple treatments with which he is familiar, or against which the medicines of the *zo* prove powerless, he turns to witchcraft as the only explanation. His logic requires the postulation of a cause, real or mystic. Similarly, there must be some hidden cause when an accident occurs, for the native does not believe in accidents. Even if a cutlass slips and cuts his foot, he attributes the event to some hidden power; the cutlass probably was bewitched.

To determine who was responsible for the witchery, the tribesman will resort to the services of a diviner, who, by one means or another, such as the use of cola nuts much as we would toss a coin, but all shrouded in mystery, will fix upon some luckless individual as the witch. The diviner will have secretly sounded out gossip, to be sure that his accusation will meet with popular approval. He knows how to control the fall of his cola nuts so as to designate the selected person. If the "witch" then confesses to his witchcraft, a medicine can be devised to undo the harm and all is well. But if he denies it, the matter is not so simple; some form of ordeal must be employed to determine his guilt or innocence. In the older days the trial by sasswood would be made. The accused would be made to drink a violently poisonous infusion made from the bark of the sasswood tree. The poison might, in exceptional cases, act as an emetic and the accused be thus acquitted. But if the result was fatal, his guilt would have been established and punishment meted out at the same time. The Government has long since prohibited the trial by sasswood, and other ordeals that do not lead to fatal results have taken its place, carried out through the services of diviners.

One of the reasons for calling in a diviner instead of making a direct accusation, when witchery was suspected, was that the accuser otherwise laid himself open to revenge. He might have to stand the equivalent of a lawsuit for defamation of character, and the penalty might be greater than that for the fault charged. But if the accusation could be made through a diviner there was no fault on the part of the accuser; responsibility rested with the medium, who, being guided by powers mysteriously beyond his control, was free to make the charge. The diviner probably had, as a rule, a pretty good idea as to the guilt or innocence of the accused and could work his trickery accordingly.

Before the Government reforms, a native who had black magic medicine made against him might in fact be facing danger much more real than could result from the mystical medicines themselves. He might have to fear possible poisoning. A person who had use for poisons could obtain them from a sorcerer. But knowledge of poisons was wide-spread among the tribal people of a generation or so ago and fear of poisoning was constantly present in the native mind. The poisons were powerful drugs, made from a gall and herb mixture, and a minute quantity could be sufficient to kill quickly or to bring about a lingering fatal illness. Enough poison to kill could be concealed beneath the thumbnail, and food would be refused if offered in a bowl so held that the thumb was within the rim. A native offering food to a friend would himself partake of it first to prove its harmlessness, a practice that still prevails.

The native formerly had another fear, not only that he might be the victim of witchery, but that he himself might be accused of witchcraft. Some physical ailment, some deformity, some irregularity in his conduct, even the unaided imagination of another, might lead to such a charge and he might have to face the dreaded trial by sasswood or the alternative of a false confession.

Fortunately, like other forms of tribal frightfulness, these fears and their causes are yielding to the influence of civilization, but the practices are insidious and are not readily eliminated. Almost as this is being written, there has been a conviction for attempted murder, not by any physical means but by the defendant's having created such fear of witchery that his victim was judged to have been in actual danger of death.

Not all witchery was evil. If the power of witchcraft was used within the rules, no blame attached. A civilized doctor, for example, because he had the knowledge that enabled him to control powerful drugs which, in over-dose, might be poison, would be deemed a witch. He would not be accused of black magic, for he uses the drugs to cure disease. It is the knowledge that would enable him to kill if he so willed that would make him a witch.

In a society where mystery prevailed and there was no formal body of laws and no restraining arm of government, there naturally flourished many secret cults or societies, given over to varying degrees of frightfulness. Probably the most savage of these was the Leopard Society, which practiced outright murder in order that its members might acquire strength by consuming human flesh. The identity of its members was never known. Its victims would be seized, their bodies horribly mutilated and left in the bush or beside a trail, to be found by their fellow villagers. The attack on a victim was made by the use of iron claws, so wielded that the wounds closely resembled those that would be made by a leopard, thus giving the impression that the death had been the work of that wild beast. Preferably the killing was done when an actual leopard was known to be in the vicinity. In Liberia the practices of the Leopard Society have for many years been effectively suppressed by the Government, but the society still has some influence. It was widespread throughout West Africa and there have been some recent indications that it may still be following its old practices of frightfulness elsewhere than in Liberia.

Somewhat like the Leopard Society was the Snake Society, formed near the coast. There were, in fact, two quite distinct snake societies. One was entirely benevolent, having for its object the control and cure of snake bites. This society tamed snakes, employed their venom as an antidote, and used the reptiles for exhibition and entertainment purposes. It was not difficult for an outsider, even a white man or woman, to be made a member of this cult and to be initiated into at least some of its mysteries. This snake society still exists.

The other snake society was far from being benevolent. It made use of poisonous snakes, cobras, vipers, to attack and kill its victims. It too has been suppressed by the Liberian Government.

Most important and widespread of the secret societies was the Poro, with its counterpart, the Sande, among the women. Primarily the Poro was an institution or "bush school" for the education of young native boys and for the continuation of their training in maturity. It was at the same time a secret organization with death as the penalty for betrayal. Ritual in the Poro sessions included highly religious rites, sometimes accompanied by human sacrifice. It represented, embodied, and gave effect to the mysteries of tribal religion. Students of the Poro have seen in the organization and in its ninety-nine degrees a close resemblance to Free Masonry, all the tribal societies being like lodges within the Poro.

For what follows in this chapter, and for much of what precedes, I am indebted to Dr. George W. Harley, who heads the Methodist Mission at Ganta, deep in Liberia's interior, and who generously made available to me so much of his great store of facts (together with their interpretation) as I was able to assimilate. Dr. Harley has spent a quarter of a century among Liberia's natives, gaining their confidence, getting to know much of their mental processes. Bit by bit, over the years, he has been able to piece together fragments of information, like a jig-saw puzzle, until the picture of tribal life, with its mysteries and superstitions, has taken shape and become fairly clear. Only recently has the doctor been able to fit in some of the pieces that had been missing.

Much of Dr. Harley's study, especially of the Poro, has centered around the masks used by the natives in the Poro ritual and hitherto little understood by the outsider. These masks are of wood, sometimes carved with great skill, sometimes crude. There are portrait masks, and masks of monstrous form. Partly they are used to conceal the identity of the wearer, but they have a deeper significance, intimately interwoven with a form of ancestor worship. In the mask, the spirit of the owner and the spirits of his ancestors are merged. Wearing it, his identity becomes one with the mask itself. It is an elusive idea, but it lies at the very heart of the old beliefs that find expression in the Poro and its ritual.

In the Peabody Museum of Harvard University at Cambridge, Massachusetts, is a collection of more than three hundred of these masks, placed there by Dr. Harley. They were acquired by him, one by one, secretly, for in the old days a native bringing one to the Mission did so at the possible risk of his life. Perhaps in the dead of night the doctor would hear a faint scratching on the screen of his window. It would be a native boy, one who had come to trust the American Medicine Man, bringing a mask. Maybe it had belonged to some relative, an uncle perhaps, who had died, leaving no one to care for it, to feed it, to keep it from rotting or from being devoured by the termites. So the boy would bring it to Dr. Harley, knowing that it would be safe in his hands.

Today so much of the mystery of the masks has become traditional only that secrecy is no longer needed. With the passing of the mystery, something has gone out of the life of the native, something that, whatever might have been its other effects, had a restraining influence on him. The replacement of what has gone out of the aboriginal religion by something better is one of today's most serious and difficult problems in Liberia. It is a task for the schools, for the missions, for the Liberian Government; a pressing task.

The Poro must be described in the past tense, for in its original form it no longer exists. Because of the savagery of some of its practices the society was suppressed a generation ago by the Liberian Government. In milder form it has been re-established on account of its disciplinary function. But the frightfulness that once characterized it is gone.

It was necessary for a boy to be initiated into Poro and submit to its training before he would be recognized as a member of the tribe. Before that, he might have great affection bestowed upon him by his parents, might even pass the age of puberty, have sexual experience, take a wife. But as a tribesman he was nil; he must first undergo the ordeals that would prove his worth.

Entrance into Poro involved the idea of the death of the boy and his subsequent rebirth into a new life. As a part of the process he would receive the tribal marks, scarifications of the skin, characteristic in pattern, that would signify his right as an initiate.

In the Poro there were three classes, reflecting the tribal status of the family from which the member had come and his own abilities. There were the commoners, the chiefs and the priests or *zo's*. There were various grades of *zo*, representing the degrees of Poro attained, but in general, while hereditary, the term *zo* indicated proficiency in the man's special calling. A native trained in Poro might travel away from home and enter the "foreign" Poro school, where he would immediately be received according to his rank, after being put through an examination by the *zo* in charge, degree by degree, until examiner or examined dropped out.

The upper degrees of the Poro and the men who made up its inner circle were a far greater power in tribal life than were the chiefs. Actually they controlled clan government. It was they who had the final say with respect to inter-tribal relations, war, politics.

The Poro leaders were called *ge's* (pronounced "gay"). The mask was an essential part of the *ge's* equipment, for without it he never appeared in public. His identity was known only to Poro initiates. Even his voice was disguised. For this he used a small wooden tube with flute-like openings in the side, over which mem-

Upper left, Liberian women spend a large part of their time pounding cassava roots or rice in wooden mortars (see page 33). *Upper right*, group on a forest trail who are much interested in the author as he trains his camera on them. One girl carries her head load in a woven basket, but the others are using the more modern metal basin.

Lower left, mother and daughter on the foot-trail between Gipu and Flumpa, who stop to stare at the strange white man and his camera. The girl is carrying a cassava root on her head and has picked up a discarded raisin box from the white man's lunch. *Lower right*, a young beauty in a coastal village near Monrovia.

Left, tapping a rubber tree. There are 10 million rubber trees on the Firestone Plantation, half of them tapped each day. The tappers, carefully trained skilled workers, begin their tapping at dawn, and in mid-morning make a second round to collect the latex from the small plastic cups into which it has dripped.

Tree tappers on the Firestone Plantation lined up with their stainless steel pails to have their morning's take chemically tested and inspected (see pages 139-141). About half the latex is concentrated in the Plantation factory and shipped to the United States in liquid form. The rest is coagulated, calendered into sheets of crepe rubber, and baled for shipment.

branes fashioned out of spider's nests were used—an instrument sometimes defined as a "blowing drum." This disguising of the voice was necessary, for ordinarily he was merely one of the tribesmen; the fact of his being also a *ge* had to be carefully concealed. To the uninitiated, therefore, he was known solely as a mysterious voice, talking at night or from the concealment of a house. He was supposed also to sing, but actually the singing was done by several assistants, each of whom would blow on a set of pottery whistles and resonators roughly tuned to a chromatic scale. By posting these assistants at various widely separated points in the bush outside of town, it could be made to appear to the credulous natives that the *ge* was flying from place to place, as one or another took up the sound in the stillness of the African night. Ability to fly was an important accomplishment of a Bush Devil, for among his duties was that of spinning the intricate and mysterious suspension bridges of vines and tendrils that carried many of the trails over the streams.

The highest ranking member of the Poro in any given region, ordinarily the oldest if qualified, was the Big Devil or Gonola. He was the Great Forest Spirit and was supposed never to leave the bush, although he, like the other *ge's*, when not acting officially, would go about his ordinary business. The Big Devil might intervene to stop the townspeople from fighting among themselves, might tell them when they had broken the law, might impose fines. But only his mournful voice would be heard, speaking in another language than that of the tribe. Gonola must never be seen by anyone except initiates, not even by the boys in the bush school until he was "revealed" to them. When he came into a village, even though he did so only as a voice, every woman and every uninitiated male must hide.

The *ge's* were believed to be spirits, ancestral spirits. There were *ge's* whose function was really that of police, enforcing the laws, collecting debts. Others were messengers; those of high standing might act as "speaker" or representative of a higher *ge*, might even act in his place. The lesser ones served to announce sessions of the Poro, to escort boys to the bush school, or to go ahead of a big *ge* and announce his coming. Some of the *ge's* were war leaders, some Poro instructors, some athletic directors in the bush school. Some had the duty of foraging for food for the bush school boys. The *ge's* were not bad spirits. Their functions were constructive, even though severe punishment, including death, might result from violation of the Poro laws. But there was no evil demon whose characteristic was to bring calamity unless appeased. It is not really accurate, therefore, to call the *ge's* or their masks "Devils." That is the term in common use, not by the natives, but by the English-speaking Liberians, tempered somewhat to distinguish them from Satan by calling them "Bush Devils."

The fitting out of a *ge* with medicine suitable to his calling was a very secret and complicated matter. A *zo* who was also a *ge* would assemble the outfit far from any habitation, usually in various parts, each part made in a different place. When they were ready to be put together the *ge* candidate would be required to furnish a human sacrifice.

An essential adjunct of each *ge* was his mask, a carved wooden face, often a portrait mask of an ancestor. The *ge* and his mask were one, for a *ge* appeared only behind his mask, and so strong was his belief in its spiritual nature that he himself came to believe that his personality was merged with that of the mask.

A *ge* was supposed never to die. His actual death would be a closely guarded secret, the more easily guarded because his mask, in which his spirit lived, survived him and served to keep up the fiction of his continued existence, for the natives of the town knew the *ge* only as a mask and a voice. The body of a dead *ge* might be secretly embalmed and kept in the loft of his hut, or it might be surreptitiously disposed of, possibly by tunnelling to an adjacent hut whence it would be carried deep into the forest to its final resting place between the buttress roots of a giant sacred bombax tree. The mask of the dead *ge* would continue in use through successive generations. It could not be destroyed intentionally. If it was accidentally destroyed it must be replaced or a small replica made, for the spirit of the mask did not die.

The tradition is that the mummy of the founder of the Poro still exists in the Loma country, his likeness conventionalized into *Go Ge*, the mask of the succeeding line of Gonolas.

Every degree of skill and imagination was represented in the carving of the masks. Some were highly finished products of the carver's art. Usually a portrait mask can be recognized as such by its human quality. But some masks, especially Gonola, were grotesque, combining exaggerated human features with those of an animal, such as the jaws of a crocodile. Dancer's masks were female and often had a winsome beauty. The dancer wore not only his mask but also a raffia dress and head covering which entirely concealed him, so that the fact of his being a human was effectively disguised. Long gloves covered even his finger tips, and he spoke in an unknown tongue in high falsetto tones.

Gonola, the highest ranking *ge* in any area, was head of the Poro school. He was also called Lekola. He was the possessor of the great fetish known as Dunuma, the very name of which had awful significance. He was possessor also of *Go Ge*, the spirit embodied in the ranking mask. Gonola was titular owner of land and forest. He might on occasion act as supreme judge of the clan. When exercising his judicial function he actually wore his mask, with costume completely concealing him, even his hands and feet, and sat inside the inclosure of his private quarters, guarded against all but the old men. He gave judgment through an interpreter, for Gonola was supposed not to talk the common language.

Yet even though Gonola exercised the highest judicial authority in the clan, custom was in the final analysis the ruling force. It tended to preserve a fixed pattern of tribal life. There was, however, room for gradual change. New masks were now and then added to the hierarchy and so new interpretations of custom by living persons could be added to the whole. But there could be no departure from established practice without sufficient popular approval. Public opinion, acting through the elders, did not hesitate to deal the death penalty to anyone who seriously overstepped the bounds of custom. Thus, while in everyday matters, Gonola, the owner of the *Go Ge* mask, had great leeway and was almost a law unto himself, the assertion of too much rugged individualism would lead to his elimination.

When a tribesman became Gonola, the sacrifice of his oldest son was required, for it was assumed that the son could best carry the message to the ancestors. When any part of the body of the sacrifice was eaten ritually it became a substance of soul-giving power. So Gonola, through the sacrificed son, became the possessor of the power of his ancestors.

As frightfulness began to be eliminated from tribal practices, substitutes were adopted for the sacrifice of the son; first a slave, later a cow, even later a chicken was made to answer. But this was when the strength of the great Poro organization was waning. One is tempted to wonder whether there is any connection, any common origin of custom and superstition, that might link the sacrifice of Gonola's son with Abraham's proffered sacrifice of Isaac.

One woman, and one only, entered into the operation of Poro. She was the ritually sexless "wife" of Gonola and was known as Wai. She took part in the running of the bush school, supervised the cooking, heard the petty complaints of the boys. Her job was not an easy one, for it was certain that some of the boys would be homesick. She must see that none ran away, and this was a responsible duty, for running away was punishable by death. A tap on the head by Wai would be the sign for execution. Wai was also a fact-finder and a spy, and she was the keeper of the mask on which the boys took oath on entering Poro, a female mask, the big *Ma,* mother of all masks and always a woman's face.

The bush school in which, under the direction of the Poro Society and its *ge's,* the young tribesmen were formerly given their training was not a continuous thing, partly because it put quite a strain on the economy of the people. The feeding of the trainees and teachers, who were removed from productive toil for a period of three or four years, was never easily accomplished. So Poro would be declared at intervals of several years, usually when the son of a big chief was ready to become an initiate. Then all the boys of eligible age would be rounded up and their induction into Poro would begin.

Practice differed somewhat among the different tribes, but in general there were two grades of the bush school, the first being preliminary and involving mainly the rite of circumcision. In some tribes this rite was performed in infancy. The Big Devil was not seen by the boys in this preliminary school.

The second grade was the real Poro, the Big Bush. For it a

grove or bush area was set aside, marked by some form of inclosure, such as a living hedge. All possible approaches would be blocked off or posted by symbols well understood by the natives. The entrance would be effectively screened off, perhaps by stakes and palm branches, perhaps with raffia curtains. For the uninitiated to penetrate into such a grove meant death or forced initiation.

Within the area fields would be cleared, huts built, and, most important of all, a hearth installed on which food was to be cooked, including the human sacrifices that would be consumed as part of ritual. Before any fire could be put on this hearth a sacrifice was required; it might be a slave, perhaps a captive from another tribe. The fire itself was kindled from a sacred flame kept perpetually burning, its origin the first of the Poro groves, probably many miles away.

When the school was ready the boys would be summoned. They, with their families, would come to the entrance of the grove. It was a serious matter for all, but the seriousness would be masked by great excitement, dancing, the beating of drums. The voice of *Vu ni*, the bull-roarer, would be heard, deep in the forest. It was the voice of the great crocodile spirit, used to terrify the women and children. The voices of the Poro *ge's* were like the growl of the leopard.

No boy dared refuse the impending initiation, although he might be in great fear of what lay ahead of him. He would not see his family again, nor they him, for the ensuing three or four years of his training. Life within the Poro was deemed to be a spiritual state, the boys existing within the belly of the Great Forest Spirit. Entrance into Poro was equivalent to death so far as boyhood was concerned. When the boy came out he would have a new name and would be assumed to be a new personality.

To signify the theoretical death of the boy entering Poro, and to give it reality to his family, he would apparently be impaled on a spear and his body tossed over the barrier at the bush-school entrance. Actually the spear would be thrust through a piece of palm cabbage under a cloth with which the boy was protected and which concealed also a bladder filled with chicken blood, the piercing of which gave realism to the act. The boy, in his flight over the barrier, would be caught from falling on the other side, but a dropping log within the enclosure would produce a most convincing thud, heard on the outside. The chief's son would be the first to go in, as he would be the leader of the group, would become a *zo*, and someday succeed to the chieftaincy.

Once inside, each boy would be subjected to a more or less severe hazing, during which he would finally have to "fight the Devil," a struggle very real to the boy, which he would mysteriously win (the natives were good psychologists). He would then pass an inner barrier into the presence of Gonola, the Big Bush Devil.

There would follow the process of scarification, the cutting of the Poro's tribal marks. This practice has, like much of the other Poro ritual, fallen into disuse, but the scars, characteristic of the tribe to which the native belongs, are still common among the adult people, the number of rows and their position varying with the different tribes. By them, cult members could tell not only the tribe to which an individual belonged but in which tribe's bush school he had been initiated. As he might be admitted to higher degrees in later life, other marks would be added. The scarifications were supposed to be effected by the teeth of the Big Devil in swallowing the novice. The rite was really performed by means of a ceremonial razor, sharpened on a sacred whetstone. The whetstone itself had a special significance. Dr. Harley tells of seeing such a stone which, from its well worn state, must have been in use for many generations, perhaps for centuries. It was passed down from father to son, could never be sold. So vital was it to the ritual of Poro that, like the mask of Gonola, its inheritance called for human sacrifice.

To cut the marks, tiny hooks set in a handle were used, two or more hooks, depending on the number of rows of marks to be made. With these, the operator, a highly skilled *zo*, would pick up bits of the boy's skin and deftly cut with the whetted razor against the hook points. The little hooks were themselves sacred. A *zo* who disregarded this and sold or revealed the hooks would pay for it with his life. Fine marks were a matter of pride to both boy and *zo*, and the *zo* who could do a neat and artistic job was in demand.

The process would proceed until the pattern was complete. It might extend around the neck, and down the chest and around to the back, or maybe from neck to navel; in some tribes, only on the forehead.

Cutting the tribal marks was not an easy ordeal for the boy. Neither was it without its dangers. The wounds might readily become infected and serious blood poisoning ensue. If that happened, the probably fatal outcome would be anticipated. The boy would be killed, his body burned, and the ashes used to make "medicine" against like trouble among the other boys.

With the healing of the wounds, the long period of training would begin. Poro was a very practical school, organized as a community, where all the arts necessary to native life were taught by actual practice. Here the boys learned how to build huts, how to cut farm. They were taught the tribal laws and customs, sexual matters, and, high in the order of importance, the management of women. Discipline was strict. A boy who misbehaved was severely punished. If he remained recalcitrant he might be flogged to death and consumed as a sacrifice for the edification of the others. If a boy, not yet admitted to Poro, allowed his curiosity to get the better of him and peeked into its mysteries, he was forthwith subject to initiation. If a girl was similarly indiscreet, she was killed.

There were no graves within the bush school, nor was the death of a boy, from natural causes or otherwise, made known to his parents while Poro was in session. Ritualistically he died when he entered Poro. But when the boys came out of Poro, a mother whose son had actually died within the bush would find in front of her hut a broken jar, her first intimation of her loss, which she must neither mourn nor mention.

At the end of Poro, Gonola revealed himself to the boys, wearing his mask only, whereas up until then he had appeared to them only while completely covered by his raffia costume. The boys would now know that the *ge* was a human being. Gonola then made sacrifice to *Go Ge*, his mask, showing them that it was the mask, not the man, that counted.

The period of training in the Poro school was now over and the boys were ready to come out of the bush. When this time came they went through a ceremonial washing in a convenient stream, were smeared with white clay, and assembled behind the raffia curtain that closed the entrance to the school.

Dr. Harley described to me the ceremony that followed, as he saw it quite accidently when he happened to come into a town just as the boys were coming out of bush. It was at sunset, a time chosen, apparently, for the weird effect lent by the waning light. There was music from a group of men blowing on pottery whistles. Then came the town crier, announcing that *ge* had given birth to the boys. There followed a period of absolute silence, about two minutes. Then just as the sunset light turned to an eerie gray the crier walked to an open space where were gathered the boys, sitting in a long row on palm mats, each boy covered head to foot with country cloth so arranged that he could peek out.

Slowly the women began to come out of their huts where they had hidden on hearing the music of the clay whistles. The crier now introduced each boy by his new name. They were treated even by their mothers as strangers. Then there began a pantomime of teaching each boy how to walk, showing him how to wrap a blanket around himself, naming to him various familiar objects, all carrying out the idea of new birth. For two days the town belonged to the boys, during which they "learned" remarkably fast. And then they were full tribesmen.

The counterpart of the Poro was the girl's society, the Sande. In comparison with Poro it played a somewhat minor part. It too was a training school, but it did not base its authority on frightfulness. As a result, it continues with little change today.

The object of the Sande society was primarily fertility. Initiation into it was theoretically optional, but a woman who had never been in the bush was despised. The instruction the girls received in the Sande school included singing, dancing, cooking, midwifery, the ways of winning a husband's affection, witchcraft and the art of catching witches, and a thorough course in the use of poisons. The "medicines" and other sacred objects of the Sande cult were not permitted to come into the hands of men, but their power could be invoked by both men and women when they failed to have the desired children.

Before the young girls go into the bush their dress consists mainly of a string of beads. Within the Sande school they may go naked or wear a simple clout. Their coming out of the bush is a time of joyful dancing and feasting by the whole town. It is preceded by ceremonial washing and the coating of the entire body with white clay. As they enter the town they wear on their heads tall cylindrical hats of mat-work woven by the men. For several days the girls dance and feast. During that time they must not talk to a male nor enter a hut, but sleep in the palaver house. At the end of the period of feasting and dancing they are again ceremonially washed. It is then that they don the wrap-arounds, head-dresses, beads and ornaments that have been given them.

In the Sande society there are women *zo's*, just as there are men *zo's* in Poro, but the status of a woman *zo* in town and tribe is of course inferior, except in the case of the *zo* who is the Sande mother, and except the Poro mother, Wai, the ritual wife of Gonola.

Poro played, in the old days, an important part in Liberian tribal life. In some respects its function was highly salutary. Its training was practical, its discipline effective. Its evil lay in its superstitions and in the savagery of its ritualistic practices, especially human sacrifice. And the rigidity of its laws and customs had a stultifying effect on tribal life, resisting every change from ancestral usage and preventing experimentation and progress.

Chapter Five

THE AMERICO-LIBERIANS

LIBERIA is in many ways a land of contrasts. Especially is this true of its population. At one end of the cultural scale are the aboriginal tribesmen, who, as we have seen, are living, many of them, very much as their savage forebears lived centuries ago and who are even today little influenced by civilization. At the other extreme are the highly cultured Americo-Liberians, who think and act on the same plane as Europeans and Americans. They may, in fact, be regarded as a part of America transferred to another land, where they have carried on the traditions of the country whence they came and where they have also developed culture of their own. A foreigner, therefore, coming to Liberia and expecting to find, in the Americo-Liberians, an inferior race, is due for a psychological jolt.

The Liberian readily achieves a comprehensive grasp of world politics. At San Francisco and in subsequent deliberations of the United Nations, the representatives of the African Republic not only won the respect of their colleagues; they were in the front rank in international councils. At Bretton Woods some of our American financial experts were astonished to find that the Liberian representatives had at their finger-tips facts for which they themselves had to look to their staff assistants. Liberian and American business men quickly acquire a mutual respect. The fact that the diplomatic representatives of the United States and of Liberia have recently been elevated to the rank of ambassador is significant. It would be unnecessary to state the case of the Liberians so emphatically were it not that they have so often been misrepresented by writers and others who have failed to obtain more than a superficial glimpse of the country and its people.

Liberians today are the product of a century or more of struggle that has given to succeeding generations both courage and fortitude and a high degree of pride and self-confidence. They and their immediate forebears had the task of winning a foothold on a difficult shore, where mere physical survival was a problem. They had to face, subdue, and finally win over hostile savage tribes. They found themselves bitterly regarded by the European overlords of adjoining colonial empires. Without experience in government, they had to establish not only a government over themselves, but a government over a horde of aborigines who outnumbered them a hundred to one. That relations with the natives in Liberia today are on a basis more satisfactory than in the near-by British colonies, governed by a power that has prided itself on its skill in colonial management, surely redounds to the credit of the Republic.

The Liberians have been forced by circumstances to specialize in the art of government. The Americo-Liberians, including those of the tribesmen who have been assimilated, have constituted themselves a ruling class. They could not do otherwise. The running of the Government became both their vocation and their avocation. It is from the Government that the greater part of the Americo-Liberians have derived their livelihood.[1]

The original emigrants from America to Liberia came, most of them, of their own volition. But many came because the idea was rather vigorously sold to them. The period of their coming was, in the main, from 1820 until the time of the Civil War. Of those who emigrated during that time, some forty-five hundred were free-born American Negroes. A thousand or so had already been freed or had themselves managed to purchase their freedom. About six thousand were slaves whose owners had emancipated them for the specific purpose of settlement in Liberia. From Virginia came the largest number, more than thirty-seven hundred, followed by North Carolina, Georgia, Tennessee, South Carolina, and Kentucky. Maryland and Mississippi each sent five hundred odd. No less than twenty-seven states, North and South, and the District of Columbia, had been their homes. Three hundred and forty-six came from the British Barbados, and from this group have sprung some of Liberia's leaders, including two of its Presidents. These were the settlers whose "love of liberty" brought them to Liberia's shores. They took with them the culture of America, largely the culture of the Southern states.[2]

There were others who must be numbered with the original settlers, Negroes who did not come voluntarily but for whom Liberia represented escape from a fate they had feared and from which they had been delivered. These were native Africans who had been torn from their homes in the last days of the slave traders and recaptured on the high seas by vessels of the United States Navy engaged in destroying the last vestiges of the outlawed traffic in human beings. More than fifty-seven hundred of these recaptured Africans were sent by the American Government to Liberia. In theory, at least, the Government entertained the hope that from Liberia they might by some means find their way to their own native tribes. They were supposed to remain in the settlement only temporarily. But most of them stayed, rapidly learned the ways of civilization, were assimilated.

The plan for an African colonization of free American Negroes originated, not with the free Negroes themselves, but with political and philanthropic leaders in the United States. The idea, however, was not entirely philanthropic. Slavery was, of course, one of the major problems with which the Founding Fathers struggled, without finding a solution. A corollary to the slave problem was the question of what to do with slaves who, by one means or another, gained their freedom. This was a growing problem. The slaves themselves had masters; the free Negroes had none. The idea that they should have legal equality with their former masters was not readily accepted. Perhaps they could be segregated, perhaps expatriated; meanwhile they were feared. Statistics showing the comparative rates of increase of the two races, white and black, caused alarm. There was dread of possible uprisings that might involve all the blacks, bond and free.

Colonization seemed to many to be the only solution. The British, who had a lesser problem of freed Negroes, were experimenting with a settlement of blacks in Sierra Leone. Before the turn of the century, this British project was being much discussed in America. Thomas Jefferson, as early as 1776, had worked out a colonization plan in some detail, but nothing came of it. Washington and Monroe had ideas along much the same line. Jefferson even tried, while President, to arrange with the British for accepting in Sierra Leone freed slaves to be sent from the United States, but without success.

Superimposed on the problem of the free Negroes was that of the disposition of Negroes recaptured by the American Navy. These were unavoidably wards of the United States Government. To return them each to his point of origin was impossible. Some disposition, at least temporarily, must be made of them.

So there came about the foundation, in 1817, of the American Colonization Society. At first it was a voluntary association, with a very doubtful legal status. In 1831 it was incorporated in Maryland. Subsidiary societies were organized in Massachusetts, New York, Pennsylvania, North Carolina, Mississippi. A charter from Congress would have been useful, but the slavery question was already so explosive politically that a move for federal incorporation might have precipitated a serious national controversy. Even so, the Society was made up of people, leaders in their various circles, some of whom held views on the slavery question as widely divergent as could be found in abolitionist New England and in the Deep South.

The purpose of the Society, as set forth in its constitution, was "to promote and execute a plan for colonizing, with their own consent, the free people of color residing in the United States, in Africa, or such other place as Congress shall deem most expedient." There was some thought of creating a settlement within the bounds of the continental United States, but this was soon abandoned as impracticable.

The motives behind the avowed purpose of the Society were various. Some of its promoters were appalled by the rapid increase in the Negro population, which in the first thirty years after the adoption of the American Constitution had more than doubled. Some were motivated by religious enthusiasm, seeing in a settlement of American freedmen on the African coast the beginning of a movement to Christianize the whole of that great continent. Some merely looked on the plan as a convenient way to rid the country of dangerous agitators, and some had ideas of the beginning of a new East India Company that would develop into a great commercial empire. Quite generally, the aspirations of the founders of the Society, whatever their motives, greatly exceeded the contents of their pocketbooks.

Legally the organization, at least during the period preceding its incorporation, was a philanthropic society. Through its operation it was hoped to achieve four objectives: alleviation of the lot of free Negroes, encouragement of manumission, riddance of a possibly dangerous and disgruntled element, and perhaps the final abolition of slavery. What the Society actually achieved, despite many difficulties, shortcomings, and dissensions, was the giving of a considerable impetus to the emancipation movement, the rendering of important aid in stopping the slave trade, and—its crowning accomplishment—the founding of an independent republic in Africa.

What the outcome would have been if a scheme of colonizing the free Negroes in Africa had been undertaken by the United States Government instead of by a private philanthropic organization, is a matter of conjecture. Had a colony been so founded, its tendency would have been toward extension of territory, perhaps toward a joining in the race for African possessions that was just beginning to manifest itself among the European powers. The result might have been far-reaching, perhaps calamitous. An independent Negro Republic would hardly have resulted. Perhaps the whole history of America would have been changed.

But public opinion in the United States at the time (or for that matter, later) would not have tolerated a proposal for the establishment of an African colony, even though the problem of the free Negro was a national one. Moreover, there were grave doubts at the time as to the power of the United States to acquire non-contiguous territory, doubts that continued up to the time of the Alaska purchase.

So it remained for a non-governmental agency, a voluntary society, to undertake the task of colonization, supported, always inadequately, by contributions derived largely from the members of the Protestant churches, two and a half million dollars over a period of half a century.

Fortunately a way was found whereby the early efforts of the Colonization Society were given support by the American Government, through an ingenious device without which their plans might have come to naught. On March 3, 1819, Congress passed an act which authorized the transportation to the West Coast of Africa of slaves captured on American vessels engaged in the illegal slave trade. An appropriation of $100,000 was made for the general purposes of the act. It was not a happily worded piece of legislation. Attorney General Wirt rendered an opinion interpreting it so narrowly that, had he been followed, it would have been practically inoperative.

President Monroe, however, took a more constructive view. Determined not to be thwarted by the legalistic view of his advisor, he sent to Congress a special message (December 19, 1819) in which he set forth his own broad interpretation of the act. No one in Congress challenged his view. With this partial equivalent of a legislative record to support him, the President proceeded to cooperate in a very special way with the Colonization Society. The theory of President Monroe's action was that the authority to transport the recaptured slaves to Africa necessarily implied authority to establish on the African coast some kind of temporary place where they could be cared for during such time as might be necessary for their final disposition.

The Society had assembled a group of eighty-eight persons who were willing to undertake the venture of settling in Africa. To transport them the 300-ton brig Elizabeth had been chartered. But there, for lack of sufficient funds, the matter rested.

President Monroe on January 8, 1820, appointed one Samuel Bacon as principal United States agent under the act of March 3, 1819, with John B. Bankson as assistant agent. Mr. Bacon was instructed by the Secretary of the Navy to board the Elizabeth, take over the charter party from the Society on behalf of the United States, load the vessel with stores and materials needed to build a "barracks" for 300 persons (i.e., for that number of recaptured slaves). He was to take with him the necessary artisans, proceed to the African coast, make arrangements for permisson to land, and then "proceed to make preparation for buildings to shelter the captured Africans and to afford them comfort and protection until they can be otherwise disposed of." He was to endeavor to return the captives "to their native places."

Although he was to take over the Elizabeth from the Society, his instructions read: "It is to be distinctly understood that you are not to connect your Agency with the views or plans of the Colonization Society, with which, under the law, the Government of the United States has no concern. You are not to exercise any power or authority founded on the principle of colonization."[3] But with these restrictions, evidently written for the record, Agent Bacon was given a free hand.

Bacon had "estimated" that to do the work required by his instructions there would be needed twenty-nine men and fifteen women. Actually he took the party of eighty-eight which the Society had assembled: thirty-three men who went as mechanics and laborers, eighteen women rated as cooks, seamstresses, nurses, and washerwomen, and thirty-seven children, the explanation being that the men refused to go without their families.

With this company, and no recaptured slaves (they were to come later), the Elizabeth, on February 6, 1820, sailed for Africa as a public vessel of the United States. The emigrants went ostensibly as employees of the United States Government. They were given transportation, provisions, and materials for houses. There was an implied obligation on the part of the Government to provide them with return transportation, but they were at liberty to stay. That of course was the purpose of their going; only a few returned.

The Elizabeth proceeded to Freetown in Sierra Leone, then down the coast to Sherbro Island, which had not at that time been claimed by the British. Agents of the Colonization Society had reconnoitered the coast previously, but the selection of Sherbro Island was a mistake. Disaster soon came in the form of sickness and death. Twenty-nine of the would-be settlers died. So did both the United States agents and the Society's agent, Dr. Samuel A. Crozer. The survivors were removed to Fourah Bay by arrangement with the government of Sierra Leone, which was willing to succor them temporarily.

In December of 1820 the Reverend Ephraim Bacon was appointed United States agent for recaptured slaves, with Jonathan B. Winn as his assistant, and the Reverend Joseph R. Andrus became agent for the Society. These, with another band of emigrants, proceeded to Sierra Leone on the brig Nautilus.

Bacon, who had United States funds with him, acquired at Freetown a small light-draft schooner, the Augusta, better able to navigate the shoal waters of the coast. In it he and Andrus set out to locate a new and more favorable site for the settlement. At Grand Bassa, about fifty miles beyond what is now Monrovia, they thought they had found it. They had a long and difficult palaver with the local native chiefs, and finally came away with an agreement for a suitable tract of land. But the natives with whom they had dealt had been acting as middlemen for ships engaged in the slave trade, collecting captives sent down to the coast from the interior and holding them for shipment. They feared interference with this lucrative business and had exacted a condition from the agents that no information as to their slaving activities was to be conveyed to warships.

When this agreement was reported to the Society it was promptly rejected because of this proviso. So the Grand Bassa deal fell through. A new agent, Dr. Eli Ayres, was appointed by the Society in January, 1821. He also received an appointment as a surgeon in the United States Navy. Ayres went to Africa, where he joined Captain Robert F. Stockton, U. S. Navy, commanding the U.S.S. Alligator. Together they embarked on the schooner Augusta and went ashore at Cape Mesurado, the site of the present city of Monrovia. Here, after several futile efforts to meet the chiefs who controlled the area, they finally succeeded in getting a meeting with "King" Peter and the other Chiefs concerned. A long and colorful palaver ensued, lasting day after day. A preliminary negotiation had been carried on before the arrival of Stockton and Ayres by a friendly half-breed, one J. S. Mill, who acted as interpreter. Mill had been educated in England, had settled near Cape Mesurado, entered trade and acquired some wealth. Through him Stockton made it clear that he was acting solely for the Society, not for the American Government, a distinction that may have been a bit vague in the minds of the native Chiefs; Stockton's status as a naval officer, together with the presence of an American ship of war, certainly did not weaken his position as a negotiator.

Finally the Chiefs agreed to "make book," as it was called, and a contract ceding the desired territory was entered into. The instrument, signed by King Peter and the others, reads as follows:[4]

"KNOW ALL MEN, that this contract, made on the fifteenth day of December, in the year of our Lord one thousand eight hundred and twenty-one, between King Peter, King George, King Zoda and King

Long Peter, their Princes, and Head-men, of the one part: and Captain Robert F. Stockton and Eli Ayres, of the other part; WITNESSETH, That whereas certain citizens of the United States of America are desirous to establish themselves on the Western Coast of Africa, and have invested Captain Robert F. Stockton and Eli Ayres with full powers to treat with and purchase from the said Kings, Princes and Head-men, certain lands, viz: Dozoa Island, and also all that portion of land bounded north and west by the Atlantic Ocean, and on the south and east by a line drawn in a south-east direction from the north of Mesurado river, WE, the said Kings, Princes, and Head-men, being fully convinced of the Pacific and just views of the said citizens of America, and being desirous to reciprocate the friendship and affection expressed to us and our people, DO HEREBY, in consideration of so much paid in hand, viz: Six muskets, one box Beads, two hogsheads Tobacco, one cask Gunpowder, six bars Iron, ten iron Pots, one dozen Knives and Forks, one dozen Spoons, six pieces blue Baft, four Hats, three Coats, three pair Shoes, one box Pipes, one keg Nails, twenty Looking-glasses, three pieces Handkerchiefs, three pieces Calico, three Canes, four Umbrellas, one box Soap, one barrel Rum; And *to be paid*, the following: three casks Tobacco, one box Pipes, Three barrels Rum, Twelve pieces Cloth, six bars Iron, one box Beads, fifty Knives, twelve Guns, three barrels Gunpowder, one dozen Plates, one dozen Knives and Forks, twenty Hats, five casks Beef, five barrels Pork, ten barrels Biscuit, twelve Decanters, twelve glass Tumblers, and fifty Shoes, FOR EVER CEDE AND RELINQUISH the above described Lands, with all thereto appertaining or belonging, or reputed so to belong, to Captain Robert F. Stockton and Eli Ayres, TO HAVE AND TO HOLD the said premises for the use of the said Citizens of America. And WE, the said Kings and Princes, and Head-men, do further pledge ourselves that we are the lawful owners of the above described Land, without manner of conditions, limitations, or other matter.

"The contracting Parties pledge themselves to live in peace and friendship for ever; and do further agree to build for the use of the said Citizens of America, six large houses, on any place selected by them within the above described tract of ceded land.

"IN WITNESS whereof, the said Princes, Kings and Head-men of the one part; and Captain Robert Stockton and Eli Ayres of the other part; do set their hands to this covenant, on the day and year above written.

"(Signed) King Peter X his mark
King George X his mark
King Zoda X his mark
King Long Peter X his mark
King Governor X his mark
King Jimmy X his mark
Captain Robert F. Stockton
Eli Ayres, M.D."

"Witness (signed)
John S. Mill
John Craig

To what extent these native Chiefs realized that they had ceded both property and political rights can only be guessed at. The consideration paid them was of course ridiculously small by civilized standards, though it had a value in their eyes, in all probability, well beyond its intrinsic worth. But these chiefs were accustomed to dealing with the trading vessels that touched on the coast. They knew something of the white man's ways. Mill was a competent interpreter. The Chiefs withdrew time and again for discussion among themselves. There was no haste. While no single Chief had general authority, all the Chiefs, or Kings, and Head-men who controlled the tribal territory involved were party to the discussion and signed the contract. The Chiefs later attempted to deny the agreement and the tribes attacked the immigrants soon after they settled on the site.

Dr. Charles H. Huberich, who made a searching and scholarly study of all the legal questions involved in the founding of Liberia, and whose treatise, on *The Political and Legislative History of Liberia,* is an authoritative work, seems to have had no great doubt but that the Chiefs understood the nature of the agreement. "Adequacy of consideration," says Dr. Huberich, "in the absence of fraud, cannot be taken into account."[5] The agreement, while it does not specifically confer sovereignty, provides that the "parties pledge themselves to live in peace and friendship forever, and do further contract not to make war or otherwise molest or disturb each other." "This," says Dr. Huberich, "shows conclusively that both contracting parties envisaged the establishment of an independent political community, endowed with the power of peace and war, one of the attributes of sovereignty."[6] This is the view of the transaction officially held by the Government of the Republic of Liberia.

On April 25, 1822, the immigrants landed on tiny Providence Island, under the brow of Cape Mesurado, and took possession of the ceded territory. Dr. Huberich concludes that upon their landing a new and sovereign state was born—not a colony but a distinct and independent political entity.[7] It is hardly to be imagined that the settlers had any conception of what their expedition, terminating at the rocky cape, would lead to: that they were in fact founding a nation ultimately to take its place proudly with the other nations of the world as the honored Republic of Liberia. Instead, they were at once faced with all the difficulties that could beset a handful of inexperienced adventurers seeking to make a new home on an uncivilized and hostile shore.

They had hardly begun to establish themselves, building houses and planting gardens that they might have food, when the natives began to assemble on the low sands of Bushrod Island nearby. The settlers found themselves under the necessity of fighting for their lives against a horde of savages who might easily have overwhelmed them.

Fortunately, a young white man, Jehudi Ashmun, dissatisfied with his lot at home, where he had run somewhat into debt, and believing that there were great possibilities in trade on the African coast, had been appointed agent for the Society and also for the Government. Ashmun, after working his way through Middlebury College in Vermont, had started life as a Congregational minister. At twenty-four he was editing an Episcopal periodical in Baltimore. He combined business ambition with religious zeal. On August 8, 1822, he arrived at the Mesurado settlement.

Ashmun was a natural leader. Despite grumblings and dissensions among the settlers he effected a military organization, built barricades, emplaced the meagre armament available, and put the embryonic colony into a state of defence.

An incident during the hostilities that ensued is cherished in Liberian history. A loaded cannon had been trained on the savages but failed to fire. A woman settler, Matilda Newport, rushed forward with an ember from a lighted pipe, touched off the recalcitrant weapon. Its unprecedented blast is credited with having broken up the attack.

Fortunately for the settlers, it happened that a British colonial vessel, the Prince Regent, passing the Cape, heard firing and came to the succor of the adventurers. A midshipman by the name of Gordon and eleven seamen volunteered to land. Their coming was a godsend. Gordon and his men remained for some weeks, but the gallant young officer and eight of his seamen died.

Meanwhile, food was getting scarce, for the gardens had been sacrificed to the defensive measures. Rationing of the insufficient supplies became necessary, and dissensions increased. There was little inclination to accept the hardships that were inevitable. When the U.S.S. Cyane, Captain Robert T. Spence, U.S.N., appeared off the coast, Ashmun wrote to Captain Spence, telling him of the conditions the colonists were facing. The plea was not in vain. Captain Spence repaired the old schooner Augusta and with it rendered valuable assistance, including vitally needed supplies. But dissatisfaction continued. Complaints as to land allotments multiplied. There was disorder, even rioting. Finally the settlers addressed a memorial of complaint to the Society. Ashmun became so discouraged that he left the settlement and started home.

When the Board of the American Colonization Society received the memorial from the settlers, they were shocked at the attitude shown. The Reverend Randolph Gurley was dispatched to Africa as the bearer of a firm rebuke. To give him added prestige, the Society arranged to have Gurley made United States agent.

Gurley, as secretary of the Society, had really been its strength. His mission proved to be the turning point. By good fortune his ship, the U.S.S. Porpoise, touched at Porto Praya on the outward voyage and there he found Jehudi Ashmun awaiting passage home. Gurley persuaded him to turn back, and together they proceeded to Cape Mesurado, where order was quickly restored. A new plan of administration was drawn up and provisionally put into effect, pending approval by the Society at home. Local officers were appointed, a scheme of price-control made effective, construction of buildings resumed. The change was rapid, electric. Gurley remained only eight days, but in that time the colonists saw the beginning of an era of prosperity. Ashmun's funk was ended. His innate abilities reasserted themselves. He became the first of Liberia's historic men.

Gurley left the Cape on August 22, 1824, on the day the new government which he and Ashmun had set up began to function. The colony numbered only two hundred, exclusive of recaptured Africans, but this little group had found themselves. And they now had a name. Gurley, before leaving for Africa, had proposed and the Society had adopted, "Liberia" as the name of the settlement, and "Monrovia," in honor of President James Monroe, as that of the town that was being laid out on the heights of Cape Mesurado.

The reorganization that Gurley and Ashmun had effected at Monrovia had, however, to run the gantlet of the Society's Board. Most of the actions these two able men had taken were at first disapproved. Of this Dr. Huberich says: "The Board were deeply convinced, despite all their outward protestations to the contrary, that the Negro race was incapable of governing a civilized state. . . . It was the smug complacency of a body of men, some bigoted visionaries, some hypocritical egoists, some irresolute, and almost all of them without practical knowledge of men and affairs. . . . The Society, dependent for its funds both on the slavocrats in the South and on the missionary and abolitionist elements in the North, was always fearsome, overcautious and wavering in its policies."[8]

Small wonder that such an organization, embracing elements that extended from Massachusetts to Mississippi in the heated decades that preceded the Civil War found trouble in dealing with the phase of the slavery problem that they had taken upon themselves.

Finally, however, in May, 1825, the plan of government and a digest of laws for the settlers were approved. The following year saw the colony definitely prospering. Indeed it was showing the beginnings of a foreign commerce, nearly $44,000 worth of exports in a six-months period, of which some $30,000 was profit.

Ashmun's business abilities were bearing fruit. But his health was failing. He had to leave Monrovia in March of 1828, and in August of the same year, at New Haven, Connecticut, he died, aged thirty-four. Very fittingly the street in Monrovia on which are located the Executive Mansion and many other important buildings, including the Centennial Pavillion, bears his name.

From the start the colony began to expand. An area along the St. John River inland from Grand Bassa was acquired and settlement started. Here and there, as opportunity offered, jurisdiction was taken over from the native tribes along the coast for a stretch of 150 miles, from Cape Mount southeastward. A succession of agents, some of them able men, some far from competent, came out to represent the Society.

A novel legal situation had been created, little understood at the time. The Society that had fostered the settlement was now acting, not as master of its creation, but as its servant. The American Colonization Society, either in its original form as a voluntary association or later as a corporation, under the laws of Maryland, had no power to exercise sovereignty. That power resided in the settlers themselves, although they had not yet realized it. The State of Maryland could not, in fact, under the Constitution of the United States, grant political sovereignty over a foreign settlement to any corporation or other body created by it. The charter of the Society contained no such grant; it did not even contain any express provision granting power to exercise governmental functions, and the relationship that was established between the corporation and the settlers may have been *ultra vires*, although that question was never raised.

However, a compact was entered into between the Society and the emigrants before their original sailing on the Elizabeth, whereby the Society undertook to perform the functions of government for the settlers, an arrangement that was reaffirmed when the Society was incorporated. This novel set-up was later challenged by the European colonial powers. It was an arrangement without precedent, but, as was demonstrated later, legally sound. The Society and its agents were acting virtually as servants of the colony, employed to run the government, while gradually, or as it turned out, rapidly, the art of self-government was being learned by the settlers.

With the colony at Cape Mesurado beginning to function more and more on its own, the various auxiliary societies began to lose interest in the parent corporation and to lay plans for colonies under their own supervision. Three major settlements resulted. The Young Men's Colonization Society of Pennsylvania, with a Quaker background, took over the problem of a group of slaves freed under the will of a deceased member. The New York Society concerned itself with another group of manumitted slaves in Savannah, Georgia. These two societies, joining their financial resources, established a settlement at Bassa Cove, but the part fostered by the Quakers had a tragic ending because of their attempt to meet a native attack with passive resistance. The Mississippi Society established a settlement at Sinoe, founding the town of Greenville, for freed slaves from Mississippi only. Both of these settlements, that at Bassa Cove and that at Sinoe, soon merged with the major colony at Cape Mesurado.

The Maryland Society effected a settlement at Cape Palmas, the far southeastern corner of what is now Liberia, and set up the independent colony of "Maryland in Liberia." It continued as a separate colony until 1856, when it came into the Republic of Liberia.

In December, 1838, the American Colonization Society raised the status of its Liberian representative from that of agent to governor. Thomas Buchanan, a cousin of the James Buchanan who became President of the United States, was appointed as Liberia's first governor. Mr. Buchanan had previously (1836-37) served with distinction as governor of the settlement at Bassa Cove, before it became part of Liberia. He took with him an important document.

The organic law of the colony dated back to 1820, when a constitution was adopted before the first group of emigrants sailed. It was a brief document, providing for the government of the colony under rules adopted by the Society and administered by its agent. It required that every settler twenty-one years of age should take oath to support the constitution, provided that the common law as followed in the United States should apply; gave to the United States extraterritorial rights with respect to recaptured slaves; and laid down the rule that there should be no slavery in the settlement.

A significant clause in the 1820 document reads: "All persons residing within the territory held by the American Colonization Society . . . or removing there to reside, shall be free, . . ." a provision that referred, not to freedom from slavery, for all the emigrants were already free in that sense, before they sailed for Africa, but to the principle that they were free from the legal, economic, and social restrictions that had limited their status in the United States.

In 1831, when the Society was incorporated, a new constitution was set up, substantially like the original. But the colony soon outgrew this rather sketchy basic law as its members gained experience in the art of government. A new corporate charter was granted the Society in 1837, specifically giving it the right to "make and ordain such constitution, by-laws, ordinances and regulations as may be necessary . . . and to do all such other acts and deeds as they shall deem necessary for regulating and managing the concerns of said body corporate."

In the colony itself a movement started for a more definitive constitution. Under Lieutenant Governor Anthony D. Williams, who immediately preceded Governor Buchanan, the colonists drew up a well-rounded and workable constitution which they transmitted to the Society. It seems to have been given slight attention by that body. But it resulted in a new and very practicable document's being adopted by the Society, known as the Constitution of 1838. This was brought to the colony by Governor Buchanan, who arrived at Monrovia on April 1, 1839.

On landing, he presented the new constitution to the settlers. It was accepted by unanimous vote, subject only to one slight change that was later agreed to by the Society. The colonists thus, for the first time, themselves in effect enacted a constitution. They might have objected to the Society's document, might have insisted on their own. That they did not do so was the act of a free people, an act of sovereignty. The Constitution of 1838 became their own constitution. The Society remained the servant, not the master of the settlers.

Governor Buchanan's administration was constructive. In particular he addressed himself to breaking up the slave trade still carried on at points along the coast, notably by groups of Spaniards who had slave "factories" at a distance from Monrovia in the direction of Cape Mount. Buchanan let his zeal outrun his authority (he was also United States agent) but he was never seriously called to account, and his actions went far toward the final destruction of the slave trade.

There were others than slavers who had a foothold on the Liberian coast. British traders had for many years maintained establishments for dealing with the natives, bartering so-called "trade goods" for ivory, palm oil, and other local products. These traders denied the right of the new Liberian Government to control trading within the territory over which the colonists claimed sovereignty. In particular, they denied the right of the colony to exact customs duties. They were upheld in their denial by officers of the British Navy, operating off the coast.

Soon after Buchanan's accession as governor, the matter of the British right to trade regardless of Liberian laws came to a head. A British subject was accused of trading in defiance of the colonial laws and was brought before the Liberian court. The legal question involved in the case (*Commonwealth of Liberia* vs. *John G. Jackson, Master of the British schooner Guineaman*) was a close one, turning on whether or not his act in taking aboard a cask of palm oil constituted trading. The case was tried before Lieutenant Governor J. J. Roberts, sitting as Chief Justice. Mr. Roberts was later to become Liberia's first President. The facts in the case were well established. Roberts' charge to the jury is remarkable for its fairness and for its clear exposition of the difficult legal points involved. It led to a verdict of guilty and the defendant was fined, protesting that he would bring the matter before Her Majesty's Government and if necessary before Parliament. The real issue was Liberia's right as a sovereign nation to govern its territory and territorial waters, a right constantly denied by the British.

Two points about this case are especially noteworthy: first, the carrying of the matter into court by the Liberians; and, second, the personality of the presiding judge. Joseph Jackson Roberts was a Negro, born free in the United States, where he had received a liberal education, which did not, however, include the law. He had, in fact, followed mercantile pursuits, establishing in Liberia a successful trading company and owning vessels. Yet his charge to the jury was a masterpiece, its legal soundness never successfully challenged.

Governor Buchanan died at Bassa Cove September 3, 1841. Lieutenant Governor Roberts succeeded him and was affirmed as Governor by the Society the following January.

The constant denial by the European powers, especially Great Britain, of the right of Liberia to exercise sovereignty continued to be the chief concern of the administration at Monrovia. The colony was still pitifully small and weak, numerically and physically. Exclusive of recaptured Africans and natives, it numbered less than three thousand. But it was strong in purpose and its leadership was acquiring formidable stature. That this little group of people should come to such a degree of political maturity within two decades is astonishing. Their task had been more than one of creating a settlement against heavy odds; they had now to face the might of the British Government. David was to meet Goliath.

The British, in the person of their naval officers, persisted in resisting Liberian sovereignty. The position of Her Majesty's Government was stated by Captain Denman, R.N., who claimed that "as British traders had for a long series of years carried on an undisturbed trade with the natives," at Bassa Cove in particular, the Liberians had "no right now to insist upon their compliance with any regulations made by the Government of Liberia."[9]

By 1843 the matter was in diplomatic channels, with the British trying to pin down American policy. The British minister in Washington was instructed to address Secretary of State Upshur, inquiring as to the degree of official patronage and protection accorded Liberia by the United States and, if such protection was extended, requesting a definition of the geographical limits of Liberia. To this inquiry Secretary Upshur replied, setting forth clearly that Liberia had no political relationship with the United States. He skirted around the question of Liberia's sovereignty, but said that the United States "would be very unwilling to see it [Liberia] despoiled of its territory rightfully acquired, or improperly restrained in the exercise of its necessary rights and powers as an independent settlement."[10]

With this mild warning to the British from Washington, Liberia was left to fend for itself. And the British resistance continued.

Governor Roberts, in a message to his legislative council dated January 18, 1845, recited the reiterated position of the British as communicated to him by Commodore Jones of H.M. Ship Penelope.[11] "The Liberian settlers," said Commodore Jones, "have asserted rights over the British subjects alluded to [traders on the coast] which appear to be . . . inadmissible on the grounds on which Liberia's settlers endeavor to found them. For the rights in question, those imposing customs duties and limiting the trade of foreigners by restrictions, are sovereign rights, which can only be lawfully exercised by sovereign and independent states, within their own borders and dominions. I need not remind your Excellancy that this description does not apply to 'Liberia' which is not recognized as a subsisting state."

In reporting to his council this statement of Commodore Jones, Governor Roberts presented an able argument in refutation and then said, "I feel, gentlemen, that the position assumed by the British officers . . . will not be sanctioned by the British Government. In the meantime, I would advise [that] a statement, setting forth the facts in relation to the misunderstandings that have arisen between the Colonial Authorities and British subjects, trading at Bassa Cove, be furnished the British Government by the people of Liberia."

But this dignified and exceedingly diplomatic position taken by Mr. Roberts, in reliance upon the British sense of fair play, was of no avail. In April, 1845, Her Majesty's brig Lily entered the harbor of Grand Bassa, seized a Liberian schooner, the John Seys, on suspicion of being engaged in the slave trade, and took it to Sierra Leone for adjudication. Here the schooner was fully acquitted of the slaving charge by the admiralty court. But the entire cost of the proceeding was assessed against the vessel and the British continued to hold the John Seys on the pretext that the Liberian settlers possessed no sovereign rights, that they were not authorized to establish a national flag, and that the John Seys was therefore a vessel having no flag, no national character.[12]

This was the last straw. Governor Roberts was now arguing on familiar ground. "I am decidedly of opinion," said he, "that the Commonwealth of Liberia, notwithstanding its connection with the Colonization Society, is a sovereign independent state, fully competent to exercise all the powers of government . . . [and that] the citizens of Liberia, as an infant Republic, entered into a league or compact with the Society, confiding to them the management of certain external concerns. . . . In this no surrender of sovereignty as a body politic was ever contemplated by the Liberians or understood by the Society. . . . That an arrangement so novel and without precedent should in its operations experience some jarrings is not surprising. . . . We have associated the idea that colonies have always commenced their existence in a state of political subjection to and dependence on a mother country, and for that reason could not be sovereign states nor exercise the powers of sovereignty until that dependence terminated. Hence we often talk as if Liberia needed to go through the same operation. But Liberia never was such a colony; she never was in that state of dependence, and therefore needs no such process in order to become a sovereign state."[13]

It is significant, and certainly speaks volumes for the soundness of Mr. Roberts' argument, that a full century later, Dr. Huberich, a world-renowned authority on international law, reached the same conclusion as did the Liberian Governor, and by the same general line of reasoning.

"That settlement," says Dr. Huberich, speaking of the landing at Cape Mesurado, "marks the beginning of a new state, not the settlement of a colony. The settlers did not retain any political connection with or remain in subordination to any foreign power. They created a state of their own[14]. . . . As an independent sovereign state the settlement had power to extend its frontiers, and acquire sovereignty over the territories acquired by it, and to subject all persons, whether its own citizens or foreigners, to its laws and the jurisdiction of its courts, in the same manner and subject to the same limitations as are imposed by international law on all states. *The British and French Governments were, therefore, wrong** in their contentions that the Settlement could not acquire additional territory, and subject the foreign traders to the laws of the Settlement extended over the new acquisitions. It had the right to subject foreign vessels within its territorial waters to its regulations and port charges, and impose customs duties on foreign imports."[15]

Certain as he was that Liberia possessed and always had possessed the rights of a sovereign power, Governor Roberts nevertheless recognized the confusion that existed in people's minds because of the peculiar relationship with the Colonization Society. He felt that the time had come to sever that relationship; that his country was now fully ready for self-government.

"That some measures should be adopted," said the Governor to his legislative council, "which may possibly relieve us from the present embarrassments is very clear, but how far it is necessary to change our relationship with the Colonization Society for that purpose is a matter for deep consideration. . . . In my opinion, it only remains for the Government of Liberia, by formal act, to announce her independence—that she is now and always has been a sovereign independent state; and that documents of this proceeding, duly certified by the Colonization Society, be presented to the British as well as to other governments, and by that means obtain from Great Britain and the other powers a just and formal recognition of the Government of Liberia."[16]

Governor Roberts was not unmindful of the fact that, sovereign or no sovereign, Liberia owed its existence to the Society. Continuing, he said: "We should remember with feelings of deep gratitude the obligations we are under to the American Colonization Society; they have made us what we are, and they are deeply interested in our welfare; and I firmly believe they will place no obstructions in the way of our future advancement and final success."

So the questions of sovereignty and independence were referred to the Society. On receipt of the Society's reply an extra session of

---

*Italics mine.

the council was called, meeting July 13-15, 1846. After a calm dispassionate discussion of the issues a call was authorized for a special election to determine whether the people were prepared to assume full responsibility for their government. The vote was taken on October 27, 1846, a slight majority voting in the affirmative, about two-thirds of the electorate participating. This result was disappointing, but it was clearly incumbent on the Governor and council to proceed.

The matter accordingly came before the next session of the legislature in January, 1847. That body seemed to be closely divided and a serious struggle impended. But Governor Roberts brought matters to a sudden head by introducing a resolution to determine whether the wishes of the people as expressed in the special election should be complied with. This floored the opposition and a resolution was adopted ordering an election for delegates to a constitutional convention.

The sessions of the convention commenced in Monrovia on July fifth and continued until the twenty-sixth. A draft of a proposed constitution had been prepared by Professor Simon Greenleaf of the Harvard Law School. Mr. Greenleaf came of an old New England family and was a leading member of the Massachusetts bar. His *Treatise on the Law of Evidence* is still regarded as a legal classic. He had become deeply interested in the Liberia project and was president of the Massachusetts Colonization Society.

The Greenleaf draft was transmitted to the convention by the American Colonization Society with its recommendation, and shortly thereafter with its request that a clause be added to the effect that title to the territory should remain vested in the Society. This draft constitution was bitterly denounced by one of the members of the convention, who presented a substitute which he represented as his own, but which was found to be almost identical with the Greenleaf proposal. The Society's request for a clause retaining title was vehemently debated and finally rejected, with the suggestion that this was a matter to be settled between the Society and the new Government.

Finally, after weeks of painstaking work, the Greenleaf constitution, with a few changes, was adopted, subject to confirmation by popular vote.

Meanwhile, and as part of the work of the convention, a "Declaration of Independence" was adopted and on July 26 was signed by all the delegates. Of this document Dr. Huberich says, "As a state paper the Declaration of Independence is characterized by a calm dignity and a clear presentation of the facts of the historical evolution of Liberia. . . . It is not a declaration of political independence, for the Liberian community was from the moment of its establishment a free, sovereign and independent State. . . . The Liberian Declaration of Independence is a political manifesto. It is an appeal addressed to the Nations of the World to recognize Liberia as a member of the Family of Nations, with all the rights and privileges of a free and independent sovereign State."[17]

Before adjourning, the convention adopted a flag, similar to that of the United States, but with eleven rather than thirteen red and white stripes, representing the eleven members who constituted the convention, and with a single star in the blue field.

An election was called forthwith, and of the votes actually cast a substantial majority confirmed the adoption of the constitution. Joseph Jenkins Roberts was elected as first President of the Republic of Liberia. The opposition to the constitution as presented had, however, continued, especially in the Sinoe area, and manifested itself by a considerable number of the colonists' refraining from voting, largely because of sympathy with the plea of the Society that it retain title to the territory, leaving the new Government somewhat in the position of a political tenant. Had all the qualified voters gone to the polls it is probable that the constitution would still have been adopted, but by a very small margin.

During the first week of the convention sessions the British sloop-of-war Favorite arrived at Monrovia. It carried authority from Lord Palmerston, Prime Minister of England, for the commanding officer, Captain Murray, R.N., in the event of a declaration of independence and sovereignty, to salute the Liberian flag and to give assurance that it would be respected by citizens of Her Majesty's Government.

Thus, with the adoption of the Declaration of Independence and the formation of the Republic, British opposition to Liberia's exercise of sovereignty ceased. But, as will be seen, the attack on its political independence was to be replaced by nutcracker tactics by both British and French, exerted upon her boundaries.

The European powers, generally, followed the lead of Britain in recognizing the new Republic, but it remained for Abraham Lincoln, in 1862, to bring about similar action by the United States.

Mr. Roberts served as President from January of 1848 until 1856, and again from 1872 to 1876. He died in Monrovia February 24, 1876, one of Liberia's truly great men. It is in his honor that Roberts Field is named, the great air base built during World War II by the United States Army Air Forces.

The period of emigration to Liberia may roughly be considered as extending to about 1867. At that time, according to the records of the Colonization Society, 13,136 settlers had gone to Liberia, including 1,227 who settled in "Maryland in Liberia." In addition there were 5,722 recaptured slaves sent by the United State Government. After 1867 emigration declined and those who then came are perhaps not to be counted as "settlers." Rather they are people who moved to an already settled Liberia to join their fortunes with those of their race who had become the proud citizens of the Republic.

• *Chapter Six* •

BOUNDARY ENCROACHMENTS

THE constitution under which began the life of the Republic of Liberia was modeled after that of the United States. It set up a government of three branches, executive, legislative and judicial, enacted a comprehensive Bill of Rights, restricted ownership of land to citizens of the Republic, and confined the right of citizenship to people of Negro blood. The race of the European powers for colonial territory in Africa had not really begun, but the founders of the young Republic sensed the danger of conquest by infiltration and effectively provided against it. If Liberia was to retain the independence that had come to it with such difficulty, it must forever safeguard its property rights; must confine them to the purposes for which the colony was founded and the Republic proclaimed.

But these internal defenses against aggression could not prevent pressure on Liberia's boundaries from without. The infant Republic was soon to find itself ruthlessly pushed back out of areas lawfully acquired by purchase or by exploration; despoiled by its neighbors of territory rich in natural resources that had first been coveted and then seized by the British and French colonial powers.

Under President Roberts the Republic set about consolidating its coastal area. By 1856, when Mr. Roberts' first incumbency as President terminated, purchases had been made from the local tribes that in effect extended Liberia's boundary westward a hundred miles or so from Cape Mount to the Sewa River, near Sherbro Island, where the first abortive attempt at settlement had been made. No objection was then raised by the British. In fact, funds with which this area was acquired came from British philanthropists.[1] The Sierra Leone boundary, along about 1825, had been brought to the Sewa by deals between the colonial authorities and the native chiefs. It seemed as though, during the period of President Roberts' administration, there had been a natural and satisfactory determination of where the Sierra Leone coast line ended and that of Liberia began.

But about the year 1860 trouble began. A British trader, John Myers Harris, had established himself on the coast between the Mano and Sulima rivers, within the area covered by Liberia's treaties with the tribal chiefs. Here he defied the Republic's authority. On his refusal to pay customs duties, the Liberian Government sent a coast-guard boat and seized two of Harris's schooners, taking them to Monrovia. Harris then appealed to the Government of the colony of Sierra Leone, and a British gunboat, the Torch, acting under orders from the colonial governor, proceeded to Monrovia and recovered the schooners for Harris by force of arms. The Liberian Government was powerless to resist. It seemed like a recrudescence of the old British trader troubles that had plagued the colonists before the Republic was proclaimed.

President Stephen A. Benson, President Roberts' successor, aware of the seriousness of the situation, journeyed to London in the hope of working out some definite settlement of the Harris trouble. There he met Earl Russell who caused to be delivered to Mr. Benson a dispatch by which the British Government recognized the coastal rights of Liberia from a somewhat vaguely indicated area known as the Mattru in the Gumbo country between the Sewa and Mongrao rivers, eastward to the San Pedro River, about sixty miles beyond the Cavalla River in what is now part of the French Ivory Coast. This eastern area, between the Cavalla and the San Pedro, had earlier been acquired by the "Maryland in Liberia" colony. It was later to be seized by the French. This acknowledgment by Earl Russell on behalf of the British Government substantially confirmed Liberia's claims in the coastal area to the west of Cape Mount.

Harris, backed by the government of Sierra Leone, now protested against the Russell document. He continued to defy the Liberian Government and himself undertook to exercise local authority much like an independent chief. This roused the opposition of the Vai tribe, on whose rights he was infringing, and they began reprisals. Harris then organized a tribal attack against the Vai, and the fat was in the fire. The Liberian Government sent an armed force of militia to support the Vai, and Harris, again with the backing of the Sierra Leone government, demanded an indemnity from Liberia in the amount of £6000. At this juncture an American warship under command of Commodore Robert W. Shufeldt appeared on the scene. Its presence seemed to have some restraining influence on the colonial governor at Freetown, who tried to get the Commodore to act as referee in an arbitration proceeding, a function that the American officer could not, under his orders as an observer, perform.[2] So the attempted arbitration got nowhere in effecting an actual settlement. It served, however, as a sounding board for the British to set up a claim to a protectorate over the entire coast as far east as the Mano River, on the grounds that the Liberians were unable to maintain order. How, the Liberians might have asked, could they maintain order when every time they attempted to do so they were faced by the armed interference of the government of Sierra Leone in support of the law-defying traders?

In 1870 President E. J. Roye went to London where he negotiated a loan of £100,000, under conditions so severe as to discounts, advance payment of interest, and so on, that Liberia realized from it less than £30,000. This caused such a reaction in Liberia that Roye had to resign. It had another unfortunate result. While President Roye was in London he received from Lord Granville a proposal that might have solved the western boundary question quite favorably from the Liberian viewpoint. The Granville plan was to fix the Sierra Leone boundary at the Sulima River, which would have involved a relatively minor concession on Liberia's part, a much smaller loss than they were ultimately to accept. But the Liberian legislature, disgusted with the financial result of the Roye negotiation, refused the boundary settlement too.

Ten years later, the Governor of Sierra Leone, Sir Arthur Havelock, determined to take aggressive action against the Liberians, to oust them from the coastal area between Sherbro Island and Cape Mount and to compel payment of indemnity to Harris.

The Governor arrived off Monrovia with four gunboats, demanded payment of £8,500 for the damages alleged to have been suffered by Harris and consent to pushing the boundary eastward to the Mafa River, which was well beyond anything that had previously been claimed, and would have given to the British colony the important promontory of Cape Mount. The Governor's demands were at first agreed to, but the Liberian Senate balked. Governor Sir Arthur Havelock then repeated his gangster tactics, again arriving off Monrovia with gunboats flying the British flag. Once more the Liberian Senate refused to ratify the steal. So in March, 1883, the colonial government of Sierra Leone took forceful possession of the territory from Sherbro Island to the Mano River, territory which Liberia had bought and paid for and over which it had enjoyed undisputed political control until the Harris disturbances began in 1860.

The American Government was disturbed at these highhanded proceedings. In 1880 Secretary of State Evarts notified the British Government of the interest the United States took in the welfare and security of Liberia. Four years later Secretary Frelinghuysen uttered a similar warning. But the American Government took no active part in the matter.

In 1885 a treaty was entered into between Great Britain and Liberia purporting to fix the boundary. The English very graciously yielded their claim to Cape Mount, for which there was no basis whatever, in return for Liberia's yielding the coastal strip west of the Mano River, territory that had cost the Liberians upwards of $100,000. That fixed the boundary at the Mano, and Liberia had to accept it, for British possession had become a fact and the Liberians had not dared to attempt by force of arms to restrain within the limits of law and order the English traders who had continued to refuse to obey Liberian regulations and whose arrogancy had been effectively supported by the colonial government at Freetown. Inland from the coast the description of the boundary was vague. So in 1903 a joint boundary commission was formed and a survey made, following the Mano River until it intersected the 10°-40′ meridian.

Soon after the completion of this boundary survey and the setting of monuments to mark it, trouble developed between two tribal chiefs in the northwestern corner of the area. Liberia at the time had no military force that could be brought to the support of Chief Fahbunde, who was friendly with the Monrovia administration, and the British offered the services of their own military from the Sierra Leone side of the frontier to quell the tribal war. This offer, which seemed at the time to be made in good faith, was accepted and the British soldiers entered Liberia with the full acquiescence of the Government. There was no suggestion of their doing so in the exercise of any political rights; rather they came offering friendly assistance, their occupancy being somewhat in the nature of a tenancy.

But soon the British began to claim this area on the pretext that Liberia was unable to defend it. President Arthur Barclay sent Mr. Charles D. B. King to London in the hope that the matter could be amicably adjudicated. Mr. King was at the time Attorney General and later became President. The British showed no willingness to yield. This was an especially valuable corner of Liberia, rich in oil palms and cola nuts. The railroad that had been built into the interior of Sierra Leone from Freetown had its terminus close to the border of the territory in dispute. Traffic in local native products was flowing across the border to the railhead.

So a "compromise" was proposed: the British would cede to Liberia an area lying to the north of the Mano River in exchange for the disputed northwest corner. Mr. King protested the unfairness of this proposal. The territory being claimed by the British was thickly settled and economically valuable; that which they proposed to give up to Liberia was dense forest, virtually unpopulated, producing no crops. His argument was in vain. The British Government proceeded to annex the northwest area to Sierra Leone, further adjusting the boundary so as to effect the exchange they had proposed, giving to Liberia the high-forest land above the Mano. Mr. King did succeed, however, in obtaining a money payment of about $20,000 as a refund of part of what the coastal territory earlier seized by Sierra Leone had cost the Liberians, an obvious confession by the British of their former aggression.[3]

This money settlement and exchange of territory had at least the color of a mutual understanding. The Republic was powerless to exact a fairer deal, much less to oust the British from the disputed corner. The Liberians saw no alternative but to accept, and a treaty was finally entered into, fixing the Liberia-Sierra Leone boundary as it stands today.

Liberia had now learned the necessity of a military force to defend its frontier. A first attempt to create such a force was made in 1908 by the appointment of a British officer, one Captain R. Macay Cadell, as Commandant. He recruited a force made up in part of British nationals. France thereupon demanded that French officers be employed too, and it looked as if a plot was in the making to sell out Liberia's hinterland. So the Liberian legislature dismissed Captain Cadell and appealed to the United States for help. A commission of three American Army officers was sent to Liberia, and with their technical assistance an efficient Frontier Force was organized. The United States Army also detailed as Military Attaché at Monrovia Colonel Charles B. Young, a splendid type of colored American.

A glance at the accompanying map will show how the Liberians were progressively pushed back by force or by subterfuge, first from the vital coastal area, then from the rich interior territory. But since the organization of the Frontier Force, there have been no further disputes with the Republic's British neighbors.

While the British were thus despoiling the Liberians of territory to the west, the French were engaged in a similar pastime to the east and north. As early as 1879 the French were proposing to declare a protectorate over the Republic. The American Minister in Paris was instructed to make inquiries as to French intentions. Perhaps the diplomatic hint was enough, for that particular proposition was dropped.

It will be recalled that the colony of "Maryland in Liberia," before it was merged into the Republic, and later the Republic itself, had obtained from the native chiefs title to the coastal area as far as the San Pedro River, the mouth of which is about sixty miles east of that of the Cavalla. Liberia's right to this area seems to have been fully recognized up to about the time when the disputes over the Sierra Leone boundary culminated in the treaty of 1885. Now the French, noting the failure of the Liberians successfully to resist the British pressure, began to assert claims to the territory along the coast from the San Pedro, not only to the

Cavalla River (the present boundary) but as far as Garawe, about thirty miles to the west, including Cape Palmas. They went farther, revived some former shadowy claims to the Grand Bassa area and even to Cape Mount.

By 1887 the French attempts on Liberian sovereignty had reached the stage where a protest was lodged by the United States,

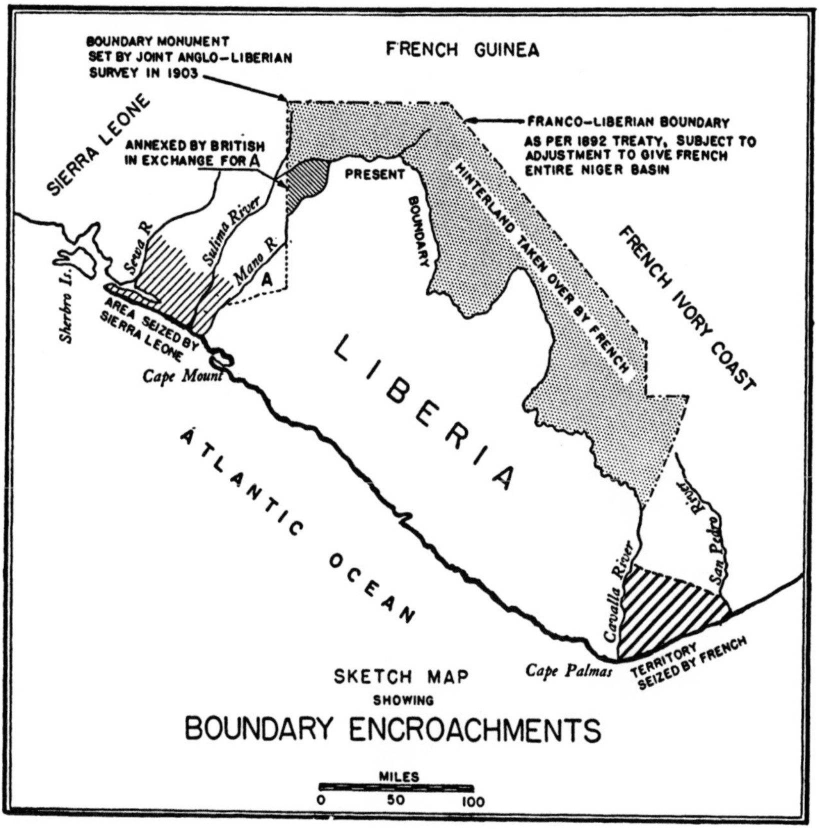

but with only partial effect. For in 1891 the French Government officially communicated to the British its intentions as to Liberian territory. But to Her Majesty's Government, British colonial aims were one thing, those of France quite another, no matter who the victim. Lord Salisbury, then Prime Minister, resisted, to some degree, the French plans, which were then modified to the extent of claiming no farther than the Cavalla River. In October, 1891, the French made formal notification, fixing the boundary between

Liberia and the Ivory Coast by unilateral action at the Cavalla River.

Again the Liberians were helpless to prevent the steal, and on December 8, 1892, entered into a treaty with France defining the boundary as following the right bank of the Cavalla to a point at 6°-30′ north latitude and inland from there by a somewhat vague description. The Liberian envoy who acted for the Republic came home from Paris believing that he had, by agreeing to the right bank, reserved the navigational rights in the river to Liberia, which would have been the case had the definition of right and left banks as understood by navigators applied. But the French insisted, with the weight of usage in their support, that the designation of the banks was determined in the descent of the river.[4] Again Liberia had to yield.

What about the remaining border, that between Liberia and French Guinea? Here the case against Liberia's neighbor as a deliberate aggressor is not so strong. Geographical knowledge of the hinterland, until well into the present century, was vague. In 1858 two Liberians, Seymour and Ash, made a journey of discovery into the interior and published an account of their explorations in London in 1860, in the *Proceedings* of the Royal Geographical Society. In 1868 another Liberian, Benjamin J. K. Anderson, made an exploration that extended well into what is now French Guinea, financed by American funds furnished by Henry N. Schieffelin, and in 1874 he made a second expedition.[5] On behalf of the Liberian Government Anderson made various agreements with the tribal chiefs throughout the territory covered by him. But although the account of his first expedition was made available to the public through the Smithsonian Institution, the Liberian Government failed to take sufficient action to consolidate the political rights to which Anderson's explorations and agreements might have entitled it. Liberia took it for granted that the area of these explorations and treaties had become part of its territory. But it had no Frontier Force, and its occupancy was theoretical only.

Then in 1899 an expedition under the aegis of the French started into the hinterland from the Ivory Coast, headed by a colonial official and a military officer, M. Hostains and Captain d'Ollone. Their exploration was extensive. It included the discovery of the lofty Nimba mountains. As a result of the Hostains-d'Ollone expedition France laid claim to two thousand square miles of territory that the Liberians believed to be theirs.

The French claim was based on an asserted right of discovery. Liberia could not establish its prior claim, and again the helpless Republic was deprived of an area that later proved to be rich in minerals, including gold and diamonds. The loss was clinched by a boundary-defining treaty in 1910. By this time the Liberian Frontier Force was beginning to function and, as had happened on the Sierra Leone side, French attempts at further seizure of Liberian territory ceased.

To the Frontier Force soon fell other duties than the defense of the boundary. Much of the troubles along the frontier had been related to the control of the native tribes. Up to the turn of the century and for a decade or two thereafter there was a more or less constant condition of so-called tribal warfare prevailing. More accurately, as has been pointed out, these "wars" were inter- and intra-tribal raids, conducted by one village or clan chief upon another. Such raids were not peculiar to the Liberian hinterland; they were characteristic of native life throughout a great part of West Africa. With boundary disputes settled, the Liberian Government was faced with the task of subduing the native tribes, stopping their warlike practices.

For this the Frontier Force was available. And for the control of the Frontier Force in the interior, as well as for the exercise of other governmental functions, District Commissioners were set up.

There were no roads in Liberia's interior at this time. Communication was a matter not of hours or even of days, but of weeks. The District Commissioners, isolated from the Monrovia Government but held by it responsible both for maintaining order and for collecting taxes, were in effect petty dictators. It was a situation that naturally bred abuse. The soldiers of the Frontier Force, small armed bands with a minimum of training and of necessity recruited from the more warlike of the native tribes, were easily made the tools of unscrupulous District Commissioners, whose acts could not, under the then existing conditions, be controlled or even reviewed by the central Government.

Nevertheless, and in spite of the scandalous conduct of some of the Commissioners, the tribes were actually and rather rapidly brought under control. Tribal warfare was effectively stopped. The vicious Leopard Society was abolished. The Poro, with its human sacrifices and cannibalistic ritual, was interdicted; then, because of its disciplinary function, permitted to be re-established, but minus its frightfulness. Peace began to reign over the hinterland. There were occasional disturbances, especially among the Kru tribe, who clung to their tribal independence; but finally even they accepted the government of the Liberians. The Kru outbreaks have generally been referred to as the "Kru Wars." They were in fact merely minor tribal troubles, hardly comparable, for example, to the cruel conflicts between the British in the Gold Coast and the Ashantis around the turn of the century and known as the "Ashanti Wars."

Now and then one can hear among the native "boys" a note of dissatisfaction, a bit of quiet and unthinking nostalgia for the good old days when civilization had not encroached on tribal life, but even that is dying out. The natives are fully aware of how much better off they are in a land where they do not live in constant fear of attack from some neighboring village or clan.

The Frontier Force has at times been charged with wanton cruelty. That their practices did not always conform to some of our rather strained and artificial ideas of "civilized" warfare is not surprising, when their origin and the conditions under which they served are considered. But today Liberia's Frontier Force, which is really its Army, is an organization of which the Republic is rightly proud. Brave, well-officered, and well trained, it is an alert and efficient instrument of the Government, making for law and order and noted for its vigor in action.

Of the Government's control of the hinterland, more will be said in a later chapter. The difficulty in effecting satisfactory control, as has been hinted at, grew largely out of the lack of communication, the absence of roads, and, fundamentally, of the capital needed for road construction. This need had long been realized, and attempts were made from time to time to solve the problem by borrowing the necessary funds.

Mention has already been made of the attempt made, as long ago as 1870, by President Roye, and of how the British money lenders sent him back to Liberia without his shirt and with less than £30,000 in his breeches pocket. This debacle, which led to Roye's resignation, was a severe blow. Locally, however, the Liberians were fairly prosperous. Liberian coffee had been a major item of export and its production had been profitable. But about 1875 Brazil began to dominate the coffee market. The price of coffee fell. Liberian coffee was not as well prepared as it might have been. Planters became discouraged, moved into town, took to politics. Government and the practice of the law became their chief occupations. No further steps were taken to obtain borrowed capital until 1906, when another $500,000 was borrowed at 6 per cent, against a pledge of the entire customs receipts. This loan was coupled with the grant of mining and trading rights to an English company. Within two years the Liberians decided that they must get rid of the company.

The American State Department was becoming disturbed about the Liberian situation, partly because of the boundary troubles and the assumption of jurisdiction in the interior. In 1909 Secretary of State Elihu Root recommended the appointment of a commission to study the entire situation. President Taft acted accordingly. The report of the resulting commission is a comprehensive treatise on Liberia. As an outgrowth of it an international loan was arranged in 1912 by American bankers in the amount of $1,700,000. An American Receiver of Customs was provided for, who also acted as Financial Advisor to the Liberian Government. The Customs Receiver was assisted by British, French, and German appointees, who served until the outbreak of World War I, when they were withdrawn, leaving the office entirely American.

This was the situation that obtained with respect to loans and financial administration until 1926, when the arrangement was entered into for the establishment of the Firestone Rubber Plantation. How that came about, how the plantation was started, how it operates and what it has meant to Liberia must be kept for a later chapter. It is necessary, however, to make brief mention here of the Firestone loan because it enters so vitally into the political history of the next few years, during which Liberia had to fight, with the British, its final battle for existence.

It was felt by the Firestone interests that the risks involved in making the investment required for the establishment of the great plantation would be better safeguarded if the then existing international loan were refinanced. The Liberian Government was agreeable, but insisted that the creditor be a separate and distinct corporate body other than the Firestone Plantation Company. So a corporation was formed for the purpose, the Finance Corporation of America, and an agreement entered into whereby it would buy the bonds of the Liberian Government up to a total of $5,000,000, although only part of that amount was to be initially issued. An important part of the agreement, one that later helped to save Liberia from the attack that was soon to be made on its right to continue to govern itself, was the stipulation that no other indebtedness could be incurred by the Liberian Government without the consent of the Finance Corporation. Interest was fixed at 7 per cent per annum and amortization provided for, and there were to be an American Receiver of Customs, a Financial Advisor, an Auditor, etc. The proceeds of the loan were used in the first instance to retire the previous international loan.

With this background of Government finance, and bearing in mind that it would take something like ten years for the Firestone Plantation to come into production and yield any substantial income to the Government, either directly or through the indirect effect of the wages to be paid to a working force, we return to the consideration of the political happenings.

The story of the events dealt with in the next two chapters has, I believe, never been properly told. It is the story of the investigations made by the League of Nations into charges that the Liberians were guilty of practices "hardly distinguishable from organized slave trade." The investigations were so conducted that the world at large was left believing that Liberia was guilty as charged. The various reports filed with the League of Nations have generally been accepted at face value. They have formed the basis of much that has been written and believed about the Republic. That there were guilty individuals among the ruling class in Liberia can hardly be doubted. But when the entire background is examined, against which the charges and the investigations were made, the matter is seen to have been not quite so simple as has generally been assumed.

At any rate, whatever may be the final judgment of the part played by the British and by the League of Nations in the episode about to be described, there resulted a series of reforms that had long been needed, and that fortunately were soon made possible by the changes beginning to take place in the economy of the country. And the attitude of the British toward Liberia has undergone complete change to cordial friendliness.

• *Chapter Seven* •

THE ATTACK

In the late 1920's Thomas J. Faulkner became a candidate for the office of President of Liberia. American born and an able business man, he had become one of the Republic's foremost citizens. An electric light plant in the city of Monrovia, a small telephone system, an ice-making plant, were among the uses to which he put his private capital. His position in the community led him to develop political ambitions.

There were many who believed that a fair count in the two presidential elections in which he stood for office would have made Faulkner president. He himself felt that he had been the victim of fraud at the polls. The repeated failure of his "People's Party" to unseat the administration of President King led Faulkner to seek some means of reprisal. Perhaps by starting a drive in the United States for reform in Liberian affairs he could at least be avenged of his political wrongs.

Circumstances played into his hand. From time to time fantastic tales hinting at the existence of slavery in the Republic had been brought home by casual travellers and had found their way into print. Missionaries returning from various parts of Africa on ships that touched at Liberian ports frequently picked up bits of gossip about Liberian natives being exported to near-by colonies. They were prone to believe whatever rumors happened to be current and to put the worst light on what they heard or saw. These stories, while they sometimes excited the missionary societies at home, generally caused only a ripple of interest on the part of the public, who knew little and cared less about Liberia.

In 1929, however, an important book on the subject of slavery in various parts of the world, including Africa, made its appearance in England and received wide attention.[1] Its distinguished author was Lady Kathleen Simon, wife of the noted British statesman Sir John Simon, who himself wrote a preface for the book. In a chapter devoted to Liberia Lady Simon made a serious attack on the Negro Republic, directed mainly toward the administration of the country by the Americo-Liberians. She bluntly demanded that the Negro government of Liberia be replaced by a government of "strong high-minded white men," a demand that had at least the sanction of her politically powerful husband, if indeed it did not originate with him. Sir John Simon was later to follow up on this demand through diplomatic means.

As to the existence of slavery in Liberia Lady Simon was not entirely specific. She accepted as authentic the hearsay then current, made no personal investigation, presented little by way of established fact. Quite naturally, however, her book, in view of its authorship and the standing of its sponsor, Sir John Simon,[2] was received as authoritative, its charges against the Liberians believed. It had a considerable effect on public opinion in both England and the United States.

At about the same time as the publication of Lady Simon's book, a feature article on Liberia appeared in the Sunday Magazine Section of *The New York Times*.[3] Its author, Caroline Singer, had actually visited Liberia, where she had absorbed some of the usual rumors. Her article was evidently inspired by Faulkner, whose praise it sang. She repeated and emphasized the stories about slavery, and combined this with ridicule of the Americo-Liberians.

About six years before the appearance of Lady Simon's book there had been published in London a volume by Henry Fenwick Reeve, entitled *The Black Republic of Liberia*,[4] which was highly critical of the rule of the Liberians; and in the United States, in 1928, Raymond Leslie Buell, who wrote prolifically about conditions in various parts of the world, came out with a two-volume work, *The Native Problem in Africa*. Buell's study contained purported information hurriedly obtained by him through interviews in Monrovia, from which he attempted to draw conclusions that have since been characterized as "factually wrong and tending to convey mistaken impressions."[5] Lady Simon had drawn partly on these two sources in the writing of her book, with its formulation of her slavery charges against Liberia, as well as her animadversions upon the ruling class in the Republic.

There was actually some ground for the various rumors concerning forced labor in Liberia, by whatever term it might be called. The aborigines of West Africa, when untouched by civilization, live a communal life. The idea of individual property rights is vague. So is that of wages, at least until an outside or foreign employer comes into the picture. The chiefs can command the labor of the natives to clear and maintain the trails, to build roads, to work away from their villages on plantations or even out of the country. Such service is not voluntary. Yet it has quite a different meaning to the native of the African hinterland than it has to the civilized wage earner. Before the turn of the century, actual slavery among the tribesmen was common throughout West Africa. Native chiefs in many of the tribes counted their personal wealth in the number of slaves they held. The raiding of villages for the purpose of obtaining captives to be held in servitude was one of the principal causes, as we have seen, of the so-called tribal wars.

At the time of the agitation fostered by Faulkner, these tribal raids had in the main been effectively suppressed, and in Liberia slavery as such had been outlawed by the Constitution of the Republic. But in the Sierra Leone Protectorate, which is the hinterland governed by the British Colony, actual slavery had the sanction of law until 1928, when the British Parliament made it illegal. Until that time, says Lady Simon, "all efforts to bring about an abolition of slave owning failed." The British Government was "confronted with great difficulties." Lady Simon tells how the system of slavery was deeply imbedded in tribal custom, with no public opinion in the Sierra Leone hinterland demanding or willing to undertake reform. In 1927 the Supreme Court of Sierra Leone, sitting in Freetown, upheld the legality of slavery in this British territory. Lady Simon gives figures showing that in the Sierra Leone Protectorate "persons in servitude" made up more than 15 per cent of the population, the proportion in some areas running as high as 30 per cent. An interesting background for her charges against Liberia!

From the standpoint of the formal outlawing of slavery the Liberians were far ahead of the British. There is no doubt, however, that the ability of the chiefs to assign tribal labor to various projects was in the past abused in Liberia, and that there were instances of such labor being performed, not merely on public works, but for private account, without compensation to the workers.

A once common practice throughout West Africa, wholly aboriginal in its origin and now outlawed in Liberia, was that of "pawning." This was an arrangement, still legal at the time of the Faulkner episode, whereby, in return for money or its equivalent, a human being, sometimes a child, sometimes an adult, would be given into servitude for an indefinite period without compensation to the person so held.

One phase of this practice, while sometimes abused, was in the main highly beneficial: the pawning of native children to civilized families. Often this was done at the behest of native chiefs for the good of the children. Such children were usually required to do household chores, but they were reared in civilized surroundings, usually received an education and often came to be numbered, in their maturity, as full citizens. In fact this was an important factor in the breaking down of the barrier between the ruling class in Liberia and the indigines.

How pawning operated among the tribal people themselves may be glimpsed from an incident in the experience of Dr. Harley that occurred some years ago, before pawning was abolished. Here is the story as the Doctor told it to me, except that I have fictionized the names.

Dr. Harley had employed two men, Yeku and Seweh, to do some work around the Ganta mission. When he came to pay them off, Yeku asked that the money for both be paid to him because, he said, Seweh was his pawn.

"How does that come about, Yeku?" the Doctor asked. The question brought out a complicated tale that started with two other natives, Gundu and Kawi.

Gundu had somehow gotten into debt to Kawi. He couldn't pay. So he gave as security for the debt a belt, which Kawi would return whenever Gundu paid up. The belt had no very great value in itself, but it served as a token, and so was quite as effective collateral as would be a negotiable bond in Wall Street.

Now along came Seweh. He was planning to go to the near-by market town and wanted to make an impression on the natives there. So for this purpose he borrowed the belt from Kawi. Unfortunately, Seweh got into a fight in the market town and the belt was broken so badly that it was no longer fit to serve as a token for the original debt; it was in such condition that Kawi would not accept its return, for neither would it be returnable in its broken condition to Gundu.

In these circumstances, tribal custom required that Seweh assume the full amount of the debt that Gundu owed to Kawi. But when the due date came, Seweh could not pay. Now tribal custom intervened again; the amount of the debt was doubled and a new due date set. Again Seweh could not pay, and another doubling of the amount made his situation hopeless. Fortunately, however, Seweh had a friend, Yeku, who offered to pay the debt provided Seweh would become his pawn. It was the only way out for Seweh. He accepted his friend's offer, became bound to him. Yeku paid Gundu's debt to Kawi and took the broken belt as token for Seweh, for when a pawn is given, some kind of a token must mark the transaction.

There were other situations that gave color to the stories about forced labor. Native villages were required to pay taxes based on the number of huts, the so-called "hut tax." When tax money or its equivalent in rice or other commodities was not forthcoming, payment had to be made in labor. This was not altogether unlike the system of working out taxes on road work sometimes followed in rural parts of the United States, but it was open to abuse by District Commissioners because of their isolation from effective governmental control. Such work on public projects, labor possibly diverted to private purposes, and pawning, were sometimes rather vaguely referred to as "Domestic Slavery." These practices were a commonplace in Africa, including the Belgian Congo and Portuguese Angola.

In Liberia, however, there was another practice, that of exporting native labor, which the British found not wholly to their liking. It had long been the custom, and still is, for Liberian natives living in the coastal area, and especially members of the Kru tribe, to work up and down the entire West African Coast on steamers, acting as stevedores and men-of-all-work. Ships took them aboard both at Monrovia and at Freetown in Sierra Leone, for service that lasted while the particular ship was on the coast, generally a month or six weeks, perhaps longer. Often, too, the Kru boys would work in the adjacent British colonies, especially the Gold Coast. There seems never to have been any question as to the voluntary character of such service. So long as this labor was available to the British, it was not objected to.

But about a thousand miles to the eastward of Liberia in the Bight of Biafra, where the African coast line makes a right angle and turns southward, is the Spanish island of Fernando Po. There a flourishing cocoa industry was in competition with the cocoa of the Gold Coast. To work the cocoa farms on this small but interesting island it had long been the practice for Spanish ships, calling along the Liberian coast, to take aboard gangs of natives and carry them to Fernando Po for what purported to be a two-year term of employment. Normally this was done by arrangement between the Spanish agents and the native chiefs, who marshaled groups of boys and turned them over to the Spaniards for shipment to the island.

In 1914, largely for the purpose of protecting the boys who were sent to Fernando Po, the traffic was formalized by a convention between the Liberian and Spanish governments. Liberia was given the right, among other things, to station a consul on the island for the special purpose of overseeing the conditions of employment. A syndicate of Liberians, mainly connected with the Government, then undertook the recruitment of a specified number of boys per year, for a fee, partly a fixed sum, partly per boy shipped.

Conditions on Fernando Po were never too good. It was not a healthful spot, even for native Africans. Many of the boys succumbed to disease and so never returned to their homes. This was true not only of boys from Liberia; in Portuguese Angola also boys were impressed for shipment to Fernando Po, where they suffered even worse than did the Kru boys. The consuls stationed on the island to protect the Kru boys from cruelty and other improper treatment sometimes had difficulty with the Spaniards, although there is evidence of their diligence in carrying out their tasks; it was to their interest to be diligent, much as it is to the interest of a traffic officer to give out a number of tickets to offending motorists. But the failure of boys to return to Liberia when the two-year period of their contract expired gave rise to all kinds of stories, many of them doubtless true.

The whole arrangement contained the seeds of trouble. It was not difficult to picture the practice of exporting labor to Fernando Po as the equivalent of slave trading. Faulkner could use such charges to stir up the American missionary societies that had activities in Africa. The Simon book, the *New York Times* article, the flood of rumors, all were well calculated to serve his ends.

The British had been constantly prodding the American Government to take a hand in Liberian affairs. They feared that a successful Negro republic in the midst of the African colonies would lead to demands for self-government by the natives under their rule, demands that they were not prepared to grant. There was therefore repeated criticism of the way the Americo-Liberians were administering their government, such as that voiced by Lady Simon.

But there was an economic as well as a political reason for British concern. The Kru tribesmen were the best workers on the coast. More and more, as the cocoa industry developed in the Gold Coast colony, the Krus were depended on for labor on the cocoa farms. The sending of workers from the Kru coast to Fernando Po tended to drain off labor on which the British were relying. If the organized export of natives to the Spanish island could be shown as the equivalent of slave trading, perhaps it could be stopped. The clamor which Faulkner had instigated and which had reached the American Department of State thus gained support from the British Foreign Office, over which presided Sir John Simon.

In the spring of 1929 Mr. Henry L. Stimson took office as Secretary of State. Almost the first thing he had to deal with on joining Mr. Hoover's cabinet was the matter of Liberia. He was horrified at the reports that the descendants of American slaves were themselves carrying on slave trading in Africa. There had been no effective denial of these reports, nor was there any channel for such denial. They seemed to come from authentic sources. The Buell treatise on the native problem in Africa, Lady Simon's book, the cumulative tales of missionaries—all seemingly told the same story. In the light of this, he needed little urging and was ready to act quickly and emphatically.

Under Mr. Stimson's direction the American Minister at Monrovia delivered to the Liberian Secretary of State, on June 8, 1929, a formal note on the matter. It read:

> I am directed by the Secretary of State to advise your Excellency that there have come to the attention of the Government of the United States from several sources reports bearing reliable evidence of authenticity which definitely indicate that existing conditions incident to the so-called 'export' of labor from Liberia to Fernando Po have resulted in the development of *a system which seems hardly distinguishable from organized slave trade*, and that in the enforcement of this system the services of the Liberian Frontier Force and the services and influences of certain high Government officials are constantly and systematically used.[6]

Although couched in diplomatic language, this was a severe indictment of the Liberian administration. It bears evidence of one at least of its sources. The words I have italicised, "a system which seems hardly distinguishable from organized slave trade," is taken almost literally from Lady Simon's book. She said: "the Liberians or American negroes are exploiting the original natives under systems . . . which are barely distinguishable from slavery." Practically the same wording appears in the report of the Christy Commission, the story of whose investigation is now to be told.[7]

President King denied the charges. Indignantly he appealed to the League of Nations, of which Liberia was a member, declaring that "the Government of the Republic will have no objection to this question being investigated on the spot by a competent, impartial and unprejudiced commission." He went further, caused the Liberian delegate at Geneva to advise the President of the League that his Government proposed to form an international commission of inquiry to be composed of three members, one to be appointed by the Government of the United States, one by the Liberian Government, and one by the Council of the League of Nations. This was agreed to by the League.

An Englishman, Dr. Cuthbert Christy, was chosen by the League of Nations to head this Commission. As it turned out, he dominated its proceedings and findings. Dr. Christy was a dentist and also practiced engineering. For a while he had lived in Nigeria, which seems to have been his chief specific qualification as a League of Nations appointee. That he was a man of intelligence and sincerity is beyond question. But he was without legal training, nor, so far as appears from the record, had he had experience as an investigator. Yet he was made both prosecutor and judge in a case of world significance, where a nation was on trial, a case where the witnesses were aborigines who readily worked themselves into a frenzy and adroit politicians whose motives were at best open to question.

Dr. Charles S. Johnson of Fisk University, an American Negro educator, became the member for the United States. Ex-President Arthur Barclay was appointed by the Liberian Government; he was the uncle of Edwin Barclay, who was President King's Secretary of State.

Dr. Johnson and Dr. Christy arrived in Liberia on April 7, 1930; the Commission was formally constituted by President King and began its work.

The inquiry lasted only about four months. During that time hearings were held in Monrovia and near-by Kakata, and visits were made and hearings held by the British and American members at various towns in the Cape Palmas region. To have made an adequate investigation of such serious charges within the short period actually consumed would have been something of an accomplishment even under ideal conditions, with ample communication and transportation facilities, a competent staff of assistants and opportunity for some pre-examination of witnesses to permit a sifting of evidence. It is hard to believe that these inexperienced investigators, under the conditions that actually existed, could have been able even to approximate the careful obtaining and weighing of testimony without which their findings would at best be of questionable validity. Travel was difficult and time-consuming. There were no railroads and few motor roads. The Cape Palmas area was reached usually by sluggish surf boats or by a casual freighter. Communication with prospective witnesses had to be mainly by such crude means as foot-messengers, perhaps even by native "talking drums." Yet the record contains the testimony of more than 250 witnesses, 109 in Monrovia, 145 in other places. Twenty of the witnesses were Paramount Chiefs, eighty-two were sub-chiefs, three were cabinet members, and there were numerous County Superintendents, District Commissioners and other public officials, an impressive list if their examination could by any means have been adequate.

The Commission acknowledged that it met with great difficulty in attempting to collect facts. Often they must have been in doubt as to the credibility of witnesses. At times they were faced with stories of a gruesome nature, conjured up, perhaps, in the lively imaginations of the aborigines. On arriving at a town to collect evidence, the Commission might be met by hundreds of natives—men, women, and children, singing and performing as a protest against the way their relatives had been recruited for export to Fernando Po.[8]

Such scenes may have been, to some extent at least, impressive. Certainly they had high dramatic effect, forming the accompaniment to tales of tribal enmities and raids inextricably mixed with the stories of forced recruiting and the use of the Frontier Force under orders of County Superintendents and other officials.

That the Commission was troubled as to the value of such testimony is evident. "A somewhat unique factor," they said, "has been the extraordinary force of rumors. The Commission feels that it should, at the outset, indicate its awareness of frequently mischievous currents of discussion. . . . The Commission further has found some difficulty in disentangling evidence of fundamental economic and social conditions from an extravagant emphasis upon politics in the Republic."

Surely this was a situation calling for the utmost skill of experienced investigators. Yet there appears to have been no formal examination of witnesses, no competent questioning, no cross-examination. The proceedings were not unlike some of the notoriously political investigations conducted now and then by committees of our own Congress.

A bare five months after the Commission began its work it rendered its report. As to slavery in what they termed the "classic sense," conveying the idea of slave markets and slave dealers, they found it no longer existed in Liberia. Pawning, they found, was recognized in the social economy of the Republic. The Commission referred to evidence that some Americo-Liberians took pawns. But they found no evidence that "leading citizens of the country" participated in domestic slavery. Indeed they said that domestic slavery was discouraged by the Government; that a slave who appealed to the courts might be freed on writ of *habeas corpus* or on direct proceedings against his master or owner.

But the Commission went on to say that forced labor, wastefully recruited, was used for road construction and other public works under conditions frequently involving intimidation on the part of Government officials and the soldiers of the Frontier Force, and that labor recruited for public purposes was in many instances devoted to private use on farms and plantations.

These findings, while they dealt with conditions in the interior that needed, and later received, corrective action by the Government, did not disclose anything that differed greatly from what was more or less common to all the West African hinterland. It was the exporting of labor to Fernando Po, however, that constituted the unique phase of the inquiry and had been the most serious of the matters that had brought about the appointment of the Commission.

Dr. Christy and his colleagues made no visit to Fernando Po. As to operations on the island, they were content to include in their report an implied indictment unsupported by evidence. It is worth note that an inquiry growing out of charges that slave trading was being carried on was directed only to the alleged participation in the traffic by the Liberians; the Spaniards received no attention. But with respect to the recruitment of boys in Liberia, the Commission was very specific, and made direct and serious accusations. The general verdict was that "a large proportion of the contract laborers shipped to Fernando Po and French Gabun from the southern counties of Liberia have been recruited under conditions of criminal compulsion scarcely distinguishable from slave raiding and slave trading, and frequently by misrepresenting the destination. "This traffic," said the Commission, "has had the support of the highest officials of the Republic, and has been organized and conducted by Vice-President Yancy, who has utilized his subordinates to further it to his advantage, he himself being the chief beneficiary."

Despite the questionable methods followed by the Commission in the conduct of their investigation, this verdict with respect to Mr. Yancy and the activities said to have been engaged in by him and under his direction has stood without effective challenge.

The Commission was not content, however, to report only on slavery, for the investigation of which they had been appointed. The entire policy of the Government with respect to the indigenous tribes became the subject of their criticism. So did the general administration of the Republic. Thus they gave voice to the thesis of Lady Simon's chapter on Liberia in her book on slavery—that what Liberia needed was "the collaboration in the actual government of the country of some capable and warm-hearted white administrators."[9]

The Christy Commission's report was dated September 8, 1930. By October, Lady Simon was making public addresses in England charging that "descendants of American negro slaves are now busy in slave owning and slave raiding in Liberia."[10]

President King himself stood ready to accept the recommendations of the Christy Commission, and communicated to the United States a program of reforms which he proposed to adopt.[11] It is to be noted that the Commission's verdict, guilty, had stopped with Vice President Yancy. No accusation against Mr. King was included nor was any intended, although the general language of the report was vague in that respect. But when it became known in Liberia that the President was not only in sympathy with the recommended reforms but was ready to proceed with them a storm of political opposition broke over his head.

It is quite possible that had the Government of the United States stood by Mr. King and shown a little patience until he could assert and make effective his leadership of the Republic, the troubles that immediately followed, and the final British attack on Liberia's independence might have been averted. But it did not turn out that way.

The American State Department received a signed copy of the Christy Commission's report on October 21, 1930. The report was accepted at its face value, not only as to the charges against Vice President Yancy but even its implications and blanket indictments of the entire Liberian administration.

When the report was received Mr. Stimson was deeply engrossed in the major problems of naval disarmament and of American relations with Great Britain. Had he been able to give his undivided attention to the Christy Commission report, so as to make allowance for its shortcomings, or had he taken more fully than he seems to have done the advice of those in the State Department who had experience in Liberian ways, he might have made some differentiation between the valid and the invalid findings of the Commission.

The report, however, appeared on its face to confirm fully what had been reported to the Secretary in the first instance. Accordingly two scathing notes were delivered to the Liberian Government, one dated November 5 and the other November 17. "The Government of the United States is profoundly shocked," said the first of these notes, "at this revelation of the existence in the Republic established in the name of human freedom of conditions not only in tragic contrast to the ideals of its founders but in denial of the engagements entered into by the Republic of Liberia through its adherence to the International Slavery Convention of 1926. . . ." Hardly was the ink dry on this note when the note of the 17th was ordered to be delivered: "This [Christy Commission] report," said Mr. Stimson, "is a shocking indictment of the Liberian Government's policy of suppression of the natives, permitted, if not actually indulged in by nearly all the high officials of Liberia. . . . While direct criminal participation in the shipment of forced labor to the Spanish Colony of Fernando Po, under conditions characterized by the report as 'scarcely distinguishable from slave raiding and slave trading' is established against Vice President Yancy, several district commissioners, county superintendents and many other officials, the President of Liberia and members of his cabinet were aware of these and other abuses. . . . Ten weeks have now elapsed since the formal submission of the report to the Liberian Government. The American Government understands that not only has no action been taken against the officials whose guilt was established therein, but apparently all of these officials continue to hold public office . . . International opinion will no longer tolerate these twin scourges of slavery and forced labor. Unless they are abolished, and unless there is instituted by the Liberian Government a comprehensive system of reform, loyally and sincerely put into effect, it will result in the final alienation of the friendly feelings which the American Government and people have entertained for Liberia since its establishment nearly a century ago."

This was virtually a demand by the American Government that "all of these officials," including the President of Liberia, resign. Meanwhile the Liberian legislature had started proceedings for the impeachment of Mr. Yancy, and the pressure on Mr. King, because of his proposed reforms, was becoming intense. The Vice President did not wait for the impeachment to become a fact. On December 2, 1930, he resigned. President King resigned the following day.

Dr. Christy, who had performed his task conscientiously within the limits of his qualifications, evidently did not realize what would be the reactions to the report of his Commission. He personally took a far less drastic view of what the investigation had disclosed than did the American and British Governments or the public. In a paper read by him before the Royal Geographical Society he outlined briefly the whole matter of the inquiry and gave a definite impression of mildness and impartiality quite different from the interpretations placed upon the official report. "The resignation of Mr. King," said Dr. Christy in this paper, "was probably not the best thing that could have happened in the interest of the Republic." But the Christy report unfortunately was magnified in the popular mind far beyond its literal statements or the intent of its authors. Fiery speeches were made in the British Parliament; editors enlarged upon it; the public, never slow to believe the worst, held Liberia as condemned.

· *Chapter Eight* ·

THE PLAN OF ASSISTANCE

On the third of December, 1930, Mr. Edwin Barclay was sworn in as President of Liberia. He was a nephew of Arthur Barclay, Mr. King's predecessor in office. On Mr. King's resignation, the Vice President having also resigned, Mr. Barclay, who was Secretary of State, became the Chief Executive.

Reporting the event to his government the British Chargé d'Affaires, Mr. Hugh Alex Ford, said: "Mr. Barclay's position will be most difficult. President King, having been forced to resign mainly on account of his professed willingness to carry into effect reforms recommended by the International Commission of Enquiry, Mr. Barclay will have either to repudiate the undertakings of his predecessor, in which case he will have difficulty with the United States Government, or else agree to be bound by them, when he will meet with opposition from his own people."[1]

Mr. Barclay chose to carry out the reforms so far as he was able. Yet both the British and American Governments refused to recognize him as President, even though he had taken office in accordance with the provisions of the Liberian Constitution. Instead, he was dealt with as *de facto* president only, fully accredited representation in Monrovia was withheld, and business with the Liberian Government was handled through Chargés d'Affaires.

It was now the turn of the British Foreign Office to put the heat on. This they did by urging action by the American Department of State. On January 13, 1931, Mr. Arthur Henderson telegraphed Ambassador Sir Ronald Lindsay in Washington instructing him to say that "His Majesty's Government will join with the United States Government in making representations in the strongest terms to the Liberian Government to induce that Government to lay before the forthcoming meeting of the Council of the League of Nations a request for the appointment of a Governing Commission." The telegram to Ambassador Lindsay went on to say that "His Majesty's Chargé d'Affaires at Monrovia is accordingly being instructed to give his full support to any representations which his American colleague may make" and to "inform the Liberian Government orally on the same occasion that failure on their part to make the request referred to above would be viewed by His Majesty's Government with grave concern, and could not but have the most serious reaction on the friendly relations at present existing between the two countries. His Majesty's Government will also exert strong pressure on the Liberian Government to persuade them to apply for a loan under League auspices."[2]

So! The Liberian Government must ask to be put into an international receivership, or else! And the initiative was to be taken by the United States with British cooperation. Furthermore, strong pressure was to be exerted to induce Liberia to violate its agreement with the Firestone interests by agreeing to a loan that would in effect give the League, and thus probably the British, the powerful position of a creditor. With Liberia facing the possibility of financial as well as political bankruptcy, such a loan might be the lethal weapon to end the Republic.

When these matters were put before Mr. Barclay on January 21, he replied to the effect that the suggestion of the appointment of an international commission might be considered an infringement of Liberia's sovereignty, but that they must bow to world opinion and would not be averse to applying to the League of Nations for assistance.

The Liberian Government then formally advised the Council of the League that it had decided to adopt in principle the recommendations of the International Commission of Enquiry, the Christy Commission, to the full extent of its resources, and expressed the desire for assistance with respect to its financial and health problems. As a result the League created a Committee on Liberia, consisting of representatives of the British, French, German, Italian,

Liberian, Spanish, Venezuelan, and Polish governments, to study how to end slavery and forced labor and to take up the financial and public health matters. The United States, which of course was not a member of the League, was invited to send a representative to sit with the Committee, and Mr. Samuel Reber, Jr., was designated for that duty by the State Department.

This formidable but unwieldy committee met at the British Foreign Office in London on March 3, 1931, under the chairmanship of Lord Robert Cecil. It did not itself attempt to devise measures for carrying out the recommendations of the Christy Commission. Instead, it appointed a third, but more workable commission of three experts; M. Henri Brunot of France, who as chairman was to elaborate a plan intended to improve the internal administration of Liberia; M. T. Ligthart of the Netherlands to study the financial problems; and Dr. Melville Mackenzie, an English physician, to plan a reorganization of the public health work.

Meanwhile, early in January, 1931, the Bank of West Africa, a British institution that operated in Sierra Leone, Gold Coast, and Nigeria, and on which Liberia had depended as the sole commercial banking agency in that country, closed its Monrovia branch, ostensibly "because of bad sanitary conditions," but believably as part of the plan to "exert strong pressure" on Liberia.

The Brunot Commission had barely started its work when there arose a situation that was quickly made use of by the British Foreign Office to attack the Liberian Republic from another angle.

Late in 1930 a disturbance broke out in the Kru country which continued for some time and was described in exaggerated terms as a war. The British Chargé d'Affaires quickly reported this "war" to London, under date of January 27, 1932. "I receive," said he, "disquieting reports concerning Kru war indicating unabated serious warfare, destruction of towns, depredations and killing of natives. Government forces appear to be fomenting civil strife, raising forced levies and establishing terror by hunting and exterminating Sasstown tribes. Abduction of men and systematic arrest, persecution and possibly death of persons charged with giving information to International Commission of Enquiry point to importance of early definite action if Kru tribes are to be saved from extermination or permanent disorganization,"[3]

The suggestion that Liberian Government forces were effecting reprisals on natives who had testified before the Christy Commission seems to have appealed immediately to Sir John Simon. Without waiting for confirmation or for further details he instructed his Chargé d'Affaires in Monrovia to go to the Liberian President, accompanied by his French and American colleagues, and say that His Majesty's Government were "satisfied that the proceedings of the Liberian Frontier Force . . . in the Kru country . . . were tyrannical and high-handed in an inexcusable degree." Acknowledging that the Liberian representative had denied before the Council of the League that these events "in any way represented reprisals upon people who had given evidence before the League Commission," the communication to the Liberian Chief Executive went on to say that "His Majesty's Government must, however, irrespective of motives underlying measures which have been taken against Krus, ask for explicit assurance that such proceedings will be discontinued immediately pending conclusion of an arrangement between the League, United States of America and Liberia for the future administration of the country."[4]

In other words, the British, arm in arm with the French and Americans, and as it turned out, the Germans also, regardless of motives and regardless of facts, insisted that the Liberian Government cease to govern, pending such time as it should be superseded by some other "arrangement."

Now, somewhat belatedly, an attempt was made to find out what had actually happened. The British Vice-Consul D. G. Rydings, who was stationed in Monrovia, proceeded to the Kru coast and actually made a careful investigation. His detailed report, while it substantiated some of the rumors of needless cruelty, failed to support the charge that the trouble grew out of an attempt at reprisals for testimony given before the Christy Commission. It had started, Mr. Rydings found, when a Paramount Chief, appointed by the Government, had been deposed by tribal authority and his reinstatement had been attempted. Disorder had followed, and when the Frontier Force was called in, it had gotten out of hand. There was cruelty, taking of prisoners, and burning of villages. Much of the disorder was inter-tribal. Villages belonging to people loyal to the Government had been attacked and burned by disaffected natives. It was not a pretty picture. But it was hardly of the dimensions of an international incident.[5]

Mr. Rydings did find, however, a serious connection between the "Kru war" and the work of the Christy Commission, but not quite the kind of a connection the British charges envisioned. "The unsettled conditions which developed on the Kru coast subsequent to the visit of the League of Nations Commission of Enquiry in 1930," said Mr. Rydings, "were due to the long standing discontent of the natives, occasioned by the oppressive acts and exploitation to which they have been subjected, and the circulation of rumors which encouraged them to believe that a change in the status of administration was imminent." According to the Rydings report, the visit of the Christy Commission was followed by the circulation in the Kru country and adjacent areas of stories of the wildest and most improbable nature that threw the entire territory into a state of unrest.

"These rumors," said the report, "were promoted primarily by the activities of a certain unprincipled adventurer . . . who moved from place to place and stirred up the natives by telling them that the white men were coming to take over the country, that the Liberian Frontier Force was to be disbanded, that war ships were coming to carry away the Americo-Liberians, that they need pay no further taxes, and similar falsehoods. These rumors were carried from place to place and, if not entirely believed, they at least had an unsettling effect." Belief in the truth of the rumors was the more easily accepted because of recollection of the visit, only a few years before, of a British warship to the Kru coast occasioned by the "Kru war" of 1915, at which time it looked much as though the French and British were preparing to take possession and displace the Liberian Government in the vicinity. The Krus at that time had remained in revolt expecting British aid, and the rebellion was not crushed until arms were furnished to the Liberians by the United States. It has even been suspected that the rumors to which Mr. Rydings referred were instigated from London, or at least that their promulgation was encouraged from that quarter. Be that as it may, the part of the report showing the origin of the "war" and the effect of the rumors resulting from the work of the Christy Commission was disregarded, the report misconstrued. The

"Kru war" continued to be a choice weapon with which to attack the Liberian Government, referred to again and again in the discussion with the League of Nations.

The three experts who made up the Brunot Commission arrived in Monrovia on June 13, 1931, presented their credentials, and went to work. They remained until the latter part of July, that is to say for about six weeks. Like the Christy Commission they covered a very difficult, involved, and vitally important situation in a remarkably short time. Their report was placed before the League's Liberia Committee in January, 1932.[6] In many respects it was a statesmanlike document. Various reforms were recommended, the soundness of which were later attested by the fact that most of them were carried out, although not under the auspices of the League but by the Liberian Government itself.

The Commission's fundamental proposal, however, was in effect that Liberia be put into a receivership. It followed closely the recommendation of the Christy Commission and gave form to the idea of a white administration, an idea that Lady Simon had developed in her book on slavery and had urged in public addresses in England, doing much to stir up distrust in that country of the ability of the Negro to govern. To be sure, under the Brunot Commission plan the form of Liberia's government was to be retained, but as a shell only. "Specialists" and "advisors" were to be appointed by the League and clothed by Liberia with authority. The country as a whole was to be districted into three provinces over each of which was to be placed a provincial commissioner and a deputy commissioner, both to be white men. Under them would come the Liberian county superintendents and district commissioners, but the real authority was to be in foreign hands. These provincial commissioners, recommended by the Brunot Commission, were relabeled by the League's Liberia Committee as "foreign specialists" to make the idea more palatable, but their authority was still to be that of administrators, not specialists.

At the seat of government was to be a "Chief Advisor," whose function it would be to tell the President of Liberia what he might and what he might not do. In the event of difficulty in the application of this program of "assistance," recourse was to be had to the Council of the League, which would in such case act by unanimous decision, "the vote of Liberia's representative not counting for the purpose of unanimity." This Chief Advisor was the invention, not of the Brunot Commission, but of the League Committee itself; the Commission did not go so far as to recommend such drastic emasculation of the office of President.[7]

Mr. Barclay had appealed to the League of Nations for financial and technical assistance to make possible the reforms the Christy Commission had recommended. Some of these he had already carried out, those that did not put a strain on the impoverished treasury. But an educational program, a comprehensive public health campaign, road building to open up the interior and make its control possible, these would cost money. The treasury was bare of funds, the external loan in default, current internal indebtedness piling up. It was to solve this problem that the President had asked for help. What he got was a "Plan of Assistance" designed to end the political independence of Liberia. Far from solving the country's financial problem, the Plan, if adopted, would have added an estimated $398,000 per year to the expenses of the Government,[8] doubling its operating budget without even providing for loan interest and amortization. Revenues had dropped, since the world depression set in, to about $450,000 per year. Where was the money to come from?

The League's answer was "Firestone." Their Committee proposed that the Finance Corporation of America agree to a moratorium on the interest and sinking fund payments and a reduction of the interest rate, and that it loan additional funds to Liberia. The League also proposed a restriction on the operations of the Firestone Rubber Plantation, the prospective competition of which with British and Dutch rubber was imminent. For the purpose of such restriction the Plantation agreement was to be amended so as to cut down the acreage available for the planting of rubber trees and to raise the rent payable by Firestone to more than eight times the contractural figure.

It was necessary that the American interests be brought into the discussion. By June, 1932, the loan of the Finance Corporation of America was badly in default. Under its agreement with the Liberian Government, service of the loan was a first charge upon revenues. The situation in Liberia was becoming increasingly critical. The world depression was seriously interfering with the already meagre customs receipts. Taxes were difficult or impossible to collect. There was a growing arrearage in salary payments. The Frontier Force could not be paid. The development of the Firestone Plantation had not yet reached the stage where there was any appreciable volume of rubber being produced and hence there was no support to the Liberian treasury from rubber export duties. As to rubber itself, the commodity that was later to become the great sustaining force of the Republic, the world price, which had been as high as $3.00 per pound, was running around ten cents; at one time it had dropped to three cents. A less bold organization than that of Firestone would have abandoned the entire plantation project, written off its losses including the loan, and gone home.[9]

Instead, when the League plan was proposed, the Firestone interests indicated a willingness to take constructive action.[10] By this time the proposal of the League to cut down the Plantation area and increase its production costs by imposing a higher rental had disappeared from the picture.[11] The Finance Corporation of America, while not yet making a definite commitment, declared itself disposed to giving favorable consideration to such proposals as might be made provided there were sufficient guarantees from the administrative, financial, and judicial angles. The Plantation Company also was prepared to make the utmost possible allowance for the general interests of the Liberian people and for their well-being.[12]

In justification of its plans for a reorganization of the Liberian Government and the appointment of "Advisors" (with power), and of its plan for the proposed increase in the Firestone loan, the Brunot Commission had said: "We believe . . . that such financial aid, for which the Liberian Government itself appeals, can only be obtained if the general situation inspires confidence, and if real guarantees can be given for the judicious expenditure of the money lent and for the service of the interest and sinking fund. We have thus, in execution of our terms of reference, been forced to take a general view of the problem of the restoration of Liberia."[13]

If it had not been for the threat to Liberia's independence involved in the Plan of Assistance this reasoning would have been unassailable. The Firestone people, because of the loan default, were even beginning to feel that the authority proposed for the Chief Advisor might be insufficient to safeguard their interests. The American State Department had endorsed the general principles laid down by the Committee "as a basis for further development of the Liberian problem through direct negotiations between the Finance Corporation and Liberia."[14] It was, in fact, just such a direct negotiation that finally solved the problem as between Firestone and Liberia. But the League did not want the matter to get out of its own hands. Instead, it urged the Firestone subsidiary to send representatives to Geneva to negotiate.

Meanwhile, Mr. T. J. Lyle, Vice President of the Finance Corporation went to Monrovia on a fact-finding mission. On December 15 he had his first conference with President Barclay. Two days later the Liberian legislature authorized the President to suspend payment of interest and amortization on the loan until such time as the Government revenue should reach $650,000 annually. In a sense this was little more than giving legislative expression to the fact that funds for servicing the loan were insufficient. But the debtor-creditor relationship was under great strain and this act did not improve it. In mid-January, 1933, the Government attempted to remove such funds as there were from foreign control by dismissing the American Supervisor of Internal Revenue, who was also Acting Financial Advisor, functioning under the loan agreement, and by cancelling the depository agreement with the Banking Department of Firestone's United States Trading Company. An attempt was also made to float an internal loan covering the floating debt, in violation of the loan agreement.

These rather high-handed steps were protested by the fiscal officers of the Finance Company with the support of the American State Department, and diplomatic relations between the United States and Liberia, already strained by the non-recognition of Mr. Barclay's administration, were at the breaking point.

President Barclay believed that he had taken the only course open to him.[15] The situation was desperate. Because the loan service was a first charge on revenues, funds for the ordinary day-to-day running of the Government were dried up. It was a condition that the President felt could be met only by drastic steps, whatever the consequences.

As was later recognized, the loan agreement was too severe and in some respects unworkable, certainly so when national bankruptcy was impending. It is significant that later, when it was revised after the League of Nations had dropped out of the picture, service of the loan was given eighth place instead of first as a charge against Government receipts.

With the moratorium declaration and the accompanying actions, the whole matter had taken so serious a turn from the standpoint of the American interests that President Hoover sent a personal representative, General Blanton Winship, to Liberia to find, if possible, a solution safeguarding American rights and "restoring a situation which will permit further efforts to assist Liberia."[16] Discussions also took place with the Liberia Committee in Geneva and London in May and June, 1933, participated in by General Winship, Mr. Harvey Firestone, Jr., Mr. Lyle, and Mr. Grimes, Liberia's Secretary of State. It had become clear that the terms of the 1926 loan to Liberia by the Finance Corporation of America precluded the possibility of obtaining financial assistance except from that corporation or at least with its consent. The key to Liberia's future and even to its independence lay with Firestone and its finance subsidiary.

By this time Mr. Barclay had come to the belief that time was playing on the side of Liberia. The Brunot Commission had predicted an increase in the Government revenues. If that should occur, the situation would grow less desperate. It might be possible to stave off League proposals until there should be enough improvement to permit Liberia to get along without the "assistance." If so, the country's independence could be maintained. So a policy was adopted of accepting in principle the League's proposals while stalling their actual adoption, a policy pursued with great skill.

At the Geneva meetings, Liberia's representative offered objection to the expense involved in the League's proposed plan. Mr. Ligthart, the financial member of the Commission, sharpened his pencil and produced more realistic figures. The cost of the "Plan" he now estimated at $150,000 per year instead of $398,000. Ordinary running expenses of the Government he thought could be reduced to $300,000, a figure the Liberians felt would inevitably lead to further salary deferments. The Finance Corporation agreed to a reduction in the interest rate from 7 per cent to five, to a funding of the then existing arrearage by the issue of additional bonds and a similar funding of interest payments in future years whenever the Government revenues should be less than certain stipulated sums. The Finance Corporation was also willing to loan an additional $150,000 to tide over the interval while the Plan of Assistance was being made operative. Definite progress was thus being made with respect to the financial adjustment with Firestone, but not as to the vital matter of Liberia's continued right of self-government.

A complete and formal "Plan of Assistance," based on these revisions in the loan agreement was now adopted by the Committee, less the Liberian representative. The Council of the League accepted the plan as "fair and practical." It was decided to send Dr. Mackenzie to Monrovia "to exert persuasion upon the Liberian Government to accept the plan."[17] The British Ambassador at Washington was also told to consult the American Government as to the possibility of joint action by His Majesty's Government and the United States in support of the plan,[18] and General Winship, who had left for Liberia, with Dr. Mackenzie, was accordingly instructed "to consult with His Majesty's Chargé d'Affaires as to the conveyance of a message to President Barclay." Meanwhile Sir John Simon telegraphed the British Chargé d'Affaires in Monrovia to advise the Liberian Government that the League plan offered an opportunity for Liberia to secure both "the assistance of the League of Nations and a reasonable composition with her principal foreign creditor." If the League plan were accepted, "His Majesty's Government will be prepared to recognize and enter into full diplomatic relations with the existing Liberian Administration."[19]

The reply to this proffer of recognition by Sir John Simon was given to the British Chargé d'Affaires in Monrovia on September 9, 1933, and telegraphed by him to London as follows: "In accepting plan Liberian President has made the following four reservations: Chief Advisor must not be American; powers of Chief Advisor must not violate Liberian Constitution; indebtedness to Finance Corporation should not be increased; amount allotted for Liberian budget is inadequate."[20]

Because Mr. Barclay believed that trade conditions, and hence customs duties, would improve, he was opposed to an increase in the country's external debt. He thought his Government's relations with Firestone might be better handled if the Chief Advisor were not an American. But his main reservation went directly to the heart of the whole matter—the powers proposed to be given to the so-called "Advisors." In arguing this point he had the very able assistance of his Secretary of State, Mr. Grimes, a lawyer of great skill, who commanded respect because of his logic and his diplomatic ability.

The Liberian delegation at Geneva now proposed a number of amendments to the Plan of Assistance, most of which were rejected. To the objection that the Plan endangered the independence of Liberia, Lord Cecil, who was representing the United Kingdom, replied that the Liberian Government was entirely free to accept or refuse the plan; nothing was being imposed on her without her consent.[21] That was in October, 1933. How sincere was the British position with respect to Liberia's freedom of action soon became evident. The following January Mr. Anthony Eden telegraphed to Sir John Simon from Geneva that the Liberian Government had authorized its local representatives to say that the Plan of Assistance was accepted with certain reservations, but that further negotiations between it and the Finance Corporation were necessary with regard to the actual terms of financial assistance. On January 19, 1934, the Council of the League again took up the matter. Sir John Simon himself participated in the meeting and reiterated a statement that Lord Cecil had made for the record: "If the Liberian Government should be so ill advised as not to carry out the scheme *in its entirety*,* then the only consequence would be that the scheme would come to an end and the Liberian Government would again be in the position that it occupies at the present moment."[22]

"The Liberian Government," Sir John went on to say, "must remember that it was that Government which had appealed to the Council for assistance." He neglected to remind the Council that three years previously the British Foreign Office had caused its representative in Monrovia to inform the Liberian Government

*Italics mine.

orally that failure to make such a request of the League "would be viewed by his Majesty's Government with grave concern, and could not but have the most serious reaction on the friendly relations [then] existing between the two countries."[23]

Sir John Simon waited about two months and then again brought up the matter of the Kru tribes. In a telegram to the British representative in Monrovia dated March 16, 1934, instructions were given to say to the President of Liberia: "His Majesty's Government are seriously concerned to receive information which indicates . . . that certain tribes are again being dispossessed and driven into the bush. . . . You should draw the President's attention to fact that barbarous treatment of tribes which Liberian Government previously denied were entirely confirmed by Mr. Consul Ryding's mission of investigation."[24]

Bearing in mind that the gravamen of the charges had been that the so-called "Kru War" had been undertaken in deliberate reprisal for testimony given before the Christy Commission and that this had definitely *not* been substantiated by Consul Rydings, this renewed misstatement by the British Foreign Secretary is a little difficult to understand. But Sir John was not through. "His Majesty's Government trust therefore," he said, "that on this occasion Liberian Government will not content themselves with an empty denial. Note should add that from point of view of Liberian Government moment at which they have laid themselves open to a renewal of the charges is singularly inopportune since May meeting of Council is to afford them what can scarcely fail to be last opportunity of accepting assistance in reform of their administration."

It was in this atmosphere that, in the words of Lord Cecil, already quoted, "nothing was being imposed [on the Liberian Government] without her consent."

Mr. Barclay denied that the assurances given in 1932 with respect to the Krus had been disregarded, and there appears to have been no effort by the British to show that their new protest rested on anything but rumor.

We come now to the Seventy-ninth Session of the Council of the League of Nations, held in Geneva on May 18, 1934. Mr. Eden appeared as the British representative and presented a comprehensive summary of the case against Liberia, from the British point of view. He again referred to the Kru disturbances, recalled that under the League Covenant its members undertook to secure just treatment of the native inhabitants of the territories under their control, and then said that "it was the view of the United Kingdom Government that Liberia had so grossly failed to observe this obligation attaching to her as a member of the League of Nations that the League would be quite entitled to consider her expulsion." Mr. Eden then proposed on behalf of his Government that if the Council decided that the League's offer of assistance must now be withdrawn the United States be approached on the subject, "since that Government appeared to the United Kingdom Government to be that most closely associated both historically and economically with Liberia."[25]

The Liberian representative made a brief reply to Mr. Eden. "The Liberian Government," said he, "had explained that what it desired most was technical assistance that did not encroach upon the sovereignty of the country. . . . Had that wish been observed? Was it not a fact that, by successive modification, the plan as it stood had departed from those principles? . . . The Liberian Government desired above all to safeguard itself against the relinquishment of its sovereign rights. . . . It was in that spirit therefore, and inspired by its desire to be able to accept the plan, that the Liberian Government hoped that the Council would not regard its reservations as a rejection of the plan. . . ." He also referred to the renewed Kru charges and suggested that "the sources of which the United Kingdom representative had availed himself and the oral information he had obtained might be tendentious."

The record had now been made. The Council proceeded to adopt the following resolution: "The Council notes that the plan of assistance requested by the Liberian Government on the 23rd January, 1931, drawn up by the Committee of the Council, and submitted by the Council to the Liberian Government, has been rejected by the latter, And decides, in consequence, to withdraw the offer of that plan of assistance to the Liberian Government."[26]

After the adoption of the resolution, the Liberian representative made a brief further statement: "The Liberian Government regretted the decision to which the Council had come. . . . So definite, however, was the Liberian Government's determination to secure the advice of specialists in its administration, that it had decided to obtain them otherwise than under the plan of assistance." On behalf of the Government he represented, he thanked the League, the members of the Council and the Liberian Committee for their efforts. His Government, he said, "would find in the plan valuable elements, guidance for the future, which it would be able to appreciate, and would remember, and for which it would be grateful to the League."

This ended the British attempt to end the independence of the Republic of Liberia through the intervention of the League of Nations. Mr. Barclay was managing to tide over his country's financial crisis and was soon to come into agreement with Firestone and with the Finance Corporation as to a workable revision of the loan agreement. He had outmanoeuvred Sir John Simon and his colleagues. He had kept intact the sovereignty of Liberia.

Sir John Simon himself wrote the epilogue. In a long communication to Sir Ronald Lindsay, the British Ambassador at Washington, he gave his own not wholly accurate version of the entire Liberian affair, and instructed the Ambassador to dump the Liberian problem into the lap of Uncle Sam. "His Majesty's Government," said he, "are aware of the deep interest which the United States Government have always taken in the fortunes of that State, which indeed owes its foundation to American enterprise and philanthropy. On the material side Liberia is rendered dependent upon the United States Government by the extent to which her financial machinery is already in American hands and organized in conformity with a contract entered into between the Liberian Government and an American Corporation. . . . His Majesty's Government are ready to cooperate to the utmost of their power in any well-considered measures which the United States Government may consider appropriate to the occasion."[27]

But the United States Government had no intention of accepting the British invitation to declare a protectorate over Liberia. In July, 1934, the State Department sent Colonel Harry A. McBride to Monrovia to study Liberian conditions on the spot, get the real Liberian point of view, and see what could be done to meet the needs of the country. Colonel McBride at the time was assistant to Secretary of State Cordell Hull. He had had long experience in the diplomatic service and some years previously had been Collector of Customs in Liberia under the international loan agreement. He enjoyed the confidence of President Barclay and was able to remove many misunderstandings that had stood in the way of a friendly adjustment with Firestone. His visit brought about recognition of the Barclay administration by Washington and opened the way for direct negotiations with the Finance Corporation. Judge Fisher, Firestone's legal advisor, guided the revision of the loan agreement. Full service of the loan was still not practicable, but by the end of 1934 the improvement in the Liberian revenues was such that a token payment of $100,000 was made, applicable to back interest, and the Government's books were closed at the year end with a balance, small but real, in the Treasury.

How the loan fared thereafter, so that it is no longer a problem to either debtor or creditor, will be told in another chapter. The rubber plantation was coming into production, Firestone was taking on additional employees to make the first tapping of its ten million rubber trees. The whole Liberian picture began to change.

A courageous and patient Chief Executive and a constructive, if at times somewhat exasperated American corporation, with its Finance subsidiary, had saved the independence of Liberia.

· *Chapter Nine* ·

FIRESTONE

THE coming of Firestone to Liberia about twenty-five years ago had gradual, but ultimately very important effects upon the entire life of the Republic. It marked the beginning of real American interest in the natural resources of the country, served to block finally and effectively the attacks upon Liberia's independence, and revolutionized her internal economy. Curiously, it all started with the British, who attempted in the early 1920's to force upward to an artificial level the price of crude rubber grown in the East Indies.

Natural rubber is obtainable from a considerable number of plants, some of them weeds. But practically the entire world's supply comes from the tree known to science as the *Hevea brasiliensis*, which grows wild in the Amazon country. Until the advent of the automobile, these Brazilian trees might have been able to supply the needs of commerce. But there were no plantations. Individual trees as they stood in the forests were tapped by the natives and the latex coagulated over smoky fires, producing great balls of black caoutchouc. The area where these trees grew, vast as it was, sustained only a sparse population. There were no roads penetrating the Amazon jungles. The entire output never reached substantial volume in terms of present-day needs. Had this crude source remained the only one from which rubber was to be obtained, it is probable that the age of the automobile would have been greatly retarded.

Every American school child knows how an Englishman smuggled a quantity of the Hevea seeds out of Brazil.[1] It was in

1876 that Henry A. Wickham took these seeds to Kew Gardens in London, where they were germinated in the hothouses and the seedlings taken to Malaya, starting one of the world's greatest agricultural industries where climate, soil and an almost unlimited supply of cheap labor made its development possible. Soon the Dutch followed suit. By the time that production of American automobiles was on a quantity basis, the English and Dutch between them were shipping from the Far East a rapidly increasing tonnage of rubber, the greater part of which was bought by American tire manufacturers.

The temptation to force an artificially high price upon the American consumer was too great to be resisted. It has been asserted that Winston Churchill fostered the idea of making the rubber industry pay off the British World War I debt to the United States through abnormal profits obtained at America's expense, thus paying Paul by robbing Paul, not Peter. Be that as it may, the British Parliament in 1922 passed the "Rubber Plantation Act," generally spoken of as the Stevenson Plan. It required licenses for the export of rubber and empowered the Governor-in-Council of Malaya to make and enforce rules for the trade, including the fixing of an official "fair price."

When the Stevenson Plan became effective, on November 1, 1922, the price of rubber was 14 cents a pound. It immediately was pegged at 36 cents. Later the "fair price" was increased to 42 cents, then to 48. In July, 1925, crude rubber brought $1.23 per pound. By that time rubber manufacturers in the United States were taking 70 per cent of the world's production.[2] It has been asserted that the Stevenson Plan cost the American car owner a billion and a quarter dollars as against the 14-cent price.

The Dutch were invited to participate in the operation of the price-fixing plan, but shrewdly declined. They reaped much of the advantages of the artificial price boosting, added to the area of their rubber plantations, and by scientific culture increased the output per acre, so that their share of the rubber grown in the Far East rose from about 25 per cent to nearly 50.

The Stevenson Plan remained in effect for six years.[3] American manufacturers were in general content to pass along the increased cost of crude rubber to the consumer. Two of them, the United

States Rubber Company and the Goodyear Company, themselves developed rubber plantations in Malaya and Sumatra and so came within the operation of the Plan and stood to profit by the high prices it had created.

There were three men, however, Harvey S. Firestone, Thomas A. Edison and Henry Ford, who were not so complacent about the British-Dutch monopoly of the crude rubber supply. They happened to be cronies, who spent their winters in Florida, at Fort Myers. There they fished together, talked and planned together, decided together to do something about the rubber problem as they sat under the palm trees on Mr. Edison's estate.

Each went about it in his own way. Mr. Ford undertook to bring the rubber industry back to Brazil. Land was acquired on the Amazon in the heart of the country whence the *Hevea brasiliensis* had come. A determined attempt was made to establish there a rubber plantation. But the daily tapping of rubber trees requires a large working force and there were not enough natives in the area to meet this need. Ford had also to cope with the "South American Blight," a fungus disease that killed the leaves of the rubber trees. No solution for this blight problem has ever been found, short of a costly and time-consuming process of double bud grafting.

Mr. Edison turned his attention to the production of rubber from plants that could be grown in the United States. Characteristically he caused thousands of specimens of flora from all parts of the world to be tested. A variety of the common golden rod was finally determined to be most suitable, and by selection and cultivation a giant strain was developed for the purpose, and machinery was designed to grind the plants and extract the latex. The Edison attack upon the problem was to avoid the use of a large labor force by resorting to mechanical means. His death came before the fruition of his plans, but at the Edison Homestead in Fort Myers today are exhibited a specimen of crude rubber produced by the great inventor and an old Model T touring car equipped with tires made from the golden-rod rubber. The rubber Mr. Edison made was good. Whether it could have been produced commercially in quantity and at a price to compete with the Hevea rubber is an unanswered question.

It remained for Mr. Firestone to carry out the successful attack on the cartel-controlled rubber industry. He experimented at first with latex-producing trees in Mexico. The results were disappointing. An attempt to start a large-scale rubber plantation in the Philippines was frustrated politically. Meanwhile a world-wide search was being made under the direction of Mr. Firestone's eldest son, Harvey S. Firestone, Jr., for a location where climate, soil, and political conditions would be favorable for the production of rubber and where an adequate supply of labor was available. Liberia conformed to these requirements. It had the additional advantage of being far removed from the Dutch and English rubber producing areas.

In 1910 a British company had planted some two thousand acres in rubber at Mount Barclay, not far from Monrovia, the Liberian capital. They had given up the project, but when two Firestone men, Donald A. Ross and William D. Hines, examined the trees, their finding was confirmed that the natural conditions were right. By September of 1926 the decision to create a great rubber plantation in Liberia had been made and Mr. Harvey Firestone, Jr., had gone to Monrovia to see what arrangements could be made with the Government there. Outright purchase of the needed land was impossible, for the Liberian Constitution restricted title in real estate to citizens of the Republic. But a long-term leasing arrangement for lands that were in the public domain was acceptable to both Firestone and the Liberian authorities.

Accordingly an agreement was negotiated with President King and his Secretary of State Edwin Barclay. It was enacted into law by the Liberian legislature in November, 1926. By its terms the Firestone Plantations Company was granted the right to lease for a term of ninety-nine years land to be selected by it from time to time as suitable for rubber planting, up to a total of one million acres, at an annual rental of six cents per acre, with the additional provision that Firestone should pay an export duty on all rubber it shipped out of the country, at one per cent of the New York price. A ninety-nine year lease has been questioned as an evasion of the law against foreign ownership of land in Liberia, but the view has held that as a Government contract, confirmed by the legislature, the Firestone lease could not be upset on constitutional grounds.

It was this lease, and the Planting Agreement, that the League of Nations, as we have seen, later attempted to attack, with the obvious end in view of increasing Firestone's costs to the advantage of its competitors in the Far East, and the emphasis was put on the rental price of six cents per acre which was criticised as too low. Some comment on this seems to be in order.

Over a long period prior to the coming of Firestone, many concessions had been granted to various groups and companies for development projects in Liberia. In these no particular set pattern had appeared except one of nonperformance. Early in the 1900's, however, there came into use a plan of land rental combined with royalties for concessions that involved a combination of timber, mining, and agriculture, and of straight land rental where agricultural development was the prime motive. For example, a company known as the Liberian Timber and Trading Company was granted land for the "planting of coffee, cocoa, kola or any other agricultural products" under a lease at six cents per acre. Land was leased to another company for thirty years for a lump sum payment of three hundred dollars per square mile, equivalent, disregarding future interest, to about 1½ cents per acre. The Liberian Rubber Company, whose plantation project antedated that of Firestone, obtained their land at a rental of six cents per acre. The Government, meanwhile, fixed a sales price on publicly owned land of fifty cents per acre for land not favorably located, one dollar for that which was more accessible.

A rental of six cents per acre on land that was yielding nothing and that had a maximum price of one dollar, was fully in line with Liberian precedent. But in the case of the Firestone Plantations Company this acreage rental was by no means the only consideration moving from the Company to the Liberian Government. The export duty, which critics of the arrangement had chosen to overlook, was in effect a part of the rental, and a very real part. At normal yield and price, it would amount to about two dollars per acre, might come to a much higher figure with an improved yield. The British precedent in Malaya was a grant in perpetuity of rubber lands at a rental of about seventeen cents per acre, with freedom from all duties and taxes, present and future.[4] So in fact the Firestone payment per acre to the Liberian Government would amount to ten or twelve times the corresponding Malaya cost. It is not surprising that the attempt of the League to saddle Firestone with a higher rental was not persisted in.

An important phase of the negotiations had to do with the Liberian Government's finances. The so-called "International Loan" of 1912 stood at a little over $1,180,000. It was administered through a customs receivership. In addition there was internal and floating debt in excess of $600,000 and $35,000 owing to the United States Government for monies advanced during World War I. Mr. Firestone felt that the entire public debt of Liberia should be refinanced, preferably by a loan from the United States Government. Back in President Wilson's time such a loan, in the amount of five million dollars, had been tentatively arranged, but had failed of approval by the American Congress. Secretary of State Hughes, with whom Mr. Firestone had discussed the matter late in 1924, was willing to extend the good offices of the United States in facilitating discussions with the Liberian Government, but not to the extent of reopening the question of a government loan. The Liberian Government, on the other hand, objected to a refunding loan being made directly by the Firestone Plantations Company, believing that the tenant corporation, which would also be liable for export duties, should not be the Government's principal creditor.

The upshot of all this was that, as already mentioned, a special legal entity, the Finance Corporation of America, was formed as a subsidiary of the parent rubber company and a loan agreement was executed between it and the Liberian Government. By its terms, Liberia would issue up to $5 million of "External Forty Year Sinking Fund Seven Per Cent Gold Bonds," of which the Finance Corporation would initially purchase not to exceed $2,500,000 at 90. The remainder could be issued when "the total annual amount [of revenues] exceeded the sum of $800,000 for two consecutive years," and must be offered in the first instance to the Finance Corporation. Certain revenues were pledged as security, the National City Bank of New York was designated as fiscal agent, and all revenues and receipts of the Government were required to be deposited in a bank jointly designated by the Fiscal Agent and the Government as the official depository. It was agreed that the President of the United States should nominate and the President of

Liberia appoint a Financial Advisor. No floating debt was to be created without his approval and he was given authority to supervise the collection and disbursement of funds.

The bonds actually issued to the Finance Corporation totalled $2,253,000, which at the purchase price of 90 netted the Government $2,027,700. This sum was applied as follows:[5]

Redemption of the 1912 external bonds, including expenses	$1,180,669.27
Repayment of debt to U.S.	35,610.46
Liberian internal and floating debt	606,234.93
Legal fees, print'g, etc.	22,350.57
Public works, incl. sanitation	168,169.73
Cash balance as at Dec. 31, 1930	14,665.04
	$2,027,700.00

The item of $168,169.73 for public works relates to one of the purposes of the new loan, which was to provide some limited funds for sanitation, roads, and other public improvements, and some of the proceeds were so allocated, although controversy developed as to the integrity of their administration.

There was criticism later of the terms of this loan, and, as has been seen, the loan agreement was voluntarily revised by the Finance Corporation following the League of Nations investigation and its proffering of a "Plan of Assistance." Interest was reduced and a much more workable scheme of priorities in the application of available funds adopted, while a liberal plan was provided for funding interest when Government receipts were inadequate for full service of the loan.

In retrospect, it may be that the Firestone Company and the Finance Corporation, being concerned not only as creditor but more importantly as the promoter of a vast commercial project that was to affect Liberia's entire economy, might have been wise to have arranged more liberal terms for the loan at the outset. But that is moot. Liberia's financial history had not been such as to entitle it to preferred consideration, and generosity, even a selfish generosity, at this juncture might have encouraged irresponsibility. Actually, the loan compared very favorably with similar contemporary international transactions. Belgium floated a loan in 1926 at 7 per cent, issued to the public at 94. Loans at 7 per cent or higher were being contracted for by Argentina, Bolivia, France, Peru, Poland, Yugoslavia. The terms of the Liberian loan were thus quite in line, and any softening in them would have been a matter of policy, not of propriety.

How the loan of 1926 from the Finance Corporation of America served to block the attack on Liberia's independence, made through the League of Nations, has already been told. How it has been administered so as to have been progressively reduced to a fraction of its original amount, until today the service of the loan is a relatively minor figure in a government budget that has the unique distinction of being balanced, will appear from the data set out in a later chapter.

Under Firestone's Planting Agreement with the Liberian Government the Company acquired not only an option to lease the land needed for its Plantations, but important auxiliary rights designed to enable it to develop the rubber project along practical lines. It obtained the right, for example, to construct, maintain, and operate roads and highways, waterways, railroads, telephone and power lines, hydroelectric plants, and a radio station powerful enough for direct communication with the United States. Within the leased areas these rights are exclusive and virtually unrestricted. Outside the confines of the Plantations the rights are nonexclusive, and, although broad, they must be related to the purposes of the agreement, that is, to the operation of the rubber plantations. The original agreement makes provision for tax exemption, including exemption from customs duties, but applicable only to the Plantation project. This exemption might appear at first glance to have been a very liberal provision. Actually what it meant was that the Liberian Government's revenue from Firestone's investment and activity in the production of rubber would be upon the simple and easily administered basis of acreage rental and export duty, and at a rate materially higher than the Malayan planter pays his government. If Firestone engaged in other and unrelated activities, they would be subject to taxation. Thus for example, should a railroad be built to haul rubber from the Plantation to the Port of Monrovia, and should it haul nothing but the Plantation's freight, it would be tax exempt, but if it served also as a common carrier, hauling goods and passengers for others, then to that extent it would be subject to tax. The agreement provided also that Plantation employees shall not be subject to any direct or personal tax, but did not exempt them from property taxes or customs duties. Neither are goods imported for resale by the Company's trading subsidiary exempt from customs duties. The tenor of the tax exemption provisions was to merge what would otherwise be taxable, so far as related to operation of the Plantations, into the general rental and export duty payments, to protect employees from possible discrimination, and then to place all else on the same basis as other property and activities. The Planting Agreement has now been so amended as to provide for the payment by Firestone of an income tax of general application. The resulting payments will be a very considerable help to Liberia.

On the leased land Firestone has exclusive rights, not only as to the growing of rubber and other agricultural products but as to all other activities. If minerals are found on the leased land, only Firestone may mine them, but it would have to pay a royalty to the government up to 10 per cent on the value of any such production, since that is not included in the rent and export payments.

The Liberian Government agrees to "encourage, support and assist the efforts of the Lessee to secure and maintain an adequate labor supply, and to that end the Lessee shall not be required by compulsion of law to maintain a scale of wages, benefits and conditions of employment in excess of (1) the average of the prevailing compensation paid (2) benefits granted and (3) conditions of employment maintained from time to time by other employers of like labor in comparable work for like hours in Liberia and other tropical countries of West Africa." Firestone, on its part, agrees not to import unskilled foreign labor except in the event that the local labor supply is inadequate, and then only as acceptable to the Government.

A very important clause protects the Firestone interests from possible cut-throat competition, such as might conceivably have made its appearance in reprisal, having in mind the causes that led to the Liberian rubber project, the Stevenson Plan, and the British and Dutch monopoly. Here is the clause:

"Upon written notice by the Lessee to the Government of Liberia of Lessee's intention to make selection of land hereunder within a named territory Lessee shall have six (6) months thereafter to select land within such territory and upon the filing by Lessee with the Government within such six (6) months of written notice of the selection of land within such designated territory the title of such selected land shall vest in Lessee for the purpose named in this Agreement.

"It is not intended hereby to deny Lessee the right to make selection of lands hereunder without such previous notification to select with six (6) months; but if such last named notification is filed the same shall have the effect of preventing others from acquiring title within such territory during such six (6) months."

This clause would seem to put Firestone in a position to prevent the starting of any other rubber project in Liberia. That its purpose was to serve as a warning against an unfair attack from without while a heavy investment was being made that would return nothing for more than a decade, may be inferred from the fact that the clause has never been invoked. Indeed, Firestone has encouraged the production of rubber on private Liberian owned plantations, and has constantly stood ready to purchase all such rubber offered to it, at prices determined by reference to the New York market. There are a number of rubber plantations owned by Liberians, whose output, in increasing volume, is handled in this way, and the technical experience of Firestone's scientific staff is at their service, all of which is greatly to the advantage of the local planters.

The success of the Firestone project in Liberia furnishes abundant proof of the soundness of a business policy that looks to the fundamental welfare of the people of the country where it operates, and to that of its own employees. There has been no paternalism in this policy, no catering to false socialistic ideas. But it has recognized that the African natives who make up the great labor force on the Plantations are human beings (a fact that has all too often been lost sight of in colonial Africa), and that the health and happiness of the workers and a gradual improvement in their economic condition are important elements in sound management.

Bearing in mind the general conditions in which the tribal people live, and the evils all too often marking the employment of native labor, the attitude of the Firestone management has exceptional interest. It was expressed at the very outset by Mr. Harvey S. Firestone Jr., in a letter he wrote on December 2, 1926, to President King, amplifying the understanding as to the recruitment of labor under the Planting Agreement. Mr. Firestone said:

"The Company may employ any labor or laborers which the Company may recruit or which may present themselves to the Company at any of its operations or offices for employment without such labor being first required to obtain permission of, or be registered by, the Government.

"Such labor so employed shall be free to bargain for its terms and conditions of employment with the Company and shall be free to sever its employment with the Company at its own will and convenience.

"We desire to point out to the Government again that the success of our development in Liberia is largely dependent upon the organization of a permanent and contented labor force. This can only be done through free and unrestricted employment and upon terms and conditions which are agreeable to the laborers themselves.

"We also desire to inform the Government that its representations regarding labor presented at past conferences received our utmost consideration and the interpretations suggested herein are put forward in a spirit of cooperation and in accord with the Government's problems."

The actual recruiting of labor for the Plantation conformed to tribal customs. Agents of the Company travelled into the interior, met and held palaver with Paramount and Clan Chiefs, and made arrangements with them for the assignment of workers from the villages. In this way groups of natives would be assembled and would travel afoot over the forest trails to the Plantation. So far as practicable every part of the country was drawn upon, in order that the effect on the villages and on their community life might be minimized and the load spread more or less evenly. Usually the chiefs would stipulate that the tribesmen should return to their villages during the dry season to "cut farm"; this, too, so as to interfere as little as possible with local food production. It had the further effect of bringing back into the interior trade goods of all kinds, bought by the workers with their wages. Today many of the workers stay, with their families, permanently on the Plantation. But Fred Helm, who pioneered in the recruitment of labor, still makes periodic trips into the hinterland, sometimes by motor car, sometimes as of old on foot or by hammock over the forest trails.

When the newly recruited workers came to the Plantation they built for themselves and their families mud-hut villages, duplicating the living arrangements to which they were accustomed, but with guidance from the Plantation staff, especially as to sanitary arrangements. These native villages are among the sights of the Plantation, the huts glistening white, the streets straight and clean-swept. As the skill of the workers increased and leaders developed among them, groups of brick houses were built for those who had attained to higher jobs.

One of the first of the installations on the Plantation was a hospital. A sanitation and health survey was made under the direction of Dr. Richard P. Strong of the Harvard School of Tropical Medicine. Schools were established, and a company, the United States Trading Company, organized to import and distribute goods of all kinds. At its store on the Plantation almost every conceivable article of merchandise is obtainable by both the native workers and the members and families of the administrative staff.

The auxiliary activities of the Plantation are numerous and impressive. They include a hydroelectric plant, an intra-company telephone system, a public-service radio system that provides direct communication with the United States, a brickmaking plant, even a carbonizing and bottling plant for coca-cola, a commodity that is spreading all over Liberia, wherever there are roads for its transportation.

On the Plantation there are experimental stations and laboratories for the study of the problems in chemistry, biology, bacteriology, agronomy which are involved in the production of rubber and the upkeep and health of a busy community. At the instance of Firestone, the Yale School of Forestry undertook a comprehensive study of Liberia's forests under the direction of Mr. G. Proctor Cooper III, a study that has recently been extended by a survey under the auspices of the United States Economic Mission. Dr. Charles Schwab's expedition, by which so much was added to our knowledge of primitive native life in Liberia, and whose report, edited and amplified by Dr. George W. Harley, has been largely relied upon in the writing of the present book, undertook his great project through Firestone cooperation.

When work on the Plantation began, in September, 1926, the only road out of Monrovia had a length of twenty-six miles. Access to the Plantation was necessary, and Firestone extended this road to Kakata, doubling its length.[6] This is the road that later was extended across the country to Ganta, Sanniquellie, and Tappita, partly by the American Army Air Forces, partly by contract with the Liberian Construction Company, a Firestone subsidiary. While the work of clearing the thousands of acres of land proceeded, a network of roads had to be built within the great Plantation itself. The total mileage built by Firestone finally reached the impressive figure of over four hundred.

The Plantation Agreement required the payment of rental on a minimum of 20,000 acres. Fifteen thousand had actually been cleared and planted by the end of 1928.[7] Within the next five years the Plantation had grown until 55,000 acres were under cultivation, with a second project well under way in the southeastern corner of Liberia on the Cavalla River. Today the Plantation includes about 110,000 acres and employs some 25,000 workers, about 15,000 of whom are skilled tappers.

It is an impressive sight to stand on the crest of one of the sharp conical hills that dot the main Plantation at Harbel, and look out over the vast expanse of tree tops, stretching far beyond the visible horizon, bright green in the tropical sunlight. One needs strong faith in the truthfulness of figures to convert this visual picture of ten million trees into terms of dry rubber tonnage, for the quantity of liquid latex that each tree contributes when, on each alternate day, it is tapped, is very small, only a couple of ounces. But when two ounces are multiplied by five million, the number of trees tapped each day, then multiplied again by three hundred or so for the working days in the year, and by a factor of something like 33 per cent to get down to the dry-rubber content of the latex as it comes from the tree, the patient mathematician will come out with a figure of over twenty-five thousand tons as the annual output, say 5 per cent of the normal demand of American manufacturers for natural rubber. The actual production of the Plantations in 1951 was 72,588,000 pounds of dry rubber. This integration of minute quantities into the impressive total output of this, the greatest single rubber plantation in the world, appeals to the imagination. Not only is the amount of latex taken daily from each tree seemingly very small, but every tiny scrap of rubber is carefully saved, even the minute film that forms on the plastic cup in which the latex has been caught; even the more minute thread of coagulated latex left in the groove that the tapper has cut in the bark; even the casual drop or two that may have dripped to the ground.

The gathering of the latex begins in the very early morning, soon after dawn. Then the tappers start their work, each tapper tending about three hundred trees. This tapping is a simple operation, but a very exact one. It must be done by cutting diagonally through the outer bark of the tree, half way around the trunk, taking a very thin sliver, about a sixteenth of an inch or less, off the scar left from the previous tapping. The latex is not the sap of the tree; it is an emulsion, tiny particles of rubber suspended in a watery fluid. This latex is secreted in the cortical tissue between the outer bark and the wood. To make the cut the tapper has a special very sharp knife. With it he must cut just so deep and no deeper, or the tree will be permanently injured. Very thorough training of the tappers is thus one of the requirements of rubber production.

As soon as the tapper makes his cut the latex begins to flow, a fine line of pure white liquid slowly moving down the edge of the cut. It looks much like the milk of magnesia with which we are all familiar. At the bottom of the cut a small V-shaped piece of metal has been stuck into the bark, acting as a spout to direct the latex into a plastic cup just below. The flow lasts only a short while, then the cut dries, and nature begins to restore the damage by growing new bark over the wound. The tapping will continue, however, on alternate days until a full panel of 39 inches is completed. Then a new panel will be started, very carefully, on the opposite side of the tree. Thus the process of cutting and healing can go on, year after year, indefinitely.

In the middle of the morning, signals are given by the clanging of bells at the section headquarters, and the tappers go their rounds a second time, collecting the latex from the plastic cups, which they empty into stainless steel pails. The tapper has with him, tied to his belt or to a cord around his waist, a bottle containing ammonia in solution, a few drops of which he has put into each cup when he tapped the tree, so that the latex would remain liquid. Without some such anticoagulant, bacteriological action would begin at once to cause the latex to solidify. He has also carefully stripped each cup of the dried film of latex from the previous tapping, and this he has put into a bag that likewise hangs from his belt. He picks up from the ground any "ground rubber" and puts it into another bag, keeping it separate, for it will have much dirt in it.

Now he comes with his pails of latex to the central station of his particular section of the Plantation. Usually he has two pails, slung from a shoulder stick. He lines up with the other tappers, his pails and scrap bags in front of him, while a chemical test is made to be sure that his latex has had sufficient ammonia put into it when it was running into the plastic cups. Inspection finished, each tapper's load is weighed and recorded. If he has slighted his work it will be apparent from this weighing, which also determines how much more ammonia must be added when the pails are emptied into the receiving tanks.

From these section stations the latex is taken to the great central factory for further processing. Part of it will be sent to the United States still in liquid form, but this will first be concentrated by means of centrifugal machines that operate much like great cream separators and remove about half the water content.

The latex that is to be converted into dry rubber at the Plantation is run into open vats, where it is treated with formic acid. This neutralizes the ammonia and promotes coagulation. The result is a great mass of pure white rubber, which is now cut up into workable pieces and then put through successive calendering machines. It comes out in sheets of crepe rubber, requiring only to be dried, first in the air, then in drying rooms, when it will be ready for baling and shipment. The finest of this, after careful inspection and the cutting out of any imperfections, is the crepe rubber of commerce, from which such articles as rubber soles for shoes are made. Other grades, including rubber made from the ground scraps and even from gleanings from the sweepings of the factory floor, are baled, for use where price is more important than quality. None of it is lost.

Both the Firestone Plantations in Liberia are located on rivers, the main Plantation at Harbel on the Farmington River about fifteen miles from the sea, and the smaller one twenty-five miles from the mouth of the Cavalla River. The Cavalla is navigable for small craft, although the bar where it enters the sea, like the bars at all Liberia's river mouths, makes entrance of ocean vessels impracticable.

The Farmington River was rendered navigable for barges by a major job of snag clearance. Now it serves as a waterway to take the rubber by special diesel-driven craft to the port at Marshall. There, it has been the practice until quite recently for ships loading rubber to anchor about a mile off-shore, the barges coming out to them over the five-foot bar where the surf is at times a bit treacherous. Baled rubber was handled by ordinary ship's gear from the barges alongside. The liquid latex, however, was transshipped at sea by hose and compressed air, portable gasoline-operated compressors being placed on the freighter's deck. A barge-load of latex could thus be forced from the tank in the small craft to the ship's deep tanks in about twenty minutes. The number of barges that could be handled by a ship anchored off shore, especially in bad weather, was limited, and the trip down the river from the Plantation and back again for another load took time. A ship would often be held off Marshall for four or five days taking on a load of rubber that could be handled in a port in a few hours. But until recently no such port was available, and the off-shore operation served the purpose. It is believed that the method of transferring liquid latex at sea by compressed air has been used nowhere else in the world.

The novelty of this surf-port operation is today of historic interest only. With the opening of the new harbor at Monrovia, where ample storage tanks for liquid latex have been built, the surf port at Marshall is no longer used. Instead, special diesel-driven lighters bring the rubber, both liquid and baled, by virtually continuous operation from the Harbel Plantation to the Port of Monrovia, via the Farmington River and the sea, accumulating the material at the port where a ship can now be expeditiously handled.

Now that the Firestone rubber project in Liberia is a proven success, there is no longer any threat of another Stevenson Plan. But a more sinister threat to the world's natural rubber supply exists. The area in the Far East whence comes the greater part of our rubber is in a state of political unrest, with an apparently advancing communistic front. It is fortunate that the problem of an artificial rubber supply has been substantially solved. But even with the advent commercially of the artificial product, America uses about the same quantity of natural rubber as it did before the war. The Firestone Plantations in Liberia are therefore of national importance. It might even be possible, should an emergency so require, to increase the Liberian output considerably, at least for a time, by tapping the rubber trees in excess of what is good practice. That was done during World War II, at some cost to the health of the trees.

Meanwhile, constant improvement in the cultivation of the *Hevea brasiliensis*, with careful selection and budding, is building up the output per acre. For the science of the rubber planter does not stand still.

· Chapter Ten ·

ROBERTS FIELD

In September, 1941, Mr. Averill Harriman was sent by President Roosevelt on a special mission to Moscow. He went by air from Scotland in a nonstop flight of 3,150 miles, a remarkable performance for that day. It had a by-product that was in no way related to the prime purpose of the expedition and that led ultimately to the American development of Roberts Field in Liberia.[1]

One of the two planes that carried the Harriman party flew east on its return trip from Moscow. The other, with Lieutenant Louis T. Reichers as its pilot, returned by flying in the opposite direction, first to Cairo, Egypt, and then over central Africa, crossing the South Atlantic to Brazil and thence to the United States. Both of these flights, the eastward one and the Africa-South Atlantic flight, were exploratory. Landings at the crudely developed airfields along the routes were hazardous. There were no weather-reporting services, no adequate communications, no reliable maps. The short runways where landings had to be made had been built for much smaller planes; they were barely sufficient to permit the heavy bombers either to land or to take off.

But these two flights, although they attracted little attention at the time, pointed the way to the development of routes across both oceans that later became of the highest importance.

England and Russia were both looking to the United States for their principal supply of planes, which were being furnished them through Lend-Lease. Many of these planes were delivered by sea, on freight ships and the decks of tankers. This was the case especially with the fighter planes, because with their great speed and power they had a short radius of action and could not attempt long nonstop flights under their own power over the oceans. But if delivery by air could be made, it would be safer, and of course much quicker.

In November, 1940, a Canadian air-line company undertook the ferrying of American-built bombers across the North Atlantic via Newfoundland, to Ayr in Scotland, an over-seas jump of 2,100 miles. Out of this operation there developed an aerial supply line that, as an instrument of logistics, has been likened in military importance to the first use of the railroad in the nineteenth century.

But the North Atlantic air route was seriously hampered in winter by weather conditions. At times it was shut down altogether. The South Atlantic, even though the over-all distance from the United States to the delivery points was much greater, had the advantage of year-around flying weather. This more than compensated for the difference in mileage.

Even before the outbreak of the Second World War the route across Africa to Cairo had been opened up to some extent by the British. A regular service was in operation between Khartoum and Nigerian Lagos. Airfields of a sort had been built at Accra and Takoradi in the Gold Coast colony, and at Freetown and Bathurst in Sierra Leone and Gambia. There were other airfields that had been cut out of the jungle or built on the trackless desert between Lagos and the Egyptian cities, some in French Equatorial Africa, some in the Anglo-Egyptian Sudan.

The United States, on its part, as early as November, 1940, had made the Pan American Airways its agent in carrying out a national defense project known as the Airport Development Program. This contemplated the building or improvement of landing fields on foreign territory in the Caribbean, in Central America, Brazil, and Liberia. During 1941 plans developed rapidly for delivery of Lend-Lease planes by the South Atlantic route, then across central Africa and through Egypt to Cairo. But the ferrying operation itself was on a small scale; there were many difficulties to be overcome, not the least of which was the scarcity of pilots competent to fly a route still in the pioneering stage.

In July, Pan American undertook a contract to deliver twenty

Lend-Lease planes to the British via the South Atlantic for use on the Takoradi–Cairo run. To carry out the plan for a landing field in Liberia under the Airport Development Program, arrangements were made whereby the Firestone Plantations Company undertook the necessary negotiations with the Liberian Government on behalf of Pan American. An engineering survey led to the selection of a site on the Farmington River adjoining the Firestone Plantation and about fifty miles from Monrovia. Without waiting for a formal contract or even a "letter of intent" that could be looked to for reimbursement, Firestone went ahead with the construction of an airfield that in theory, since America was still at peace, was to be developed as a commercial airport.

Soon hundreds of natives were at work over an area of two square miles, clearing away jungle. A runway was built, and on January 18, 1942, just six weeks after Pearl Harbor, the first plane landed on what had now been named "Roberts Field" in honor of the first President of the Republic of Liberia. Just before the Field was turned over to the Army Air Force, a formal contract was signed between Pan American and Firestone. Meanwhile all of the construction of the airfield, much of the engineering, and all the financing up to near completion were done by Firestone Plantations Company and its staff in Liberia, acting theoretically as a subcontractor of Pan American, who in turn, through the Airport Development Program, were contractors with the U. S. Army Air Force for the construction of this Field.

Meanwhile the British suggested to the United States that their transport service between the African West Coast and Egypt be hooked up with the South Atlantic airplane ferry. This was agreed to, and in July Pan American took over the combined operation. Public announcement of this was made by President Roosevelt on August 18, almost at the same moment that work began in the building of Roberts Field.

With Pearl Harbor and the entry of the United States into the war, the air route across the Narrows of the Atlantic to the West Coast of Africa and thence to Cairo took on a new significance. It continued to be of great importance for the ferrying of Lend-Lease planes. Very soon it became the principal line of communication between the United States and the South Pacific. The

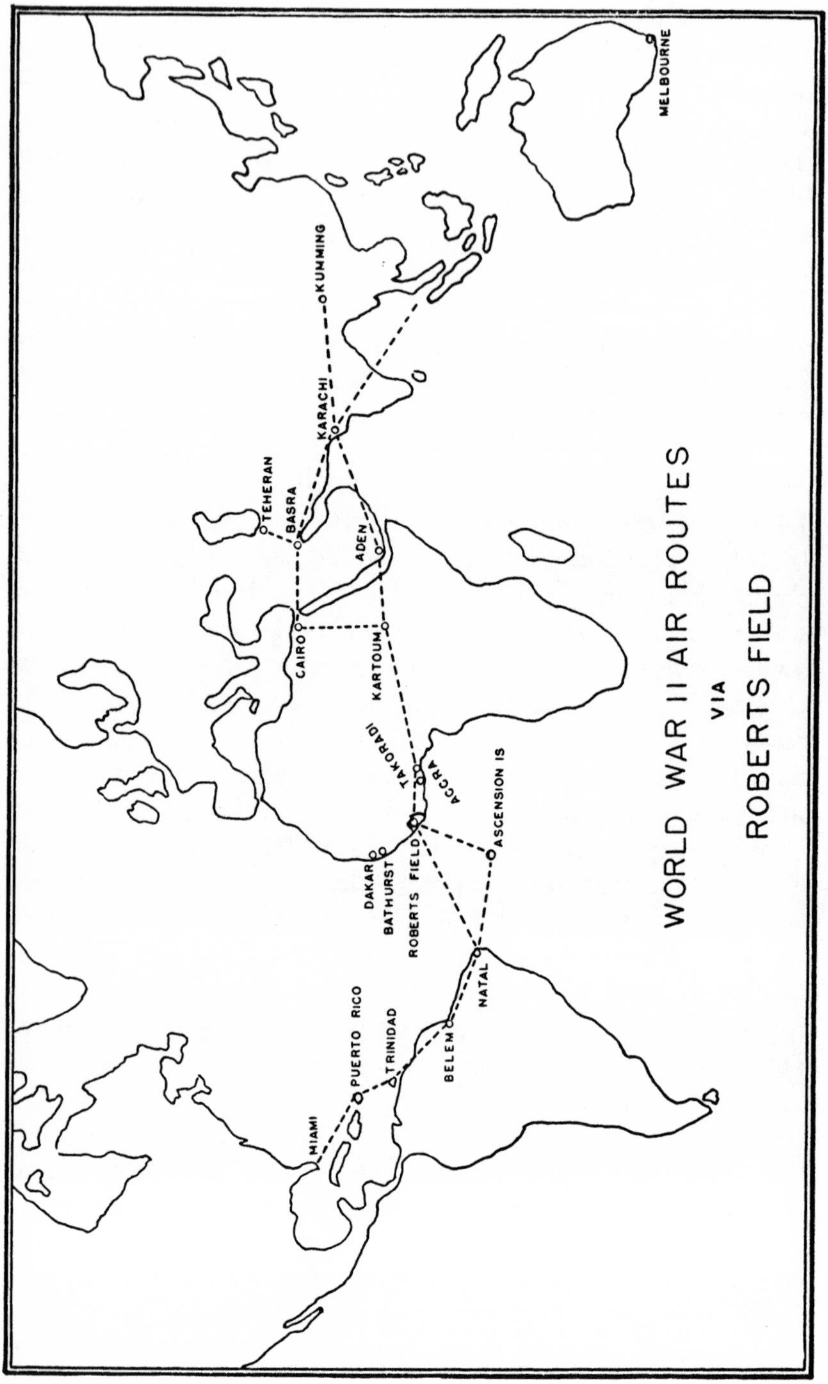

WORLD WAR II AIR ROUTES
VIA
ROBERTS FIELD

normal air route over the Pacific from Hawaii through Midway and Wake to Australia and New Guinea had been cut by the Japs. It was necessary, in order to reach the South Pacific area, to fly east, instead of west. Cairo became the focal point of an air route that nearly encircled the globe. American control of the Narrows of the Atlantic was a MUST of the highest order.

A glance at the accompanying map will give an idea of the strategic significance of this great pathway through the air. From the Florida peninsula to Puerto Rico, thence to Trinidad and British Guinea, to Brazilian Belem and Natal, the planes followed a route that was relatively safe from attack. But the landing points in Africa and the route across the continent were within possible striking range of the Nazis; would be very definitely so if Hitler succeeded in the attempt to seize North Africa. Cairo was the distributing point, where the air-stream divided, part of it flowing toward Southern Russia, part toward India, China, the Straits, and Australia. It was being threatened by Rommel. If Cairo were to fall the entire air route would have to be shifted far to the south, crossing Africa through the Belgian Congo and Tanganyika to Mombasa in the British Kenya colony.

The very fact that Rommel's threat to Cairo might force the line hinging on Natal to be swung southward made the securing of an American-controlled base at the eastern portal of the Atlantic Narrows imperative. The distance across the Narrows is about 1600 nautical miles. From Natal, the oversea hop is about the same to Dakar in French West Africa, to Bathurst in British Gambia, or to Monrovia in Liberia.

Long before Pearl Harbor the danger of an unfriendly occupancy of Dakar was troubling minds in Washington. Already under control of Vichy France, Dakar was infested with Nazi agents. There was the possibility that the German westward thrust that had overwhelmed France might be extended to include the entire Iberian peninsula, that Gibraltar might be invested, Spanish Morocco seized, and all the French territory in northern and western Africa be overrun by Rommel's troops. Dakar could then become a Nazi base for submarines and airplanes, and might seriously threaten both sea and air routes through and over the South Atlantic.

An American base in Liberia was the answer. Strategically,

Monrovia had a slight edge over Dakar, for while it had, geographically, almost the same relation to Natal as did the French town, it was nearer to the sources of important materials that were moving in quantity by sea from Africa to the United States, materials vital to our war production—chrome, copper, uranium, from the Belgian Congo; manganese from the Gold Coast; rubber from Liberia itself. We already had a toe-hold in Liberia, the small landing field that was just being completed by Pan American. But more was needed.

So a special representative of the President was dispatched to Monrovia, Colonel Harry A. McBride, who knew Liberia and its people well from years of service in that country. It will be recalled that Colonel McBride had not only been the Collector of Customs under the International Loan, but had later helped greatly in the restoration of relations between Liberia and the United States after the League of Nations episode. His task was to negotiate an agreement with the Government of Liberia whereby the United States would be able to create and use, in that country, whatever facilities were needed for the support of its operations in the war.

Our envoy, at the outset, met with resistance from some of the Liberians.[2] Their country was not in the war, was a neutral. Communication between the African Republic and the outside world had not been good. War news was reaching Liberia imperfectly; often it was fragmentary, garbled, or deliberately misstated. The Allied situation seemed to the Liberians to be on the verge of collapse. France had fallen; England looked to be helpless under the constant destructive bombing; German armies were threatening Moscow, their eastward push as yet unchecked; Singapore had been lost, a substantial part of the American Navy sunk. Even though Liberia had always looked to the United States as its one real friend among the nations of the world, why should it now subject itself to possible engulfment by becoming needlessly involved?

Colonel McBride had a difficult task in changing this very understandable attitude. He had to convince President Barclay and his colleagues that, discouraging as things seemed at the moment, the real interest of Liberia was still tied to that of the United States.

In the First World War Liberia had found it necessary to

sever relations with the Imperial German Government. The Kaiser's consul at Monrovia had attempted to intimidate the Liberians, threatening them with reprisals "after the happy ending of the war." In fear of the fate that then seemed to await small and weak nations by reason of German aggression, they had sent the consul home and had thrown in their lot with the Allies, only to be shelled by a German submarine. Colonel McBride reminded the Liberians of that unhappy episode and suggested that without the help of the United States Liberia might again find itself face to face with possible annihilation at the hands of the Germans, who had always looked upon Liberia as of great intrinsic value in any attempt they might make to regain their lost African colonies.

He reminded the President that Moscow had not yet fallen and that the Germans might meet the same fate in Russia as Napoleon had met a century and a quarter before; that it was the entry of the United States into World War I that had turned the tide in that conflict; that the British traditionally lost many battles but never the last one; that the great power of the United States must ultimately crush its enemies in this war as it had in the other.

His diplomatic battle was a tough one, but finally he won. The task was made easier by the foresightedness and traditional friendship of the Liberians, who in such dark days decided to cast their lot with Uncle Sam, as they had done in World War I. On behalf of the Government of the United States Colonel McBride concluded a comprehensive agreement with the Government of the Republic of Liberia that became known as the "Defense Areas Agreement."[3]

This document, sometimes mistakenly called a treaty, opened with a preamble reciting that the situation of Liberia was rendered critical by the danger of attack and aggression in the then-existing war, that it needed protection to safeguard the independence and security of the Republic. It then requested aid from the United States. With this general basis for the agreement, the Liberian Government granted to the United States the right, at its own expense, to construct, control, operate, and defend such military and commercial airports in Liberia as might be mutually considered necessary, and to assist in the protection and defense of any part of the Republic which might be liable to attack. The grant included the right, specifically, to construct access roads from Monrovia to the airport which Pan American had built at Roberts Field and to Fishermans Lake, some miles northwest of Monrovia, where a seaplane base was to be established.

The right was included to improve and deepen channels, to construct connecting roads, communication services, fortifications, repair and storage facilities, housing for personnel, and generally to do any and all things necessary. The matter of sovereignty over the occupied defense areas was defined, the exercise of police powers by both governments suitably provided for, and the United States agreed to withdraw at the end of a six-months period following the termination of the war.

The actual provisions of the contract as to the building of roads were permissive rather than specifically obligating the United States to undertake a highway construction program in Liberia. There was, however, something more than an implied obligation for such a program. Liberia, still technically a neutral, was taking a serious step in permitting the creation of an American military base on its soil and its garrisoning with American troops. President Barclay felt that there should be some direct compensation, and in the correspondence that preceded the signing of the Defense Areas Agreement it was made clear that the intention of the United States to make a major contribution toward the solving of Liberia's road problems was part of what moved the Republic to conclude the negotiation with Colonel McBride. The road-building that resulted is reserved for another chapter, but it had its inception in the contract for the construction and use of Roberts Field.

With the signing of the Defense Areas Agreement in Monrovia on March 31, 1942, by Secretary of State C. L. Simpson for Liberia and Colonel McBride on behalf of the United States, the way was open for the development of a major air and military base. The start that Firestone and Pan American had made in determining the best location and in laying out and constructing a runway, even though it was inadequate for the great bombers, was helpful; it avoided lost time in preliminary surveys and the selection of a site and in much of the work of clearing the jungle. But to accommodate planes of the type that would use the field and to make possible the heavy volume of traffic for which it was intended, it was necessary to build much longer runways and to provide facilities for an adequate garrison.

Meanwhile use was made of Fishermans Lake, a large land-locked and shallow body of water just inside the Liberian coast-line some fifty miles northwest of Monrovia, about as far in one direction as Roberts Field was in the other. Here temporary facilities were quickly provided to permit the landing of seaplanes, and a short runway was built for small planes on shuttle service to Roberts Field. An access road from Monrovia to Fishermans Lake was started, as contemplated by the Defense Areas Agreement, but its construction was discontinued when the completion of the major air base made the use of the lake no longer necessary.

The work of rebuilding Roberts Field began actively in the middle of June, 1942, with the arrival on the 16th of that month of the 899th Engineers (Aviation) Company. The first undertaking was the clearing away of the bush and the erecting of tents and then of semi-permanent buildings for Task Force 5889, the 5000 Negro troops who were to be stationed there for the duration of the war. The runway that Pan American had built was repaired. A second, 7000 feet long and 200 wide was completed on Christmas Day, 1942. As traffic increased the original runway became inadequate; it was rebuilt to equal in length the other, and a taxi-way, 8000 feet long was also built, with a roomy dispersal area. Waterworks were provided, an electric plant, a radio beam, and radio communication. Crude in general appearance, Roberts Field was nevertheless adequate and efficient.

The matter of supplying aviation gasoline presented a bit of a problem. It was solved by running a pipe line from the airfield some fifteen miles to the sea, opposite the "surf port" of Marshall, at the mouth of the Farmington River. Tankers could not enter the shallow port any more than could freighters; so the pipe line was extended out to sea on the ocean floor and buoyed, to be picked up by ships loaded with gasoline and coupled to their cargo-discharge pumps.

The Army Engineers were greatly helped by the Firestone organization. The Plantation was right next door. Its hydroelectric plant was in operation and current from it was made available, pending the installation of generating equipment at the air base.

It had a well equipped hospital and a very thorough knowledge, learned the hard way, of the peculiarities of the Liberian natives. Not the least of its contributions to the undertaking was the provision of recreation facilities: a club house with a moving-picture projector; a golf links; a ball field. Life at Roberts Field, even during its most active period, was rather dull. It was one of those spots, essential to the conduct of a great war, where remoteness from the actual combat areas makes it difficult to maintain morale. About the only diversion available at the new airfield, not provided by the Firestone people, was the 307th Army Service Band, which furnished music not only for the forces at the base but also for the civilians in Monrovia, a distinct contribution to amicable relations.

Life at Roberts Field was not altogether without its diversions. There was constant trouble with stealing on the part of the natives. The African aborigine knows little of the theory of property ownership; but he has highly developed acquisitiveness. He will take to himself anything he can lay his hands on, especially if he can do so surreptitiously. It was necessary for our troops, at intervals, to stage extensive raiding parties, which searched the native villages and recovered quantities of stolen goods that ranged all the way from surgical instruments to airplane parts. In dealing with this problem of thieving our Army had the full cooperation of the Liberian Government, which meted out severe punishment to any native caught stealing.

By the time the first 7000-foot runway was completed Roberts Field began a period of activity that was to make it one of the world's busiest staging fields. Before the entry of the United States into the war the South Atlantic route was important mainly because of the ferry service, delivering lend-lease planes to Britain and Russia. Soon after Pearl Harbor, however, Ascension Island, a British possession in the South Atlantic, became available to cut even the short hop from Brazil to Africa in half.

Before the opening of the base at Ascension Island nearly all two-engined planes that were capable of making the Atlantic crossing at all took off from Natal and landed either at Hastings Field in Gambia or at Roberts Field. Heavy bombers were able to fly directly to Accra, but many stopped to refuel at Hastings or Roberts Field. With the assistance of the mid-Atlantic staging point on

Ascension Island, however, not only bombers but fighter planes could make the crossing under their own power.

The all-out struggle to stop Rommel was in progress. The campaign that started with the amphibious landing at Casablanca was in the making. The South Atlantic air route assumed outstanding importance, not only as a supply route but as a support to combat operations. Roberts Field became a base for tactical flights as well as a refueling station.

But the ferry service continued as a major activity of the Liberian base. From a monthly average of about 200 planes in the early part of 1943, the total rose to as high as 600. The traffic moved from Roberts Field in easy stages across Africa by way of Accra and Khartoum, where the route divided. Planes bound for India went, some by way of Cairo, Habbaniya and Basra to Karachi. Others flew across southern Arabia to Karachi via Aden. Planes for Russia went by way of Cairo, and were delivered at Basra or Teheran. Aircraft destined for China, after crossing central India, flew over the Himalayas to Kunming.

Roberts Field became a global Times Square, a real crossroads of the world. The great air route in the operation of which it played so vital a part has been called the "Life Line to the Middle East." It was a route that was held and operated throughout the war.

After VE-Day the military need for Roberts Field rapidly diminished. There was still a certain amount of traffic; one or two military planes a day continued to use it throughout 1946. But after the Army Air Forces were withdrawn, the field was neglected. The two great runways began to show the effect of the tropical rains. Cut here and there by gullies that were not repaired, they were soon in a condition that made their use hazardous.

In 1948 Roberts Field was rehabilitated. The gullies were filled, the landing strips smoothed out, proper fire-fighting equipment was installed, the field brought into conformity with the exacting standards of American practice.

It was first planned to operate a shuttle service to Dakar, connecting with the trans-Atlantic planes. But Pan American World Airways has now made Roberts Field a regular stop on its through service between the United States and South Africa. Two flights a week each way put the Liberian airport within twenty-four hours of New York. Mail service is fast and dependable. Business men have been able to fly to Liberia, attend to their affairs in Monrovia, and be back in New York within the week.

Air France continues to call at Roberts Field on its flights from Dakar to Abijan and Doualla. A regular local Liberian service is operating to the Cape Palmas area and Sinoe. Landing strips in the interior of Liberia are planned; there is one about ready for use at Sanniquellie, and it should soon be possible to reach most of the hitherto inaccessible hinterland in a matter of minutes. When that comes about, political control of the interior, where government has been difficult, will cease to be quite so great a problem.

So by bringing the boon of air communication to Liberia the United States has, in part at least, repaid the Republic for the vitally important rights granted to our Army Air Forces in time of war. It is a repayment that is a benefit to both countries in time of peace, for it is facilitating almost beyond calculation the development of commercial relations between the United States and Liberia and making possible projects of mutual importance.

Meanwhile, Roberts Field remains as a potential military air base, capable, with the consent of the Liberian Government, of again on short notice playing a major part in world strategy. Its value in case of war can be summed up by a remark that President Roosevelt made to Colonel McBride when the Defense Areas Agreement had been concluded. "Never again," said Mr. Roosevelt, "shall the Bulge of Africa be allowed to become a menace to the Western Hemisphere."

• *Chapter Eleven* •

THE ROAD TO GANTA

About thirty years ago, in 1919 to be more exact, a Model T Ford car was landed at Monrovia from a ship anchored off the mouth of the Mesurado River. It belonged to a British firm, Woodin and Company, who had "factories" at all the principal cities of the African West Coast. This automobile had been shipped from the United States and was intended for the Woodin agent in Nigeria. But the crate in which it was packed had been labeled "Liberia." So, because of the mistake of a careless shipping clerk back in the States, it was hoisted out of the ship's hold and sent ashore at Monrovia.[1]

The crated car was much too large and heavy a piece of freight to be handled with safety by the only means then available, the surf boats that were rowed by the natives out to anchored ships and carried whatever had to be moved between ship and shore. But over the side and into the surf boat went the Model T.

Fortunately, by what amounted to a miracle, the boat that was given the job of landing the big box managed to get it through the heavy surf over the treacherous bar, and land it without mishap on the customs wharf. There the agent of Woodin and Company found himself with a bit of a problem on his hands. Bringing the heavy crate ashore through the breakers had been risky enough. To get it on board another ship when one might happen along bound for Nigeria would be tempting Providence. It would again have to run the gantlet of the dangerous surf, would probably be lost. But on the other hand, there was no use for the car in Liberia, or so thought the Woodin agent, for there were no roads—none in all the country.

But there was an American in Monrovia, Harry A. McBride, serving as receiver of customs under the provisions of Liberia's foreign loan, the same McBride who, later, was to negotiate the Defense Areas Agreement of 1942, under which the military base at Roberts Field was created by the United States Army Air Forces. Now, in 1919, this opportunity to get a bargain was too much for him to resist. He offered to take the white elephant off the hands of the discomfited agent—at a price. A deal was made. McBride found himself the possessor of a brand-new Model T Ford car, complete with tools and spare parts. All it lacked was gasoline and a place to go.

In those days the streets of Monrovia were, most of them, impassable for wheeled vehicles. Some were streets in name only, blocked by protruding rocks between which meandered the paths by which the foot-traffic of the city moved. But around three sides of the house where McBride made his home (it now houses Liberia's Treasury Department), was a graded street, and here the first automobile to be seen in Liberia made its debut. Duly assembled, and supplied with gasoline obtained from a passing ship, it could travel back and forth over a course of several hundred yards. It was a real event when the completion of the street on the fourth side of the house made it possible for the Receiver of Customs to drive around and around the block to his heart's content and the wonderment of the populace.

But the energetic McBride soon tired of this. The route and the scenery seemed a bit monotonous. So he talked the matter over with the Liberian authorities and got them interested in the idea of something more of a road, something over which not only his Ford, but other cars that would some day appear in Liberia, could travel with a little more freedom.

Unfortunately there was no money in the Liberian treasury that could be devoted to road construction. Indeed, in those days, there was very little money at all, hardly enough for the bare requirements of running the Government. But that did not daunt the ingenious McBride. He found a way.

In addition to being Collector of Customs, McBride was acting for the Liberian Government as Alien Property Custodian. In his charge was a quantity of goods, textiles, cutlery, tobacco, and so on, taken over from a German trading company when Liberia had entered World War I as a belligerent. This property, especially the tobacco, could be used to pay the workers needed for road building.

So the first automobile road in Liberia was built with German tobacco, thirteen miles of it, extending from Monrovia along what had once been a native foot trail and connecting the capital city with the village of Painsville. Now the Acting Collector of Customs, Alien Property Custodian, and Financial Advisor to the Liberian Government could really step on the gas; he could drive his Model T a good baker's dozen miles along Liberia's coastal fringe. It was a proud day when he could drive President Howard to Painsville.

The total lack of roads, until recently, in this country of 40,000 square miles has probably had more to do, directly and indirectly with its slow development than any other single factor. Only the native foot trails reached into the hinterland. Travel over them was slow and arduous. A journey that by automobile consumes a few hours sometimes took weeks. Transport of goods was confined to head-loads, and the distance that goods could thus be carried was limited. The trails are picturesque and to the inquisitive and venturesome explorer they are interesting. But as arteries of trade they are wholly inadequate.

Now, however, with the episode of the McBride Model T in their minds, the imagination of the Liberians with respect to road building was excited. But there were difficulties in the way. No maps of the country were available with which to plan a system of highways. There was no road-building equipment. There were no engineers in Liberia and no one had any knowledge, other than the crudest, of either road location or construction. Worst of all, there still was no money for such projects. The best that could be done was to put the matter up to the Paramount Chiefs, persuade them to provide the needed labor and let them go ahead, each in his own bailiwick, according as he saw fit, under the general direction of the District and County Commissioners, who might also raise funds for the work by taxing the natives.

So in 1923 President King called the Chiefs into a big Palaver, and the idea was put before them. The program of the Government was to build in each of the five coastal counties a road running from the sea into the interior, five separate roads, each conceived as an artery from the back country to a surf port.

With this general idea as a guide, the work began. Each Chief, either on his own volition or under pressure from the District or County Commissioner, built his own bit of road, pretty much as suited his fancy. Fortunately the tendency was to follow the lines of existing trails, which had the logic of demonstrated travel use. But the result was quite often an isolated bit of highway that could not be reached by any vehicle and hence was almost useless.

The actual work of road building was naturally crude. It was strictly a manpower operation. In lieu of shovels, small metal scoops or even sections of bamboo were used to dig up the earth. Grading was done by native boys who carried the material on their heads in woven baskets. In rare instances there might be a wheelbarrow or two; they would be used, like as not, merely as containers, to be carried, loaded, on the head of a worker. When boulders intervened, they were laboriously broken by building a fire, then quenching it with water to split the rock and permit the removal of the fragments, repeating the operation again and again until the obstruction was finally demolished. The tendency was to straighten out, somewhat, the zigzags of the old trail, but often there were scenic-railway-like grades remaining.

When the great Firestone rubber project was undertaken, road construction became imperative. By that time the highway from Monrovia had reached Carysburg, twenty-seven miles from the capital city. With the help of the Firestone organization it was now pushed on another twenty-nine miles to Kakata, a town that became known, for a period, as the outpost of civilization. Within the Plantation itself a great network of roadways was built, surfaced with the laterite that is easily available throughout most of Liberia, a red iron oxide that packs hard, withstands the torrential tropical downpours remarkably, and makes an excellent road.

Motor traffic over the Monrovia–Kakata road began to grow. Other local roads near the capital were built. Foreigners in and around Monrovia, especially the owners and managers of the trading companies, began to ride in automobiles. Leading Liberians became the owners of cars, in which they took great pride. The road from Monrovia was extended from Kakata to Salala. It now totaled seventy-two miles.

By this time the need for a real arterial highway that would tap the deep hinterland, crossing the country to the Franco-

Liberian frontier, had become apparent. Beyond Salala a series of unconnected bits of road had been built, products of the older project carried out by the native Chiefs. These fragments of road lined up fairly well with what could be a through route from Monrovia to Ganta, on the border between Liberia and French Guinea. But Salala was just at the edge of the coastal plain. Beyond it was the great escarpment that borders the plateau of the interior. It was a serious barrier. The native Chiefs knew nothing of grade contours. The steep slopes and rugged ravines of the escarpment were too much of an engineering problem for their crude methods of road building. And there would have to be bridges, several of them quite long, if the road was to go beyond Salala. So at Salala the lower road stopped, at least for a time.

What followed, looked at from the viewpoint of engineering, was not an especially noteworthy achievement. But politically and economically the story of the building, by the United States Army Air Forces, of the trans-Liberian highway, past Salala, up the hill and on to the St. John River at Ganta, has in it the elements of an epic.

Harry A. McBride, hero of the Ford car episode, again appropriately appears in the picture. It was he, it will be recalled, who negotiated with President Barclay the Defense Areas Agreement that permitted the construction of the air base at Roberts Field. During these negotiations the Liberian President had brought up the pressing need of his country for motor roads.[2] He had pointed out that Liberia, then still a neutral in the World War, would be taking serious risks in permitting a belligerent power to establish, within Liberia, a military base and to garrison it with armed troops. It was reasonable that there should be compensation to Liberia for granting this extraordinary privilege. American assistance in meeting Liberia's need for roads would be an appropriate consideration.

So, although no specific provision was included in the Defense Areas Agreement under which the United States might be required to construct a given mileage of roads in the country, a moral obligation was incurred by the Army for highway building, spelled out quite definitely in collateral correspondence filed by President Barclay with the American Department of State.

The Defense Areas Agreement itself was primarily a grant of

rights to the United States to build and man the air base, although it also required the United States to aid Liberia in defending itself. Included in its grants was the right to create other military works and to build "access roads" as well. Such an access road, extending from Monrovia northwestward toward Fishermans Lake, the large landlocked body of water in the Cape Mount area that was used for a while by American seaplanes while Roberts Field was under construction, was partly built by the engineers of the Army Air Forces, then abandoned, when the seaplane landing was no longer needed. This road, had it been completed, would have connected Monrovia with Robertsport, the county-seat of Cape Mount, and would have brought that whole important area into contact with the capital.

The road-construction obligation of the Americans, however, was thought to have survived the abandonment of the Fishermans Lake project. Now the real objective of President Barclay could be achieved, the extension of the Monrovia–Salala road across the country to the French Guinea border at Ganta, where it would join an already existing piece of unconnected highway that ran on from Ganta to the important town of Sanniquellie. At the President's instance, Engineer Aviation Company 899 went to work on what came to be known to the Army forces as the Salala–Sanniquellie road.

There was no military reason for the building of this road by the American army, or in fact for any further road building. Roberts Field already had adequate access roads, connecting it with Monrovia by the highway that Firestone had caused to be improved, supplemented by the roads within the Plantation which the air base adjoined. But if our Army Air Forces were actually obligated, as indeed they were, to continue their road building regardless of any need on our own part, it did not matter much where they expended their effort and funds. And the completion of a motor road directly across the country would have great economic value for the Liberians.

Work was begun on this project in March, 1944.[3] "The job of the 899th," says one of the official reports, "is to build a road from Salala to Baila, on the St. Johns River, and then throw a bridge across the river, linking the road with the road that runs through French Guinea, thus forming a continuous trade route through

Liberia to the sea." A little mixed geographically, but then the road hadn't gotten as far as Baila. "When the road is opened," the report goes on to say, "that event will mark the finish of one of the toughest, contrariest, cussedest and most onerous jobs ever done in the history of the United States Corps of Engineers"; a bit of hyperbole, forgivable, perhaps, in view of the relief the corps found in facing an active job to break the monotony of hanging around the completed airport.

The road work had to be halted for a while, soon after it was started, because of the heavy rains, but was resumed the following January for another eight months, by which time a total of eighty-six miles of road had been built.

But the 899th Engineers never really finished this road. VE-Day came, and Roberts Field was no longer needed by the Army Air Forces. The garrison was withdrawn, and with it the engineer company, its highway construction work half done. They had gotten quite a kick out of it, for, as one of them reported, they had built through "eighty-six miles of the God-awfullest country that ever improved a G. I.'s cuss vocabulary."

When the 899th Engineers went home, American funds were made available for the completion of the work and the Liberia Construction Company, a Firestone subsidiary, took over. Thus the road was finally put through, reaching the boundary in November, 1947. Its total cost is bound up in the mysteries of Army finance.

The new road soon began to carry an ever-increasing stream of motor traffic, trucks from French Guinea, busses carrying natives packed in about as tightly as possible, jeeps, pick-ups, gasoline trucks, every type of vehicle, working an astonishing transformation throughout the hinterland area affected.

This road building in an aboriginal country had not been without its lighter side. During the regime of the 899th Engineers, a gigantic cottonwood tree had been found lying across the right-of-way just at the far edge of the town of Gbarnga. It had been a sacred tree, so held by the natives of the town because it was a landmark. But an inconsiderate District Commissioner had caused it to be felled, against the protests of the villagers, and it had been left lying just where it fell, a great log eight feet or so in diameter.

Over this enormous tree trunk the medicine men had cast their spell, and to this the natives attributed the fact that the District Commissioner had been unable (perhaps he was unwilling) to remove it. So there it was when the Army Air Forces Engineers reached Gbarnga with their road construction. And there it stayed, for VE-Day came just then, and there they halted their work. But the natives believed that the failure of the Americans to move the tree trunk was due to the potency of the medicine that their *zo's* had worked over it.

Later, when the Liberia Construction Company took over the work of completing the road, the fallen tree had to be removed. Again the natives called in their medicine men to perform the magic. But the Company's engineer ("Jumping Joe" Waller, by name) boasted that his medicine (it was TNT) was stronger than theirs. The villagers all stood around expectantly while Waller went to work. His first charge was preparatory; it stirred the obstruction but did not throw it out of the way. The natives were delighted; their medicine was stronger than that of the white man! But when the second charge was detonated, the great trunk upended, teetered for a moment, then fell clear. The medicine of the American engineer had proved too strong for the spirits of the bush.[4] Today the bulky log may still be seen, lying just off the motor road at the edge of the town, mute witness to the triumph of TNT over the native medicine.

By the time the road was finished, the timbers that the Army Engineers had put in to span the smaller streams were breaking down under the pounding of the motor trucks, many of them brakeless, driven by mad-cap natives who raced down the grades and hit the bridges at the bottom like battering-rams. So the Liberia Construction Company replaced many of these bridges with more permanent concrete structures. One such bridge, spanning the St. John River at Baila, gave them trouble. The river was too wide for a single concrete span and a pier in the middle of the stream was necessary. But the river at that point had been bewitched. The builders were warned by a native witch-woman that a pier in the river at this point could not stand; medicine had been made against it. However, the construction gang went right ahead in the face of the witchery and put in the pier. No sooner had it been completed than it settled about two feet, breaking the back of the viaduct it was supposed to support. The pier itself had created a scouring current in the river that had washed out the foundation. But again the medicine of the American engineers proved stronger than that of the native *zo's*. The foundation was reinforced and protected against the eroding currents; the viaduct was jacked up; the space between the old top of the pier and the superstructure was filled in with concrete, the bridge restored to full usefulness despite the witchery.[5]

How the natives of the hinterland have welcomed the opening up of their country by the road to Ganta can be judged from a report made by President Tubman of an executive council convoked by him in the Central Province in June, 1949, some eighteen or twenty months after the opening of the road. "The Chieftains and People of this Province," said Mr. Tubman, in his sixth annual message to the Liberian legislature, "are taking full advantage of the motor roads that have been built through the Province and are buying sedan cars, pick-ups and trucks. They are further showing an admirable spirit of enthusiasm to have each of their principal towns linked up with the main motor road by access roads and are making application to the Government for tools which Government supplies at their request."

The Monrovia–Ganta road has now been extended to Tappita, in the Eastern Province and deep in the interior. As this is being written, a branch road from Gbarnga to Zorzor in the Western Province lacks only a few miles of completion. Until now, Zorzor has been reached only by trail or by a long detour from Ganta over roads in French Guinea. The Zorzor road has been pushed on a few miles beyond that town to the Wanigisi range of hills, where the grades become an obstacle; when these are overcome, the road can go on to Voinjama and Kolahun, opening up the rich agricultural area and directing the flow of its products toward the Port of Monrovia instead of Sierra Leone, where they now go.

· *Chapter Twelve* ·

THE FREE PORT OF MONROVIA

LATE in January, 1943, President Roosevelt visited Liberia. His stay was a short one, merely a luncheon date with President Edwin Barclay. But it had important results.

Mr. Roosevelt had come by air to Africa for the Casablanca conference. His journey had been across the Narrows of the Atlantic, from Belem in Brazil to Bathurst in British Gambia. He would return over the same route. Just a year earlier there had been brought about the building of the great American air base at Roberts Field. Now, with the exploring curiosity that seems to be a family trait, the President was determined to see, even if for only a few hours, the spot on Liberian soil which had become the center of American air traffic over Africa. Perhaps, too, he was thinking far ahead—of Africa in a post-war world. On his way to Casablanca, flying from Bathurst, he had deviated from the beeline air route, to have a look from aloft at Dakar, that trouble spot on the West African bulge. Now he wanted to see the Liberian airfield, the location of which gave it the same strategic value as Dakar. It was a four-hour flight each way. He could leave Bathurst at seven in the morning, lunch with President Barclay at Roberts Field at noon, and be back at the British airfield in time for a late dinner and a midnight take-off for the trans-Atlantic hop.

At the time of the Roosevelt visit to Liberia, Roberts Field was in full operation, handling thousands of planes. It was even serving as a shipping point for rubber from the Firestone Plantation, for rubber had become so badly needed in the United States that tons of it were going by air. Mr. Roosevelt had heard some discussion of the handicap to operations at Roberts Field because of the lack of any harbor on the Liberian coast. Ferrying supplies for the airfield from ship to shore through the surf that broke over the bar at the mouth of the Farmington River was at best hazardous. Tankers bringing the great quantities of aviation gasoline needed for the planes fueling at Roberts Field had to land their fluid cargo through a submarine pipe line buoyed a mile or more off shore.

The matter of a harbor was, of course, always uppermost in the minds of the Liberians. When Firestone was granted its original concession for the rubber plantation, part of the deal was that the American company would cause a harbor to be built; such a facility was needed for the shipment of the rubber and would have a national usefulness. A study was made by a leading engineering firm, but their report indicated that the cost would be prohibitive; so nothing came of the Firestone harbor project except the absorbing by that company of the cost of the engineering survey.

When Colonel McBride visited Monrovia in January, 1942, to negotiate the agreements for the building of Roberts Field, President Barclay brought up the harbor matter and suggested that the United States do something about it, but it was beyond the scope of McBride's mission.

Now, as President Barclay sat down to lunch with his distinguished guest, he sensed the opportunity to urge again the need for a harbor. He could tell Mr. Roosevelt of the barrier to foreign trade presented by the shifting sands at the mouths of Liberia's rivers, sands that would still be shifting when the war activity at Roberts Field had become a thing of the past, making difficult or even impossible any real development of his country. Mr. Barclay wanted to suggest to the American President the propriety of aid from the United States so that Liberia might have a safe harbor and adequate port facilities, not only on the grounds of the historic relationship between the two republics, but because the strategic location of Monrovia made a prosperous and healthy Liberia a matter of concern to the United States.

But it was Mr. Roosevelt who brought up the matter. Turning to President Barclay he said, "I understand you want to have a harbor built at Monrovia." Naturally Mr. Barclay replied in the affirmative. "Well," said Mr. Roosevelt, "I think it can be arranged." Evidently the seed sown by President Barclay in his talks with Colonel McBride had fallen on fertile ground. The idea had a natural appeal to the American President. His visit to Roberts Field gave emphasis to strategic ideas already in his mind. He was not the first American chief executive to sponsor help for Liberia, but other Presidents had been thwarted by the Congress in their attempts to give assistance to the African Republic. Now Mr. Roosevelt had it in his power, through the Lend-Lease Act, to proceed on his own initiative.

Little more was said at the luncheon about the suggested harbor, but during the meal Mr. Roosevelt remarked to his host that he hoped Mr. Barclay would visit him in Washington. The Liberian President took this as intended to be merely a gesture, a casual courtesy not to be taken seriously. But it was not casual. Soon a formal invitation came from the White House, and Mr. Barclay, after consulting his legislature, made the trip to the United States, accompanied by Mr. Tubman who, as President-elect, would soon succeed to the presidency of Liberia.

While President Barclay and Mr. Tubman were guests at the White House, the matter of the harbor was thoroughly discussed. Mr. Barclay wanted the harbor to be built by the engineers of the American Navy, that is to say, by the Bureau of Yards and Docks. But that could not be; the Navy had a war on its hands, and besides there was a legal question as to whether it could be so employed on foreign soil, working, in effect, for a foreign power. So it was arranged that the Liberan President would nominate some outstanding private American engineering concern to do the work under contract with the Liberian Government, backed by lend-lease funds.[1]

The project quickly became the subject of official action. The Joint Chiefs of Staff were favorably impressed. The Navy Department was strongly in favor. The State Department, working closely with the Lend-Lease Administration, undertook its sponsorship. On June 16, 1943, Secretary Hull addressed a letter to the President in which he said:

"In view of your recently expressed interest in the construction of a port in Liberia, particularly for naval purposes . . . we are of the opinion that it would be advisable to have an official survey made as a first step in determining the site which would best serve our naval purposes and the economic needs of Liberia. . . . The Office of Lend Lease Administration included a provisional estimate in its budget for the fiscal year 1944 of $6,000,000 for allocation to Liberia for the possible construction of a port and for other purposes, and a lump sum appropriation embracing this amount along with funds for certain other uses has been approved by the Congress. . . ."[2]

The "other purposes" mentioned in Mr. Hull's letter contemplated an economic survey of Liberia and its resources, with the ultimate objective of inducing private American capital to seek investment there. If that should result, it was the hope that revenue would be derived from commercial projects that could be applied toward the repayment of Lend-Lease funds employed in building the proposed port. "If the amount needed should not be considerably in excess of the figure indicated," said Mr. Hull, "it is anticipated that port revenues would cover amortization within a reasonable period of time, provided the economic development program envisaged by the Department should be carried forward. . . . Thus managed, and unless unforeseen factors arise, there should be no ultimate cost to the Government, as both projects should pay for themselves, and meanwhile many advantages, commercial, strategic and political would accrue to this country as well as to Liberia. . . ."[3]

Mr. Barclay's visit to the United States was nearly over; he would leave for Liberia on the eighteenth of June. On that date the President sent to the State Department an informal note on White House memorandum paper, unsigned, but with typed "F. D. R." (a frequent practice of Mr. Roosevelt's) as follows:

> Memorandum for Hon. Cordell Hull.
>
> I have referred your letter in regard to a port in Liberia to the Navy Department. I agree with you that they should make a survey. You can tell this to the President of Liberia.
>
> F. D. R.

This was followed, on July 3, 1943, by a formal letter to the Secretary of State in which the President records the recommendation of the Secretary of the Navy that the construction of the port be proceeded with and that provision be made in the port for the establishment of an outlying base for submarines and patrols. "The interest of the Navy Department," said Mr. Roosevelt, "is associated with the security of South America, particularly Brazil. . . ."

By September 4, preliminary surveys had been made by the Navy Department. Two possible sites were suggested, one at the estuary of the St. Paul River, some five or six miles north of Monrovia, the other at Momba Point, which is the end of the peninsula on which the capital city is built. By the time this survey was reported on, the estimate had risen to $8,580,000. Lend Lease said it had funds available for the project on receipt of a directive from the President. The Secretary of State recommended that the work be proceeded with as soon as possible.[4]

The requested directive from the President was forthcoming in the form of a letter to the Secretary of State dated September 14, 1943. It read:

> Dear Mr. Secretary:
>
> The recommendation in your letter of 4 September 1943 for the construction of a port in Liberia meets with my approval. In concluding your negotiations in this matter with the Liberian Government provision should be made for protection of United States military, air and naval interests in the port, with particular reference to our future operational rights there.
>
> Allocation of Lend-Lease funds for this project within the general limitation outlined in your letter is authorized. It is to be understood, however, that the work shall be performed by private contractors since military and naval personnel cannot be assigned without detriment to the war effort.
>
> Very sincerely yours
> (Signed) FRANKLIN D. ROOSEVELT.

On receipt of this authorization Mr. Hull informed Mr. Edward R. Stettinius, Jr., the Lend-Lease Administrator, of the decision to proceed and advised him that the Liberian Consul General in New York, who was the African Republic's only diplomatic representative in the United States at the time, had been requested to consult with him concerning procedure in requisitioning funds.[5]

The American minister to Liberia, Lester A. Walton, was now instructed to negotiate with the Liberian Government an agreement for the construction of the port and for its control. A draft agreement was sent for his guidance, accompanied by a "Full Power" signed by the President authorizing him to "negotiate and sign an agreement between the Government of the United States of America and the Government of the Republic of Liberia relating to the construction of a port and port works on the coast of Liberia." Mr. Walton was thus constituted "Minister Plenipotentiary and Envoy Extraordinary."

The agreement between the two Governments was signed in Monrovia on December 31, 1943, Mr. Walton executing it on behalf of the United States, and Mr. C. L. Simpson, the Liberian Secretary of State, on behalf of his country.[6] Like the Defense Areas Agreement, it has sometimes been referred to as a treaty. Actually it was an "executive agreement," a contract between the two governments. A treaty would have required the approval of the United States Senate.

By the terms of this Port Agreement the United States undertook to make funds available for the surveying and construction of a "port and port works and access roads at the estuary of the St. Paul River, to be built under a contract between the Liberian Government and an American Company," and under the direction of American engineers.

Liberia, on its part, agreed to provide the site and also agreed to the establishment of the port as a "free port or foreign trade zone, to be operated for the mutual benefit of the United States of America and the Republic of Liberia and all nations with which the United States of America and the Republic of Liberia maintain friendly relations, under such conditions and by such means as may be hereafter provided."

Actual administration of the port for commercial purposes, it was agreed, should be through an operating contract with an American company to be formed for the purpose, with equitable Liberian representation.[7]

The Liberian Government agreed that upon request it would

grant to the United States the right "to establish, use, maintain, improve, supplement, guard and control . . . at the expense of the United States of America such naval, air and military facilities and installations at the site of the port and in the general vicinity thereof as may be desired by the Government of the United States of America for the protection of the strategic interests of the United States of America in the South Atlantic."

Provision was made for amortization payments to the United States out of net revenues derived from port charges and from other port income, until the cost of constructing the commercial port and port facilities (excluding military or naval installations) should have been reimbursed to the United States. Thereupon operating control, except for the military and naval installations, should pass to the Government of Liberia.

Estimates, like healthy children, have a way of growing. The estimates for the port were no exception to this law of nature. When the project was first proposed the estimated cost of port and access roads was put at $5,000,000 and provision was made in the over-all appropriation for Lend Lease in the sum of $6,000,000 so as to be on the safe side. The estimate was soon to grow to something over $8,000,000. On November 28, 1944, Mr. Stettinius, who had now succeeded Mr. Hull as Secretary of State, informed the President that "although the site of the port has not as yet been definitely determined . . . construction of a suitable port with a minimum of facilities cannot be accomplished within the amount of $8,665,000 now allocated. The Navy Department believes that a total of $12,500,000 will be required."[8]

These estimates reflect the somewhat vague ideas of the State Department, which had no engineering personnel, and of the Navy Department's Bureau of Yards and Docks whose engineers, part of the armed services waging a great war, were hardly in a position at the time to give to the Monrovia port project the detailed study it needed.

President Barclay, before he left New York to return to Liberia, had instructed the Liberian Consul General, Mr. W. F. Walker, to determine what American engineering concern could best undertake the harbor project.[9] This was in accordance with the understanding arrived at in the White House between the two

Presidents. The result was that the Raymond Concrete Pile Company of New York was called in. A tentative design for a marine terminal to be built, presumably on the banks of the St. Paul River, had been prepared some time before for the Raymond Company by an engineer, C. S. Christopher. During the summer of 1944 the Raymond people made a comprehensive survey of the area in the vicinity of Monrovia and determined upon the southern end of Bushrod Island as the best site for the harbor. And the estimate grew again, with the result that $15,000,000 of Lend-Lease funds, three times the original estimate, were allocated to the building of the harbor, its facilities, and access roads. The amount turned out to be insufficient.

Bushrod Island, named after the brother of George Washington, is separated from the city of Monrovia by the Mesurado River, a relatively small stream whose estuary accommodated the wharves and surf boats handling the traffic that passed through the surf port. North of the island, about five miles from the Mesurado, the St. Paul River flows into the sea. It is an important stream, serving as a traffic artery for native canoes. Both rivers are blocked at their mouths by shifting bars over which the water is only a few feet deep. The entire coast in the vicinity is characterized by these treacherous sands, the movement of which under the strong tidal currents is such that not only are the bars constantly altering but even the configuration of the island shore changes, almost from day to day. The building of an artificial harbor in such an area was a costly undertaking.

The island, however, was ideal as a site either for a free trade zone or a naval base. It had the obvious advantage of isolation, coupled with proximity to the city. A bridge could readily connect the port with Monrovia. The St. Paul River could also be bridged and railroad connection be established over it with the valuable iron ore deposits of the Bomi Hills, some forty miles away. A narrow stream known as Stockton Creek meandered from the St. Paul River to the Mesurado, forming the eastern boundary of the island and serving as a moat to complete its isolation.

All parties concerned, including the President of the United States, approved the proposed location. The engineering problem presented by the shifting sands, with the consequent high cost, might have been a deterrent, but this condition must be met no matter where the harbor might be built. The green light was therefore given to the Raymond Company, the Navy's Bureau of Yards and Docks, and the Liberian Government, for the construction of the harbor, its wharf, warehouses, and other facilities.

A vast quantity of rock was required for the two great jetties that were to reach out a mile and a half to sea and enclose an area of 750 acres of protected water. Granite was available near by, the stuff that Cape Mesurado is made of. Geologically it was rock of great age, perhaps as old as any in the world, and consequently so hard that its quarrying was difficult. But even the hardest granite gives way to TNT, and the entire side of the cliff was blasted away to provide material for the jetties. Across the Mesurado River a steel and concrete bridge was built, and over it a temporary railroad, the first that Liberia had seen, carried the rock to the harbor site.

The heavy blasting at the quarry shook the entire city of Monrovia violently; led some of its more litigious citizens to threaten suits for damages, until ex-President King, who was looked upon as an "Elder Statesman," somewhat as Bernard Baruch is in this country, suggested, "You cannot have an omelet without breaking some eggs."

It was at first planned to bring in Brazilian labor for the construction gangs. But at the suggestion of the Liberian Government this idea was abandoned and native help employed instead. These Liberian natives had never seen a steam locomotive, or other major construction equipment. With no inherent aptitude, they had to start from scratch. The Raymond Company learned that in an undeveloped country construction men must first of all be teachers. An apprentice system was established in cooperation with the Liberian Government, conforming in general to American practice. It was soon found that many Liberian natives learned the simple tasks readily. Some local employees even became qualified technicians. There were 1800 natives employed on the port project. The American force numbered only 225.

The building of the harbor took about three years. Within the area enclosed by the jetties some 150 acres were dredged to provide safe anchorage for sea-going vessels. A sea wall along the land side gave 2000 feet of wharfage, sufficient to permit four ships to lie alongside. A storage shed more than 800 feet long, a power plant, tanks for petroleum products, cranes, and railroad trackage, and, finally, elevated tanks for liquid latex, were provided. A road was built from the St. Paul River to the Mesurado and extended up and along the cliff of the cape on which Monrovia is built, connecting the port with the city and with the group of modern houses that were constructed for the use of the port officials. The term "access roads" was thus given broad and very practical interpretation.

The cost estimate grew as the work progressed. On March 30, 1946, the Secretary of the Navy advised the Secretary of State that "the present estimated cost of the work as made by the construction contractor and concurred in by the Chief of the Bureau of Yards and Docks is $17,884,200." A further sum of 2½ million dollars for contingencies was recommended, and after some adjustments an additional allotment of funds was approved by President Truman which brought the total to $19,275,000.[10]

This, at last, was a realistic figure. But a new difficulty appeared. By the first of January, 1948, the harbor itself was substantially finished, with something over $5,000,000 of the $19,270,000 Lend-Lease allocation still unexpended. Unfortunately the important bridge over the St. Paul River, which would make railroad access to the harbor possible and permit the iron ore from the Bomi Hills to reach ship-side, was not yet started, had not even been contracted for. By law, the availability of all unexpended Lend-Lease funds was to lapse on June 30, 1948. Worse than that, the authority to make new contracts under Lend-Lease had expired two years previously. It looked as though someone had been asleep, and that the harbor on which so many millions of American dollars had been spent would be seriously handicapped by want of a railway bridge.

Congress, at the instance of the State Department, came to the rescue.[11] Provision was made in the First Deficiency Appropriation Act, 1948, approved May 10, 1948, whereby the funds, up to $4,000,000, which had been allocated for the construction of the Monrovia port, port facilities, and access roads would remain available for another two years, or until June 30, 1950. The authority to enter into contracts was likewise extended. A contract for the bridge was promptly let, by amending the Raymond Company agreement so as to include the additional work. Construction of the bridge piers was started at once, and the harbor was opened for commercial use on July 26, 1948, the Liberian Independence Day.

The building of this artificial harbor in Liberia by the use of Lend-Lease funds, even under the theory that income from its commercial use might ultimately repay the cost, required a considerable stretching of the purposes for which Lend-Lease had been created by the Congress when the Act authorizing it was passed in March, 1941. Of course it was desirable to have proper port facilities in support of the operations at Roberts Field. But the use of Lend-Lease funds for the harbor project was not determined upon until long after our Army Air Forces were at peak activity in Liberia. The timing of the scheme to build a harbor at or near Monrovia was such as to have made it obvious that it would not be likely to play any part in the prosecution of the war then in progress. When the port construction contract between the Raymond Company and the Liberian Government was signed, North Africa had passed into Allied control, Italy had changed sides in the conflict, Normandy had been invaded, and the collapse of German power on the continent of Europe was imminent. Clearly, therefore, the harbor at Monrovia, even though started before VE-Day, was a post-war project. From a military viewpoint it was a provision against possible future needs in the event of another war involving the United States in the Eastern Hemisphere.

In its sponsorship of the harbor the State Department was doubtless influenced largely by its desire to encourage the economic development of Liberia. That country's strategic value as an ally of the United States had been amply demonstrated. If history should repeat itself, a Liberia strong economically, with its natural resources fully developed, would have enhanced value. A policy of assistance to the African Republic is therefore not difficult to justify. But it is a long way from Lend-Lease, a creature of the war. Fortunately Congress, in passing the 1948 Deficiency Appropriation Act with its special provision relating to the port at Monrovia, gave its blessing to the use of the funds for that project and for the bridge that would make possible the railroad to the iron mines. At any rate, we now have a nineteen-million-dollar investment in Liberia, approved by Congress, which it is definitely in our interest to convert into a paying proposition.

No one can see the harbor as it is today without feeling pride in the way the Raymond Concrete Pile Company carried out their work, a result in which our Navy engineers who supervised the construction had a major part. Perhaps the port could have been built for less money, especially if a fixed price contract had been possible, rather than the cost-plus-fixed-fee form. But it is hardly likely that any reputable engineering firm would have been willing to risk everything on a fixed total under the conditions that prevailed. The Raymond people worked conscientiously and well, and the result speaks for itself.

To administer the harbor and its facilities the Monrovia Port Management Company, Ltd., a Delaware corporation, was organized to carry out the provision of the agreement under which the harbor was built, namely, that it should be operated under American management. The stock of this Port Management Company was issued to the interests mainly concerned with the efficient operation of the port, which were two steamship companies, Farrell Lines and the Mississippi Shipping Company that had just established services to the West Coast of Africa; Firestone; two American oil companies, Socony Vacuum and the Texas Company; the Liberia Company which Mr. Stettinius had formed to promote the development of Liberia's resources; the Liberia Mining Company which was engaged in opening up the Bomi Hills iron mines; and the Liberian Government. This corporate set-up, unfettered by government red tape, was designed to insure that the operation of the port would be along sound business lines, and that is just what is being done.

With the opening of the port a contract went into effect between the Port Management Company and the Liberian Government. Under it the Government appointed the Company as its agent to "manage, operate and administer the port and harbor of Monrovia and the appurtenances thereof," and the Company agreed to administer the port and harbor "in the public interest and in a non-discriminatory manner."

Under the contract the Port Management Company is given

broad authority, subject to certain limited governmental veto rights, to fix port fees and charges and to promulgate and enforce rules and regulations for the operation of the Port. It is empowered to appoint and remove personnel without being subject to Liberian civil service rules, and to determine their duties and compensation. Thus the Port Management Company is given very full and free control of the port area and facilities, with what would seem to be a minimum of possible interference.

As to personnel, it is provided that the Company may not bring into the country any unskilled labor, but may "bring in under contract and engage from time to time skilled workers for employment by it in administrative, supervisory, technical and expert mechanical capacities whenever it is necessary in its judgment." The contract declares, however, that "it shall be the policy of the Port Management Company to train Liberians as employees and employ Liberian citizens whenever possible."

A general right is given to carry on "activities incidental to or desirable in connection with the operation of the port, within the port area," and with the approval of the Liberian Government to "operate and maintain public utilities and furnish services thereunder in other areas." Under this clause, the broken-down electric light plant that had served Monrovia prior to the opening of the port has given way to a somewhat more reliable generating plant, operated by the Port Management Company and utilizing machinery left over from the harbor construction.

An important right is given to the Port Management Company to "make contracts with third parties involving the grant of concessions customary or desirable in free port districts, for furnishing services in connection with the port and its appurtenances and utilization of the same, and contracts for refining, storing and selling products of Liberia and for carrying out functions performed by bonded warehouses." This provision might, conceivably, lead to very interesting activities connected with the free port area in the processing of crude products such as palm kernels or cocoa.

As a fee for managing the port, the Company is allowed 5 per cent of the gross revenues until January 1, 1953, and 10 per cent thereafter. After salaries, wages, other administrative expenses and the cost of acquiring equipment and gear and making repairs and replacements are paid from gross revenues, a reserve fund may be set aside in an amount to be agreed upon between the American and Liberian Governments. The balance is defined as "net revenue," and may be used in the discretion of the Management Company, in agreement with the Liberian Government, for improvements, but only to the extent approved by the Government of the United States. All remaining net revenue must be delivered to the Liberian Government for transmission to the Government of the United States on account of amortization of the cost of the harbor project, until the entire amount shall have been paid.

Such, in essence, is the port management agreement. It is to remain in force until the cost of the harbor project, exclusive of military installations, has been recovered. There are other more or less routine provisions covering tax exemptions, disputes, arbitration and so on. But fundamentally it gives to the Management Company the right and the obligation to operate the Free Port of Monrovia in accordance with commercial business principles, in the public interest, without discrimination, and with the interested Governments consulted or advised on all matters of policy, high or low.

It is too early to attempt any prediction as to the financial results of the port project. Nineteen million dollars is a lot of money to recover from such an operation, even without interest. Yet in the relatively short time since the port was opened, its activity has materially exceeded expectations. The freight (imports and exports) handled through the port is rapidly increasing. During the latter part of 1948 (the port opened late in July of that year) an average of 6,180 tons per month was handled. In the first half of 1949 it had increased to 6,403 tons, and in the second half of that year to 9,350. These are not large figures, but their trend is significant. It is worth noting that the increased traffic is mainly incoming goods. Until about the middle of 1950 only part of the Firestone output, the baled rubber, could be shipped through the port; liquid latex, for which special tanks had to be constructed, still went by way of the surf port at Marshall until May, 1950, when the tanks were finished. The effect will be another increase in the tonnage of the Monrovia port. So too, with the Bomi Hills iron ore movement, which began in 1951, the figures will reflect that operation.

It was expected that the port would show a deficit for some

time after its opening, and a cash fund was underwritten by the stockholders of the Management Company to prime the operation. But income has kept pace with tonnage. Port charges during the second half of 1949 were nearly double those collected in the five months of 1948 that followed the opening of the harbor, and a substantial cash fund has been built up, part of which may be devoted to further improving the port facilities.[12] Firestone's liquid latex shipments through the port and the iron-ore movement will cause the revenue to show a material increase. If Liberia's hopes for the building up of an important export trade in such things as cocoa, palm oil and kernels, and coffee are realized, there will be a further increase. So there may be some actual recovery of the American investment, perhaps a substantial recovery. That the Free Port of Monrovia will be of great value to American commerce along the entire West Coast of Africa needs no demonstration.

But whatever may be the financial outcome, and whatever the usefulness of the port to American commerce, the completion and opening of the harbor and its facilities marked a new day for Liberia. It was more than appropriate that the event should have occurred on the Republic's Independence Day.

Chapter Thirteen

THE BOMI HILLS

ABOUT forty miles from Monrovia, almost due north, where the coastal fringe of Liberia gives way to the area of high forest, a great cliff juts out of the surrounding plain, its bare rocky face glistening with a reddish tinge in the light of the tropical sun.[1]

The cliff is part of a series of ridges that have come to be known as the Bomi Hills, the rock a singularly high-grade iron ore, averaging from 66 to 68 per cent pure iron, the equal of the famous Kiruna ore that has given the Swedish metal its reputation as the finest iron in the world. The ore of our own Mesabi range in the Great Lakes region, where for years America has found its principal supply of iron, averages 51 to 53 per cent. And the Mesabi range is nearly exhausted.

The Bomi Hills are of more than usual interest to geologists, for they contain two varieties of iron that originated in distinctly different ways. As we see them today, the main deposits are in an irregular basin about six thousand feet long in the granitic rocks of the region. The high-grade ore consists of massive magnetite and hematite, great lenses that form the bottom and sides of the basin, like the shell of a gigantic bowl. This bowl or basin is filled with itabirite, a layered iron formation that contains about 42 per cent of iron. In most places the two varieties of ore are separated by a zone of relatively soft altered rock; in other places they are mixed.

The iron deposits are products of ancient mountain-building earth movements in Liberia. Itabirite is found in many parts of the country, and probably accumulated on a prehistoric sea bottom as iron-rich mud. After these iron-rich muds were deeply buried under sands and other muds, the rocks were folded and broken under great pressure, and at about the same time granite came up from wherever granites come from.

If you try folding several sheets of paper into the form of a cup, you will see that the inner sheets tend to slide outward over the others. In a similar way, the rocks in the Bomi Hill basin slipped along shear planes near the bottom of the itabirite, and when hot solutions rose from the advancing granite they followed these breaks. The solutions soaked into the rocks along the fractures, depositing iron which they brought from below and carrying off lime and other elements. In this manner, the high grade ores literally took the place of the rocks along the fractures and formed the ore bodies that we see today.

During the folding, the iron-rich muds were changed to the very hard layered itabirite. Most of the folding movements were over before the high-grade ore was deposited, but a few later adjustments caused minor breaks in the ore bodies. The hills we see today are due to the resistance of the iron ore and itabirite to erosion. The granites and gneisses around the basin weather rather rapidly to clay, but the iron ores, because they are essentially iron rust already, erode very slowly.

The massive magnetite-hematite ore now rears in high vertical cliffs, below each of which is a great accumulation of fragments that have broken off as the ore bodies were worn down. This mantle of talus appears almost as though it were buttressing the cliffs. It represents, itself, a substantial amount of ore.

Until a few years ago the Bomi Hills were hidden treasure. There had been rumors of the possible existence of iron in Liberia, based in part on erratic behavior of magnetic compasses observed by navigators along the shore. The natives, too, had for ages smelted iron, some of which may have come from the Bomi Hills, some from deposits elsewhere in Liberia. Even the laterite, a low-grade red oxide of iron that is found throughout the country, was used by the natives for smelting in their crude clay furnaces.

It was not until about two decades ago that the actual existence of workable deposits of iron ore in Liberia became established, for the Bomi Hills, although only a short distance from Monrovia, were deep in the high forest and in an area sparsely inhabited and penetrated only by a few difficult trails.

In the early 1930's, however, a syndicate from Holland obtained from the Liberian Government a right to make explorations. This group included an able geologist, H. Terpstra. Their interest was chiefly in the discovery of diamonds, reported to be found in Liberia, and possibly of other minerals. A careful examination of what purported to be a diamond field in the Kongba area was discouraging. But in the course of their explorations the Hollanders came upon the Bomi Hills and at once Mr. Terpstra and his colleagues recognized the value and the extraordinary purity of the iron ore. Engineer Englebert van Bevervoorde, chief mining engineer of Messrs William H. Muller and Company, of Rotterdam, became associated with the undertaking, and negotiations were begun with the Liberian Government for a mining concession.

But the lack of harbor facilities presented a serious obstacle to the development of the ore deposit, and the negotiations with the Government broke down over questions of royalties and taxes. The plans of the Holland syndicate, therefore, while not entirely abandoned, were held in abeyance.

About 1935 another and quite distinct Dutch group, the Noord Europeesche Ertz en Pyriet Maatschappy, commonly referred to as NEEP, became interested in the Bomi Hills. During 1936 and 1937 they undertook extensive magnetic and geological surveys and made drillings totalling some 6500 feet, and even pushed a road through to the Bomi Hills. Suspicion arose that there was a Nazi interest in the background of this undertaking, and as a result the Liberian Goverment called off the NEEP project.

Then, at the suggestion of the American State Department, the United States Steel Company was given a six-months exclusive right to make a geological exploration in the Western and Central Provinces. In 1938 a group from that company visited Liberia, made a somewhat superficial inquiry into the Bomi Hills matter, saw the difficulty of shipping such a material as iron ore by surf-port operation, and made an unfavorable report. So the United States Steel Company dropped the matter.

There things rested until 1943, when President Barclay took the matter up with the American Government and requested that a survey be made with American help to determine the possibilities with respect to iron ore in Liberia. Congress had granted authority for such a survey as Mr. Barclay was requesting, by an act approved May 3, 1939, (Pub. 63, 76th Congress), applicable to Latin American Republics and the Philippines. This authority President Roosevelt, by Executive Order 9190, dated July 2, 1943, so broadened as to include Liberia, and the Department of the Interior was directed to organize and send to Liberia a geological mission.

In December, 1943, a group consisting of Dr. Walter N. Newhouse, Dr. Thomas P. Thayer, and Dr. Arthur B. Butler, Jr., proceeded to Liberia, where they were joined by Mr. Arthur Sherman, a Liberian mining engineer educated in the United States, who acted as the representative of his Government and whose knowledge of the country and of native customs gave valuable assistance to the American Group. Mr. Tubman was just taking office as President. He suggested that the geologists direct their attention first to the Bomi Hills area.

It is significant that the arrival of this geological mission coincided almost exactly with the conclusion of the negotiation conducted with President Roosevelt by Mr. Barclay and Mr. Tubman, jointly, for the building of the harbor at Monrovia, the completion of which would make possible the shipment of ore from the Bomi Hills.

Dr. Newhouse and his associates spent four months examining, testing, and surveying the Bomi Hills deposits and reconnoitering an iron deposit of less value in the Kpandemai Hills, far to the north of Bomi. The Liberian Government gave them full cooperation, assuming their living and travel expense and supplying all needed labor and transportation. The survey of the Bomi Hills deposits was as complete as possible at the time, and fully corroborated the findings of the earlier Dutch explorations. It only remained for someone to be found bold enough and with the needed energy to turn the geological data into a going venture.

It so happened that an ambitious young American by the name of Lansdell K. Christie was casting about for a new field of activity. Some years before, he had organized a marine transportation company with extensive operations in connection with engineering projects in and around New York Harbor. During the war he had served with the American Army in Africa mainly in the establishment of a chain of airfields extending from Monrovia across the continent to Cairo and south to Capetown.

Christie was a man of pioneering type. Two years at West Point, and the intimate contact with construction work that his business interests led to, had given him a taste for engineering. In his earlier life he had worked in lumber camps and in mines in the West. At seventeen he had left home and sought his fortune in the Klondike. While in Africa he learned of the iron in the Bomi Hills, sensed its possibilities, sat down with President Tubman and worked out with him an agreement. To operate under the resulting concession he organized the Liberia Mining Company, Ltd., and later brought the first group of Hollanders in as stockholders.

The Christie concession, which dates from August, 1945, runs for a period of eighty years. It gives to the Liberia Mining Company exclusive mining rights for all minerals except gold, platinum and diamonds, within a radius of forty miles of the Bomi Hills, which means an area of about three million acres. It provides for a fixed royalty to the Liberian Government of five cents per ton of ore taken out, plus a variable amount based on the New York market price of Bessemer-grade pig iron. Under this arrangement the Liberians might receive as much as twenty cents or more per ton of ore exported.

The original group of Hollanders, with their valuable accumulation of data and the even more valuable experience of their personnel gained in the earlier exploration, were an important contribution to the Christie undertaking, and Mr. Hendrik Jordense, one of the original Netherland prospectors, entered the employ of the company. The undertaking rapidly grew to major proportions. The road that the NEEP people had put through to the mining area and then abandoned had gone back to bush; its bridges had long since vanished. A new motor road had to be built, no mean job in itself, but it was only the forerunner of a more serious project, the railroad that would be essential for moving the ore from the mine to ship-side. There were no railroads in Liberia; this one would be the pioneer. It would have to be built through difficult country, through the mapless, unsurveyed, trackless bush and forest.

Fortunately the harbor project was well under way when

the mine development began, and in July, 1948, it was opened for commercial use, greatly facilitating the work of railroad construction. But the island location of the Monrovia port made necessary a bridge over the St. Paul River, without which the harbor would be of little use for such an undertaking as the mine and railroad. For a while there was doubt as to whether the bridge could be built as part of the harbor project, because of legal complications, but finally it was authorized by Congressional action, as already told, and the 980-foot reinforced concrete structure, designed for both railroad and highway use, was completed and opened to traffic late in 1949. As soon as the bridge was authorized, the Bomi Hills railroad became a possibility.

Meanwhile a railroad location survey was being made over an area ten or more miles wide, through the Liberian swamps, jungles, bush, and forest. The work of grading, with its heavy cuts and fills, was started. Some of this had to be done by primitive methods until modern equipment could be gotten onto the job. Concrete bridges had to be built over many small streams that were subject to flash floods and worse during the rainy season. Two large steel bridges were required, one over the Kpo River, the other over the Maher.

As the dimensions of the undertaking grew, Mr. Christie was able to interest the Republic Steel Company, not only as a prospective purchaser of ore but as a possible active participant in the project. If they would come in, it would add both technical and financial strength. A conference was held on the ground at Bomi Hills in February, 1949, participated in by the Liberia Mining Company, The Republic Steel Company, and the Export-Import Bank. Dr. Thayer, of the geological mission, was present also, serving as a disinterested but enthusiastic consultant for the three interests involved. Largely as a result of this conference the steel company decided to participate in the venture, the Export-Import Bank agreed to assist with a loan of $4,000,000, and the future of the project was thus provided for.

The success of the undertaking was now assured. Much of the grading for the railroad had been done, the laying of rails proceeded rapidly, bridges were completed, the remaining cuts and fills were rapidly finished, and on April 16, 1951, the first train went through from the Port of Monrovia to the Bomi Hills.

Meanwhile the Robbins Conveyor Belt Company had been installing a modern ore-handling plant at the Port, designed for the continuous receipt of ore from the railroad, and capable of loading a ship from the stock-pile at a rate of 3000 tons per hour. That meant a quick turn-around for the ore vessels; only one day in port. And on June 23, 1951, the first shipload of Liberian ore, 10,000 tons, arrived at the Port of Baltimore, some of it destined for products that had previously required Swedish iron.

The total cost of the project has been around eight million dollars, about half of it the cost of the railroad, the other half represented by crusher and loading plants, conveyors, housing, water supply and sanitation, equipment of various kinds, the construction of the motor road, the cost of the organization before the beginning of ore production, and the miscellaneous other items that are involved in such an undertaking. It is a substantial contribution to the economic development of Liberia, quite aside from the actual mining of the ore. As activity at the mines builds up, important income will result for the Liberian Government, and, as happened when the Firestone Plantations were started, there will be a permanent effect on Liberian life.

The construction phase has already brought wage-money into the country. The regular working force will probably ultimately be upward of 750 Liberians, some of whom will have administrative jobs, and from thirty-five to fifty Americans and Europeans. Already native towns are growing up near the mines and along the motor road and the railroad right of way. Life is coming to the previously almost uninhabited area. Farms are being "cut"; rice and cassava planted. Not only is the mine project itself causing this, but the mere fact of highway access is creating change, just as it is doing elsewhere in Liberia. It is possible that in the final analysis the motor road and the railway will prove of more importance to the Liberians than the working of the ore. Advancing civilization has by-products like that. The entire project offers a striking example of how private enterprize, government cooperation, the initiative of an individual, the strength of a great industrial corporation, and the peculiar ways of aborigines can be combined to the great advantage of all.

The movement of the ore from the Bomi Hills mine is planned at the rate of a million tons a year. At least 30 million tons have been proven in the deposits; probably much more will ultimately be disclosed. Six to eight trains a day, each of ten 50-ton cars, will make the forty-five-mile haul to the port. These are not very large figures compared with the production and consumption of iron ore in the United States, but they are impressive, nevertheless, with respect to a single operation. The fact is that every addition to America's iron ore supply is important.

The dwindling supply of high-grade domestic ores has led far-sighted steel executives to seek every means for widening the ore supply lines. In 1949, for example, 8,300,000 net tons of foreign ore were brought into the United States, from eighteen countries, the largest tonnage coming from Sweden, Chile, and Canada. That was an increase of 22 per cent over 1948, when 6,800,000 tons were imported. In 1947 the figure was 5,492,000 tons and in 1946, 3,085,000.[2] This rapid increase in ore importations is an indication of the welcome that the million tons per year of Liberian ore will have, especially in view of its high quality.

Vast quantities are available of taconite, the low-grade ore stripped from the Mesabi range and occurring elsewhere in the United States. But taconite contains only 25 to 30 per cent of iron and is mechanically very difficult to handle. It must be processed, or beneficiated (that is, processed so as to make it usable for smelting), before it can be used in the furnaces of our steel mills, and its possible commercial use is still in the research stage. Estimates of the capital investment required in a taconite program run from $15 to $20 per ton of annual capacity for producing taconite concentrates.[3] Even so, the steel companies have found it worth while to invest millions of dollars in new facilities and experimental work looking toward the utilization of the low-grade taconite.

Of the itabirite that lies inside the great iron bowl of the Bomi Hills there is an unmeasured quantity, many times the tonnage of the magnetite-hematite ore. It assays from 40 to 45 per cent iron, is stratified with quartz, and is much coarser than most taconite. Before it could be used in a converter it would have to be beneficiated. At the present time that would not pay. So, like the taconite of the Mesabi range, it will be put aside, or, where possible, left untouched. It has a much higher iron content than the American taconite and probably, some day, will have a commercial value.

The structure of the Bomi Hills ore deposit is such as to

simplify its working. The great cliffs of the outcrop extend as much as six hundred feet in elevation above the railroad yard. The operation on the massive deposit will thus be principally a blasting away of the face of the cliff. The fragments will go by gravity conveyors to the crusher below. But when railroad and crusher are ready, the vast accumulation of float ore, the pieces that have already broken away from the cliff, are simply waiting to be picked up and shipped. Several million tons of this material,

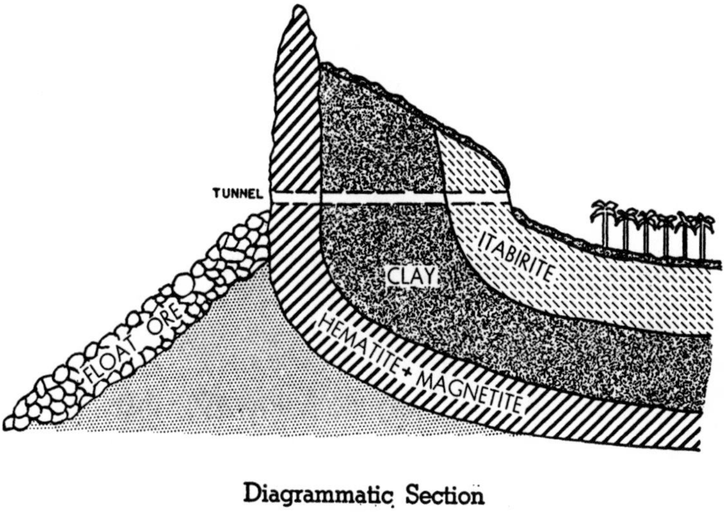

Diagrammatic Section
of the
BOMI HILLS IRON ORE

in pieces ranging from the size of a hen's egg to that of a moving van lie piled against the base of the cliff in a layer fifteen to twenty feet deep, forming a steep incline up which a hairpin road permits a jeep (but only a jeep) to climb.

The visitor to the Bomi Hills today can gain from the rocks an illustrated field lesson in geology. At the top of the pile of float ore, where its steep slope (up which the jeep climbs) meets the face of the cliff, below the crag of ore that forms Monkey Hill, its highest outcrop, a horizontal tunnel has been blasted out, as part of the exploration. It penetrates the vertical part of the great bowl from the south side for a distance of nearly five hundred feet, and comes out inside the bowl on the slope of its inner forest-covered surface. Traversing the tunnel, the light of the visitor's acetylene lantern is first reflected from the gleaming crystals of the hematite and magnetite ore, metallic gray with a tinge of red; this for the first fifty feet of tunnel. Then there is an abrupt change. The ore has given place to a clay formation that has to be shored up with heavy timbers. Two hundred and fifty feet of this; then the itabirite, highly stratified and weathered soft enough to be easily pulverized with the fingers. This for a hundred and fifty feet, and then the forest.

The strata of the lower-grade and soft ore show clearly the deformations that have taken place through the ages, while the great bowl of ore was being molded into its present shape.

Transporting the ore from the Port of Monrovia to the United States is an important shipping operation. Two ore carriers, each a ship of 22,000 deadweight tons, have been built, to be operated by a company organized for the purpose jointly by Republic Steel and the States Marine Corporation. These ships, each making about twelve voyages a year, will account for half the output of the mines. The balance of the tonnage will be carried by chartered ships or by contract haulage, with the possibility that the special fleet may be increased to four. In any case, a ship a week will leave the Port of Monrovia for the United States with Bomi Hills iron, adding materially to the activity of the port.

Republic Steel has the right to purchase from the Liberia Mining Company somewhat more than half of the million tons a year of Bomi Hills ore. Whatever Republic does not take will be available on the open market at the best prices obtainable.

Will the Bomi Hills railroad be extended so as to tap the presently isolated northwest corner of Liberia? That seems doubtful, at least for some time. A motor road from the railhead into the Voinjama and Kolahun area might serve the immediate needs of that part of Liberia, bringing it into direct communication, in conjunction with the railroad, with the Port of Monrovia. Such a road could change the flow of products from this rich agricultural area toward the Liberian port, instead of to Freetown via the Sierra Leone railroad where they now go. Perhaps some day, too, the rails will extend into French Guinea, a thing greatly desired by the French, whose motor trucks are already pounding the road that was opened in 1947 from Ganta, on the Franco-Liberian border, to Monrovia. These projects are for the future, perhaps for the far distant future.

Meanwhile the Bomi Hills mine and its railroad constitute the second great project of private enterprise to be undertaken in the development of Liberia's natural resources: Firestone in the agricultural field, the Liberia Mining Company in the mineral. A third great undertaking, the re-establishment of Liberia's lost cocoa business, is in the making, under the aegis of The Liberia Company. But that is another story, and must have a chapter to itself.

• Chapter Fourteen •

MONROVIA, CAPITAL CITY

BEFORE the opening of the new harbor in 1948 the visitor to Monrovia gained his first impression of Liberia's capital city from the deck of his steamer as it came to anchor a mile or so from the land. As he looked toward the shore he saw the imposing headland of Cape Mesurado, clad in the bright green of the tropics; against it the white houses of the city, mounting one above another up the steep hillside, glistened in the sun, their red roofs adding their color to the altogether lovely scene. At the foot of the great bare cliff where rock for the harbor jetties had been blasted away from the granite mass of the cape, the white line of surf breaking on the shore framed the picture.

At the highest point of the promontory he saw the Cape Mesurado lighthouse, it, too, glistening white and silhouetted against the cloudless sky, while beyond it, prominent against the background of green, was the American Embassy.

It was a satisfying view on which the eyes of the visitor rested as he waited, more or less patiently, for the customs and immigration officers and the port doctor to come off in a great surf boat flying the Liberian flag, which he at first mistook for the American national emblem that it so closely resembles.

When finally he got ashore, however, after crossing the treacherous bar, perhaps in a surf boat, perhaps in a motor launch, and landing at the uninviting customs wharf, the illusion of beauty was quickly lost. The houses that from the sea had looked so picturesque now appeared as grotesque masses of concrete blocks, the red of their roofs, so colorful from the ship's deck, only the rust of disintegrating corrugated iron. Here and there, to be sure, were attractive houses, some of them quite handsome, and surrounded with brightly flowering gardens. But half-finished structures, often pretentious in their architecture and embellishments, seemed to predominate; their owners, perhaps, had met with misfortune before their ambitious building plans had reached fruition. Everywhere he saw decrepit corrugated iron shacks, deep red in rust.

His first impression ashore was gained from the then unpaved Water Street, or Waterside as it is sometimes called, Monrovia's principal business thorofare, its roadway rough and, in the rainy season, almost impassable. The streets, if such they might be called, leading up the steep hill to the better part of the town above, seemed more suited to mountain goats than to human beings, much less to automobiles. Some of them were only foot-paths that wound their way around obstructing rocks.

But if this same visitor had again come to Monrovia a year or two after the opening of the new harbor, say in early 1950, he would have found great changes. Quickly he would have sensed a new spirit pervading the city, a spirit of progress. Water Street he would have found paved, its whole aspect changed by this improvement. True, at its far eastern end, beyond the old post office, there would still be dismal shacks where the charcoal vendors plied their trade. There, the paving work had not yet been done. But soon this section, too, would give way to change.

The visitor would have ridden up the hill in a bright new automobile, a Ford, a Studebaker, perhaps a Buick, over a smooth paved street. He would have noticed that other streets climbing the hill were being improved. He would have come from the harbor, where his ship had been moored alongside the quay, driving over the new road that runs the length of Bushrod Island, from the St. Paul River to Monrovia, and enters the town over a handsome concrete and steel bridge, built as a part of the harbor project. All along this road he would have seen activity, where formerly there was only waste land and swamp. On his way he would have passed a wood-working plant, an automobile service station, oil storage tanks, restaurants. He would have noticed the gangs of workers grading the right-of-way of the railroad that would soon join the harbor with the Bomi Hills iron mine, crossing the bridge over the St. Paul River which was also a part of the harbor work.

As he toured the city he would have discovered another new road, hard surfaced and handsome, leading from the Mesurado River bridge to the top of the great granite cliff and skirting the edge of the Cape until it comes to the American Embassy. From this road he would have had a splendid view of the ocean and the beach, far below. Few towns can boast of a more beautiful cliff drive than this.

Broad Street and Ashmun Street, in the upper part of the city, had already been paved and curbed when our visitors first saw Monrovia. Now, on this second visit he would have found the work of surfacing being continued beyond the city proper, the beginning of an improvement that is to be carried on for fifty miles to Roberts Field and the Firestone Plantation.

These rapid changes within the city are an indication of what is occurring throughout Liberia, at least wherever the effect of the new roads and harbor extends. Everywhere in Monrovia building is going on, some of it new construction, some the finishing or remodeling of the previously half-built structures. Here and there a once forlorn and rusty hovel of disintegrating sheet-iron is being enclosed within masonry walls, the old shack being removed when the new structure is far enough along. Many such buildings are being fitted with metal window and door frames, imported from the United States.

Broad Street, with its tree-shaded parkway, and Ashmun Street, where are the Executive Mansion, the Bank of Monrovia, the really beautiful College of West Africa, and various government offices, need no apologies.

On Water Street the trading companies cater to the needs of the populace and their places of business are thronged by the mixed crowds of natives, Liberians, Europeans, Americans. The Liberia Trading Company, the Cavalla River Company with which Lever Brothers handle their Liberian business, the English firm of Paterson and Zachonis, the Dutch house, Oost Afrikaansche Compagne, the Syrian and Lebanese traders, all are doing an active business, greatly helped by the new contacts with the outside world resulting from the completion of the harbor.

Today Monrovia has a modern motion picture theater, the

first in Liberia. It, like so many other improvements, dates from the harbor opening. In the same new building with the theater is a small but excellent library and reading room, run by the United States Information Service. The building that houses the Bank of Monrovia is new and very modern in its appointments. It, too, is doing an increasingly active business.

The old electric power plant, which so often was powerless, has been replaced by generating sets that had been part of the contractor's plant during the construction of the harbor and were made available for operation by the Monrovia Port Management Company for the account of the Government. Still inadequate to care fully for the growing load, this newer installation is a welcome replacement, even though somewhat of a makeshift, to serve until the improving fortunes of the Liberians enable them to turn to account the power of the St. John or the St. Paul River.

The opening of the harbor brought with it to Monrovia a traffic problem, contributed to also by the completion of the motor road that now crosses the country to the Franco-Liberian frontier. Automobile traffic has increased greatly. Motor trucks come down the road from French Guinea, bringing products for export. Imported goods, including gasoline, are moving by truck into the interior, to the towns that formerly were reached only by foot-trails. There were traffic officers in Monrovia before the opening of the port, stationed at a few of the more important street intersections; they led a quiet life, their drowsiness disturbed only now and then by a passing vehicle. Now this, too, is changed. Water Street, in particular, has become a congested thorofare. At every strategic corner there is a busy traffic officer, and every approaching car must signal to him its driver's intention of continuing or turning. The control is by individual vehicles rather than by stop-and-go signals, but is very effective and is rigidly enforced. It resulted from the services of an American police officer invited by the Liberian Government to come to Monrovia for the purpose.

But Monrovia is still a city without a water supply or a sewerage system. There are no telephones or taxicabs. Communication and transportation are difficult problems without these facilities and the transaction of business is consequently a time-consuming affair. How the health of the city has been brought

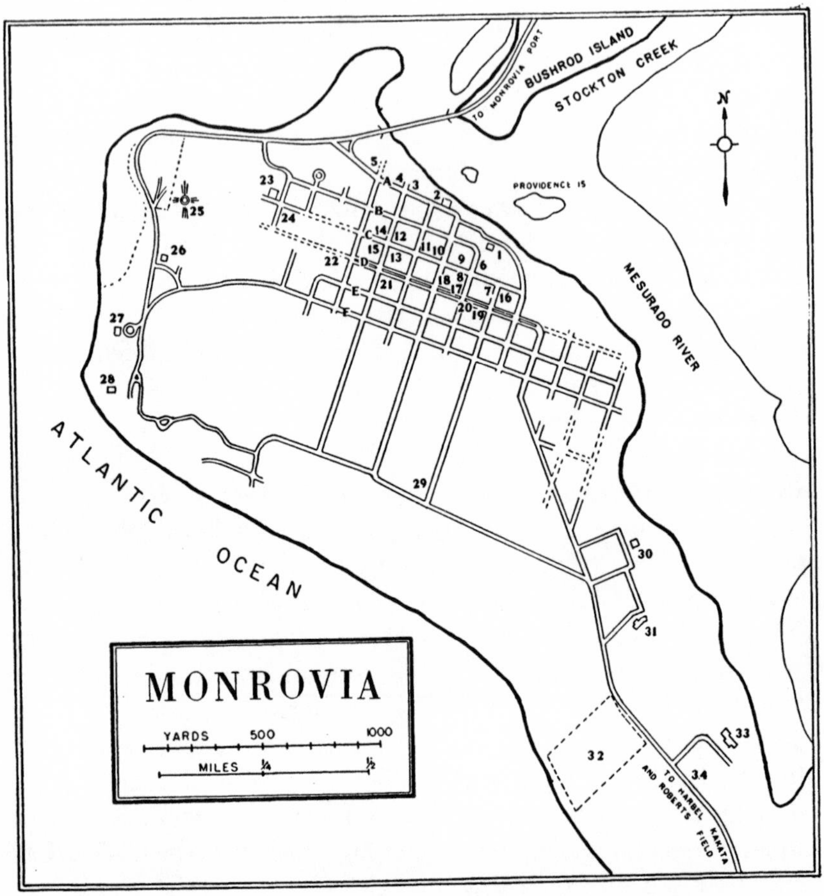

1 Farrell House
2 Post Office
3 Cavalla R. Tr. Co.
4 Liberia Trading Co.
5 Native Market
6 Immigration Office
7 Treasury Department
8 Centennial Pavillion
9 Dep't of State
10 College of West Africa
11 Methodist Church
12 Dep't of State
13 Executive Mansion
14 Bank of Monrovia
15 Bishop Harris House
16 Gov't Radio Station
17 Old Legislative Bld'g
18 Baptist Church
19 U. S. Info. Service
20 Motion Picture Theatre
21 Office, The Liberia Co.
22 Trinity Church
23 Gov't Hospital
24 Catholic Church
25 Lighthouse
26 French Consulate
27 American Embassy
28 British Consulate
29 U. S. Pub. Health
30 Baptist Hospital
31 New Capitol Bld'g
32 Camp Johnson
33 New Liberia College
34 U. S. Econ. Mission

A Water Street
B Front Street
C Ashmun Street
D Broad Street
E Carey Street
F Benson Street

Across the Mesurado River from Monrovia, on the tip of Bushrod Island, is this picturesque Fanti fishing village. The low white cylindrical objects are furnaces for smoking fish.

Below, the Free Port of Monrovia. This modern artificial harbor (see pages 164-178) gives to the growing American trade with Liberia a strategic commercial facility and is of great economic value to Liberia.

Ashmun Street in Monrovia. The white building with the arches is the Liberian Department of State. On the ground floor is the Government Printing Office. The Bank of Monrovia is on the far corner beyond the State Department Building.

Below, House on Broad Street, Monrovia, owned by former President Charles D. B. King, Liberia's Ambassador at Washington. It is now being used as an office building. Its porticoes and wide central hall reflect the influence of the American South.

to its present relatively high level, and there maintained, with such crude sanitary arrangements, is a bit of a mystery, and speaks well for the effectiveness of the educational work of the public health authorities.

Monrovia has also a slum problem. Many of the natives who have left their bush villages for life in the city exist under distressful conditions, sometimes in the shelter of half-built houses the completion of which has long since been abandoned, sometimes in the crudest kind of shacks, contrived from old pieces of corrugated iron or even from flattened-out kerosene tins. A definite attempt is being made to correct these conditions. But the process is bound to be slow. A modest minimum standard for dwellings within the city has been set, and a date fixed, not too far in the future, when structures not conforming to it will be razed. But finding or creating housing, even of the simple kind that will suffice, will be difficult for those that have to be dispossessed.

These problems of housing and of public services, difficult as they may appear to the newcomer to Monrovia, have existed for years, and until the dawn of the new day in Liberia were accepted as inevitable. Now they are looked upon as problems that must be solved. This dissatisfaction with conditions that were once acceptable is the very foundation of progress.

The striking thing about Monrovia today, if one looks beyond the superficial, is the relatively great progress that is being made, and especially the accomplishments within the past two or three years. Monrovia, from being a sleepy old town, content with its inadequacies, is developing into an active commercial city. Business is booming. Everywhere there is construction work going on. The paving of the city streets is proceeding, a surfaced highway reaching out beyond the city itself. Modern houses have been built for the Americans and Europeans stationed in Monrovia, some of these on the magnificent sites that look out to sea from the new cliff drive, and these houses, with their modern plumbing, refrigerators, electric stoves, and other amenities of American home life, are setting examples eagerly being followed by the Liberians.

New buildings are under construction for Liberia College, buildings of excellent architecture and appointments. A new capitol building is planned, on a splendid site overlooking city and sea; its foundations have been laid, its corner stone set. A new office building for the American Embassy is among the improvements. There is a feeling throughout the city of progress, optimism.

Monrovia is, of course, still far from being a Mecca for the tourist. In that respect it is not to be greatly distinguished from other towns on the West Coast of Africa, for there are no tourist cities today in all that area. But it is no longer necessary, as it was only a year or so ago, to post a notice at the head of a ship's accommodation ladder, as it came to anchor off Monrovia, warning passengers not to go ashore because of lack of accommodations for visitors.

The Hotel Mesurado, American owned, is excellently run, although small and not too conveniently located. There is a French hotel also, centrally located but small and much less modern in its accommodations. Transportation, even from the port to the city proper, remains a problem. But Monrovia is no longer impossible for the traveller who has the urge to go ashore while his ship is in port.

It is the growing commercial activity of Monrovia that is most worthy of note. Already the capacity of the harbor is being taxed. As new projects become active—the iron mines, the cocoa plantations, palm oil, coffee, perhaps bananas and other tropical fruits, mahogany, pulp wood—the city of Monrovia seems destined to become a trade center of outstanding importance. It is, of course, the key to the development of Liberia's resources. It promises also to be the focal point for America's growing commerce with the West Coast of Africa.

Chapter Fifteen

MISSIONS AND EDUCATION

It may be doubted whether any other country has as many missionaries to the square inch as Liberia. The very circumstances that led to the founding of Liberia made of it a natural field for missionary effort. The Colonization Societies were not only philanthropic; they were to a great extent fired with religious zeal. Their officers were nearly all clergymen. The settlers themselves were led to feel that they had a great God-given task to perform; that their colony, on the edge of the Dark Continent should be the center from which the light of the gospel was to spread out until all Africa became Christianized.

This was, of course, an unrealizable ideal, but it led to a deep and continuing interest in Liberia on the part of the foreign missionary boards of the American churches. Fortunate it was for Liberia that this was so, for the missionaries sent out from the United States have been responsible for most of the educational work throughout the Republic, and for much of the medical work as well. In the main they have been earnest, able people, some of them outstandingly so, many living deep in the interior in locations reached only by days or even weeks of exhausting travel by foot or hammock over the native trails.

The visible results of their work must often have seemed to these missionaries discouragingly slight. Yet it is they who have laid the foundation for what is being accomplished in bringing the life of the aborigines of Liberia into accord with civilization. The ending of cannibalism, of the frightfulness of the Poro, of the savagery of tribal wars, would hardly have been possible except for the knowledge of the ways of the natives, the understanding of their mental processes, gained bit by bit by the missionaries, and except also for the confidence built up by them, sometimes only with a few individuals, but enough to leaven the whole.

The churches that have undertaken work in Liberia are the Methodist, Lutheran, Baptist, Episcopal, and Roman Catholic. To these should be added the Assembly of God, a group little known in the United States but very active in the West Africa field.

In the main, these several denominations work each in a different area. There is, of course, some overlapping, but duplication of effort and the confusion in the native mind that might result from the fine theological distinctions that plague our churches at home have largely been avoided.

The Americo-Liberians themselves are a religious people, and the Liberian Government gives to the missions the fullest cooperation. In return, it is required that each mission station operate a school, thus making of the missions the backbone of the Liberian educational system. There has resulted a sprinkling of small elementary schools throughout the hinterland and counties, and the establishment of schools for the Americo-Liberians, including some of high-school status.

Although there has been no attempt to assign specific areas to the several denominations, it has come about that the Methodists and Episcopalians are mainly on the coast, the Lutherans in the interior along the St. Paul River in the Western Province and to some extent in the Central Province where the St. Paul touches it. The Baptists reach out from Monrovia through the coastal fringe to Cape Mount. The Assembly of God is active mainly in the Cape Palmas area. The Catholics have missions at Cape Palmas, Sanniquellie, and elsewhere. There are some exceptions to this geographical grouping, notably the Methodist Mission at Ganta, the Cuttington College and Divinity School of the Episcopalians at Suakoko, and the Episcopal Mission at Bolahan. All the denominations have activities in Monrovia, where, perhaps unfortunately, various less responsible sects are tending to set up shop and complicate the picture from both a religious and an educational standpoint.

The Baptist organization in Liberia is of especial interest because it stems entirely from the Negro race, being sponsored by the "National Baptist Convention, Inc.," which is the Negro Baptist

Church organization in the United States with more than four million members. This branch of the Baptist Church has taken on itself the special task of missions in Africa, under three supervisions: South, East, and West Africa.

Administration of the West Africa Baptist Missions, including Sierra Leone, Gold Coast, and Nigeria, is centered in Monrovia under the Reverend John B. Falconer, who during the war served as chaplain with the American troops stationed at Roberts Field, became deeply interested in Liberia, and returned to that country to supervise the work of his denomination along the African West Coast. Support for these missions comes wholly from Negroes in the United States, a fine example of what members of that race are undertaking for the uplift of the nations in the continent whence they sprang.

In Liberia the Baptist Mission Board supports three schools and a hospital, together with a training school for nurses. The schools, one at Suehn, about eighteen miles from Monrovia in the fringe of the interior, one at Bendu on the eastern shore of Fishermans Lake, and one, known as the Bible Industrial Academy, in the Bassa country, near the inland town of Hartford. These schools are organized on the Tuskegee principle of "teaching by doing." At the Suehn school, for example, which was organized in 1912, some 200 acres are planted in rubber, contributing to the support of the institution. Here a staff of five women have under instruction about 250 students, boys and girls, half of them day students. Forty boys and 85 girls are housed in dormitories, and when construction now under way is completed, 200 additional will be cared for. The school makes a charge for those students who can pay, $25 per year, but many are taken free. Both native and Liberian children are accepted. Aside from teaching the three R's the emphasis at Suehn is on industrial training as the foundation on which evangelical work must be built. The Bendu school and the Bible Industrial Academy are administered along similar lines.

The Baptist Hospital is in Monrovia. At present it is somewhat makeshift, but a new building is contemplated whenever funds being raised for it become sufficient. It now has sixty beds and a staff of Liberian nurses; Dr. Schnitzer, Monrovia's leading private medical practitioner, is the physician in charge. Primarily the hospital is run as a private institution, charging for its services, and relied on by the leading Liberians. But 30 per cent of its patients are free patients, mission personnel are not charged, and there are always some patients whose bills are not paid and are, for one reason or another, not collectable. Expenses, therefore, are not quite met, the deficit being defrayed as part of the mission budget. About a thousand patients are treated annually, and in 1948 the maternity ward recorded 184 babies.

In connection with the hospital there is a nurses school where fifteen student nurses receive training, the technical instruction being given at the U. S. Public Health Mission. An interesting fact with respect to the Baptist Hospital and its nurses training school is that the Superintendent is none other than the wife of the Secretary of the Treasury, Mrs. M. L. Dennis, who is herself a graduate nurse, trained in the United States and who, in devoting herself to this constructive undertaking, is unselfishly rendering an important service to Libera, both directly and by example.

Liberia is one of the fifteen American Episcopal districts outside the United States. The Episcopal Missions there are under the supervision of the Rt. Rev. Bravid Washington Harris, D.D., Bishop of the District of Liberia, an outstanding American Negro, with headquarters in Monrovia.

The Episcopal missions, like the Baptist, are well organized and efficiently run, their efforts largely directed toward the foundational work of education and health. Churches are maintained at the principal towns in the coastal area, two in Monrovia, including Trinity Pro-Cathedral. There are forty-two parishes and missions, plus eighty "preaching stations," sixty church schools, and thirty-four parish day schools.

One of the most important undertakings under Bishop Harris is St. Timothy's Hospital at Robertsport, an institution that is rendering much needed service to the people of the Cape Mount area. This hospital has quite recently been enlarged, has fifty beds and modern equipment, including X-ray. It, like the Baptist Hospital at Monrovia, operates a nurses training course, a very important function, for there is a serious shortage of nurses in Liberia.

The physician in charge is Dr. Henry W. Loskant, who studied medicine at Leipzig and other European Universities, served during the war as a German army doctor, briefly in France, Holland, and Belgium and for two years in Russia, escaping from the battle of

Stalingrad. His history is an interesting example of how conditions in Europe have made it possible for a country like Liberia to obtain the services of doctors who find in Africa a security they can no longer have in their home land. Dr. Loskant, in addition to being in charge of the hospital, is Health Officer for Cape Mount County and also has supervision of the Massatin Leper Colony supported partly by the Liberian Government, partly by the American Mission to Lepers. He conducts a series of clinics in the interior in connection with some of the mission schools, where he makes weekly visits, a most important service, since most of the natives who come to these clinics for treatment would otherwise be without medical care.

At Robertsport, in addition to the hospital, is the House of Bethany, an Episcopal elementary school for girls, the Saint John's School for boys, and the Episcopal High School. The boys' school, in addition to academic training, gives instruction in carpentry, tailoring, printing, bookbinding, gardening, and elementary engineering.

Cuttington College is the most ambitious of the educational activities of the Episcopal Church. It was established in 1888 in the Cape Palmas area, where for many years it did excellent work as a divinity school. An entirely new institution has now been established at Suakoko, near Gbarnga in the Central Province, about 119 miles from Monrovia on the Ganta road, replacing the school at Cape Palmas. The new Cuttington comprises a Liberal Arts College and a School of Theology. Its Principal, the Rev. Seth C. Edwards, is a graduate of Morgan State College and of Union Theological Seminary. The small but able faculty includes graduates of Haverford, Cornell, the University of California, Lincoln University, Teachers College of Columbia University, Hunter College, the University of Cincinnati, the Episcopal Theological School, and the Philadelphia Divinity School. Bishop Willis J. King of the Methodist Episcopal Church is associated with the Cuttington College as a special lecturer.

The college property includes 1500 acres of excellent soil, well suited to the practical agricultural program that is a feature of the new institution. Cocoa (cacao) is being started, as well as oil palms, citrus trees, and coffee. As this is being written, there are 8000 cocoa trees about two years old and 20,000 one-year-old trees in the nursery, about to be set out. Ten thousand palms, grown from Nigerian seed obtained through the United States Economic Mission, have reached an age of two years, and so have 5000 citrus trees. Three hundred acres are being planted to coffee. These products, when the trees reach maturity, should go a long way toward the support of the institution, as well as serve as an educational laboratory, where Latin, Greek, Theology, cocoa and palm oil can all be compounded into a practical mixture for the uplift of the people of Liberia.

The Lutherans have missions at Dobli Island, about forty miles from Monrovia in the St. Paul River; at Sanoyea and Belefanai in the Central Province; and at Totota along the Monrovia-Ganta highway. At Zorzor they have had a mud-hut type of hospital which is being improved by cement construction and will be operated as a maternity hospital. A hospital is projected at Kponita, near Zorzor to cost about $150,000.

Each Lutheran mission station has three departments, medical, educational, and evangelistic. The Lutheran objective is stated to be the creation, finally, of an indigenous church, self-supporting, self-governing, and self-reproducing, the last of these objectives to be achieved by the training of a native ministry.

The principal station of the Lutheran missions is at Muhlenberg, where there are a school for boys and girls and a seminary and Bible school. Until recently there was also a Lutheran hospital at Muhlenberg, called the Phoebe Hospital, with a nurses training school. It has now been moved into the interior, since the Muhlenberg people have access to the medical facilities at Monrovia.

A by-product of the Lutheran mission organization in Liberia is the attack being made on illiteracy, with the cooperation of the Government, by the Laubach method. Dr. Frank Laubach, who has had notable success among aboriginal people in opening their minds to the idea of a written language, has worked out for President Tubman a plan for the Liberian natives, and Miss Norma Bloomquist, of the Lutheran staff, has been released from the mission work to direct this important undertaking.

It is difficult for a person brought up in an educated community to comprehend the problem involved in the first step of an African native in learning to read. He has no idea whatever of the significance of such symbolization as letters imply. The fact that strange marks on a piece of paper actually convey *ideas*, and especially ideas that he himself expresses verbally in his own language, seems to him incredible. Once he understands, however, that the written symbols are not just marks, but have a meaning, he has conquered the most difficult problem of his learning process. It is this fact that is the basis of Dr. Laubach's method. By means of charts, simple pictures of familiar objects are used to fix in the native mind the forms of the letters of the alphabet and to associate their forms with sounds and words.

In Liberia the task is fundamentally difficult because of the number of different languages and the fact that pitch and inflection affect the meaning of words that are otherwise similar. Notwithstanding these difficulties, Laubach primers have been prepared in eleven of the twenty-odd tribal languages, and experimental work, extending over a period of two years, has served to convince many among both Liberians and sceptical foreigners of the practicability of the Laubach method for use with the aborigines of the Republic.

The creation of each primer was the work of a group consisting of a foreigner who knew phonetics and from two to six natives, at least one of whom, knowing both the native and the English language, served as "informant." The Laubach method is directed primarily toward adults, in the belief that by teaching the grown members of a family to read, even if only in their own tribal dialect, the teaching given in the schools to the younger generation will be less likely to wither in the uncultivated ground of their home life, when they leave the school and go back to their native villages.

President Tubman, in commenting on the Laubach plan in his fifth annual message (November 1948), said, "As a matter of policy I have directed that each lesson that is taught in a dialect be also taught in English so that not only will the tribesmen learn to write and read in their own dialects but they will simultaneously learn these lessons in English, which is the language of the Government."

An important part of the Laubach technique is the building up of a pride of accomplishment in the learner, inducing him to spread his newly acquired art among others in his family and village. The simple form in which the lessons and primers are cast, and the great aptitude of the native for imitation, lend themselves to this idea.

The Methodist mission work in Liberia, aside from churches in the coastal towns and a mission at Gbarnga run by the natives, is centered at Monrovia and at Ganta. Bishop Willis J. King, who heads the Methodist Church in Liberia, is, like his Episcopal colleague, Bishop Harris, an American Negro of outstanding character, combining theological and religious competence with great ability in the field of education.

The College of West Africa is a Methodist institution. Its excellent building on Ashmun Street is a feature of Monrovia. Actually the term "college" is not quite an accurate designation, since its courses correspond in general to those of an American high school. But it is one of Liberia's few really excellent schools above the elementary and primary level. In 1947, to meet the serious need for teachers of Liberian birth, Bishop King, with the cooperation of Bishop Harris, undertook to establish in the College of West Africa, a teacher-training course. Until that time no facilities existed in the Republic for the training of teachers, dependence having been entirely on teachers educated in America, Europe, or other African colonies such as Sierra Leone. This teacher-training project has now passed the incubation stage and is being made a part of the rejuvenated Liberia College.

The Methodist Mission at Ganta is by far the most significant of the missionary activities in Liberia, mainly because of its remarkable head, Dr. George W. Harley, who with his gifted wife Winifred has worked as a medical missionary among the natives of the interior for a quarter of a century, and has gained a knowledge and understanding of the tribal people, their customs and mental processes, that has had a profound influence upon nearly every undertaking in Liberia, whether in the field of missions, health, social betterment, governmental relations or agricultural or industrial developments.

Anyone who still carries in his mind a picture of a missionary among the heathen of Africa as a lugubrious frock-coated, battered-silk-hatted individual, ending his days in a vast iron kettle surrounded by dancing cannibals, will do well to begin his re-education by a review of what Dr. Harley did to prepare himself for his career in Liberia.

He is a graduate of what was Trinity College, now Duke University, where he won his Phi Beta Kappa key. His medical degree came from the Yale School of Medicine. At London he studied tropical diseases, receiving the Diploma of Tropical Medicine and

Hygiene. Today he is one of the world's experts in the field of tropical medicine.

But the embryo missionary was not content to qualify himself only in medicine. He took advantage of his stay in London to pursue a special course in map making at the Royal Geographic Institute, and as a result was able, after traveling many miles by hammock and on foot over the intricate native trails, to make what for years was the only authentic map of Liberia. Dr. Harley describes it as a "sketch map," but even the latest maps of the country are still based on his work, even repeating some of his now-known errors.

To prepare especially for the missionary field, Dr. Harley worked with Dr. Grenfell in Labrador and studied at the Hartford Seminary where he received his Ph.D. degree. While at the Seminary at Hartford he took a night school course in machine shop practice. In various ways he learned the art of brick and tile making, trades he has introduced among the natives at Ganta while utilizing the product for the physical building of the mission plant. Somehow, too, he acquired a knowledge of stone-cutting, which he taught to the natives, and of electricity, enabling him to set up a generating plant and supply the mission with current.

Dr. Harley is a Fellow of the Royal Society of Tropical Medicine and Hygiene (London), Field Associate in Anthropology (Harvard), Fellow of the American Geographical Society, member of the American Economic Mission to Liberia, Consultant of the U.S. Public Health Service in Liberia, Medical Consultant of the Firestone Plantations Company, and has been decorated by the Liberian Government. He has written extensively on Liberian ethnology, on native African medicine, and on the secret native societies of Liberia. His collection of Liberian ceremonial masks in the Peabody Museum at Harvard has been commented upon elsewhere in this book.

Near the Ganta Mission is a leper colony under Dr. Harley's care, where live some 250 natives who are afflicted with the dread disease. Here they live much as they would in any native village, but apart, of course, from other tribal people. Native technicians trained by Dr. Harley administer their weekly hypodermic injections, a painful experience for most of them and painful to watch, but alleviating in its effect.

The mysticism attached to the smelting of iron and to the trade of blacksmith among the natives has already been referred to. Dr. Harley happened, some years ago, while excavating for the foundations of one of his mission buildings, to unearth an ancient sacred native iron tool, the kind known as a *kune*, a lump of metal about the size of two fists. Because his finding of this *kune* was deemed by the natives a miracle, the doctor was made a *zo*, and thus ranks in the Liberian hinterland as a medicine man, an aboriginal degree that he proudly adds to that received from Yale.

To the clinic at the Ganta Mission come thousands of natives, sometimes two hundred or more in a single day. Five days a week it serves the medical needs of an area with a population of 175,000 people, the only clinic and dispensary within a radius of seventy-five miles. Many of its patients come from across the French Guinea border. For years Mrs. Harley, who also had medical training before she came to Liberia, presided over the clinic. Recently a trained nurse has been in charge. Meanwhile Mrs. Harley, who is a botanist, has contributed to scientific knowledge by her study of the ferns of Liberia, identifying many new species and embodying her hobby in an extensive herbarium.

An elementary school, dormitories, machine and blacksmith shops, a saw mill, brick and tile works, a service garage presently swamped with repair work for the big trucks using the Ganta road, all devoted to vocational training, plots of land where advanced methods of agriculture suited to the natives are being developed, a church under construction, all serve to make of the Ganta Mission an exceedingly busy and useful institution.

The importance to Liberia of Dr. Harley's work as a whole, derives not merely from the multiplicity of the mission's activities, nor from the service rendered by the clinic, great as that is. Rather it derives from the Doctor's deep understanding of native life. No ordinary man, even after two decades or more of devoted service in the Liberian hinterland, could have acquired such a vast and useful fund of knowledge. Fortunate indeed for the Republic is this comprehensive appreciation of the native ways by a man who is not only the exemplification of what an American Christian missionary among a backward people should be, but who is also a competent scientist, whose hungry mind satisfies itself only by diligent inquiry into every mystery it encounters; and who has made his mature judgment and expert knowledge available to those who seek to assist in the development of Liberia. It is not too much to say that back of whatever American skill and American capital can do in and for Liberia, lies the work of the Harleys at the Methodist Mission at Ganta.

Not all the missionary and educational work in Liberia is denominational. The Booker Washington Institute at Kakata stands out as a fine piece of philanthropic work, providing vocational training for the Liberian natives. It, too, like the College of West Africa and Cuttington College, has recently raised its sights to meet the increasing needs of the Republic for something more closely related to the daily welfare of the people than purely academic education. It resulted from a survey of education under the auspices of a group known as the Advisory Committee on Education in Liberia, and from the work of Mr. James L. Sibley, who went to Liberia at the request of President King to serve as Educational Advisor to the Government. The Liberian legislature granted 1000 acres of land at Kakata for the proposed Institute and President King suggested that it be developed undenominationally. It was incorporated in New York in March, 1931, as the Booker Washington Agricultural and Industrial Institute, having been made possible by a bequest of Miss Olivia Phelps Stokes, supplemented by funds from the Methodist Mission Board. Since its incorporation the support of the Institute has come from its endowments, from the Phelps-Stokes Fund, the American and New York Colonization Societies, cooperating mission boards, and Mr. Harvey S. Firestone, Jr. A number of substantial grants were made by the American Department of State for specified projects.

The Institute is managed from New York by a Board of Trustees, in cooperation with a Board of Managers in Liberia, the latter under the chairmanship of Secretary of State Gabriel L. Dennis. The Institute's principal, Mr. Walter C. Wynn, works closely with the American Economic Mission, especially with respect to such forest products as palm oil and the development of methods of oil extraction suited to the abilities and resources of the natives. Classes are conducted in grade six through grade eleven, with a total of about 175 students, half in the general course, the others specializing in agriculture, carpentry, cabinet-making, masonry, mechanics, and handicrafts.

The Institute is giving instruction in tropical tree crops with special reference to methods of propagation and field planting. It maintains nurseries of oil palms, citrus and mango seedlings, has a number of acres planted in oil palms, bananas, cocoa, and rubber, and is experimenting with pedigreed chicks introduced from the United States, and with the breeding of native cows to recently imported Brahman and brown Swiss bulls. The staff of the Institute has recently been strengthened by the addition of an American agriculturist and by a specialist in home economics, both from Tuskegee.

In Monrovia, the Catholic Church, presided over by Bishop John Collins, has an important school that carries to and includes the high school. The Seventh Day Adventists, too, have a school in Monrovia, and there are grammar schools run by the Government, although the missions are mainly relied upon for schools of elementary, primary and high school grades.

The Firestone Plantations Company early assumed the task of educating the children of its workers. At Harbel it operates eight schools for Liberian children, and two at its Cavalla River Plantation.

It has been a Government requirement that all mission stations throughout the country have elementary schools as a condition to their franchise. This in the main has had good results. Most of the mission stations have looked upon their educational activities not only as a Government requirement but as a very fundamental part of any effective religious effort, and so have employed or developed competent teachers. In a few cases, however, a well-meant but misdirected emphasis on the evangelistic phase has led to a perfunctory compliance with the school requirement, and in other cases it has not been realized that the teaching of aboriginal children, even when only the simple fundamentals of the three R's are attempted, requires unusual skill and aptitude, and pedagogical training of a high order. Even in the higher grades, the problem of educating the tribal people is a difficult one and sometimes baffling. Natives have remarkable memories and powers of imitation, but unless skillfully taught they lack understanding, and cases have occurred of natives' passing excellent eighth grade tests, yet not knowing what it was all about; they had simply memorized the textbooks.

There has been a tendency for some of the less responsible sects in the United States to establish missions in Liberia, without the background and technical ability that the mission boards of the organized denominations possess. In consequence, there has been some confusion in both religious and educational fields. Because of this, President Tubman felt it necessary to say, in his sixth annual message to the legislature (October, 1949), "I think that the time has now come when Government should exercise greater control over and concern with the nature, kind and extent of work that all missions are conducting in the country; to make assignment of the different missionary groups, according to their financial, moral and other standards, to places for operation, so that there might be no overlapping; . . . to set the educational standard and qualification to be required of missionaries who would be permitted to enter or remain in the country . . . and such other requirements as may be considered necessary."

The Government, and in particular President Tubman, are of course, in fullest sympathy with competent missionary work, deeply appreciative of the help that is coming to them through the missionary boards, and determined that the standard of educational and religious effort shall be kept on a high plane.

In Liberia College the educational ambitions of Mr. Tubman and the Liberian Government are centered. For years it has been a struggling institution in Monrovia, occupying property owned by the Methodist Church. A destructive fire served as the signal for a fresh start. A building fund of $50,000, (which in Liberia, with its low labor cost is a substantial sum for such a purpose) was provided, half by the Government and half by the Methodists. With it, a new college building has been erected on a site overlooking the city, near where the projected capitol building is to be. An experienced educator from America, Dr. J. Max Bond, has come to Liberia to be head of the college. The teachers college, organized under the aegis of the College of West Africa, is being made part of Liberia College with its present head, Mr. Draper, as Dean of Teachers College.

Immediately adjoining the new Liberia College are the grounds and buildings temporarily occupied by the American Economic Mission and owned by the Liberian Government. This property, once the German consulate, will eventually become part of the college plant.

It is President Tubman's ambition that Liberia College shall some day become the University of Liberia, with all the diversity of courses and departments that the word implies, in arts, sciences, professions. Such a consummation is probably a long way off. To staff and support a full-fledged university among a civilized population of only fifty or sixty thousand, possibly a third of whom, at most, might be concerned with higher education, would be quite an undertaking. But the rejuvenation of Liberia College and the determination to make of it a really important institution of higher education are significant of the new spirit that is pervading Liberian life.

Because of the close cooperation that exists among the various religious, philanthropic, and governmental activities in the educational field, a general pattern is beginning to be evident, the rudiments of an integrated educational system. The College of West Africa, striving to attain a standard corresponding to an American accredited high school; Liberia College, reaching toward academic standing in the higher educational field with Cuttington College as a divinity school also at college level; Booker Washington Institute being built up to where it can fill part, at least, of the need for vocational training—these all now appear as parts of a logical plan.

The leaders among the Liberians have long been noted for their natural bent for classical education, often obtained by study abroad. There has been in the past, as a result, some tendency to direct the effort of Liberian schools toward training of a clerical character. The great need of the country today is for people educated along scientific and mechanical lines. This need, fortunately, is beginning to be understood, and the Liberian Government is sending increasing numbers of young men and women to the United States for practical training. They should, if they apply themselves with a diligence commensurate with their opportunities, form the nucleus for real progress in education in Liberia.

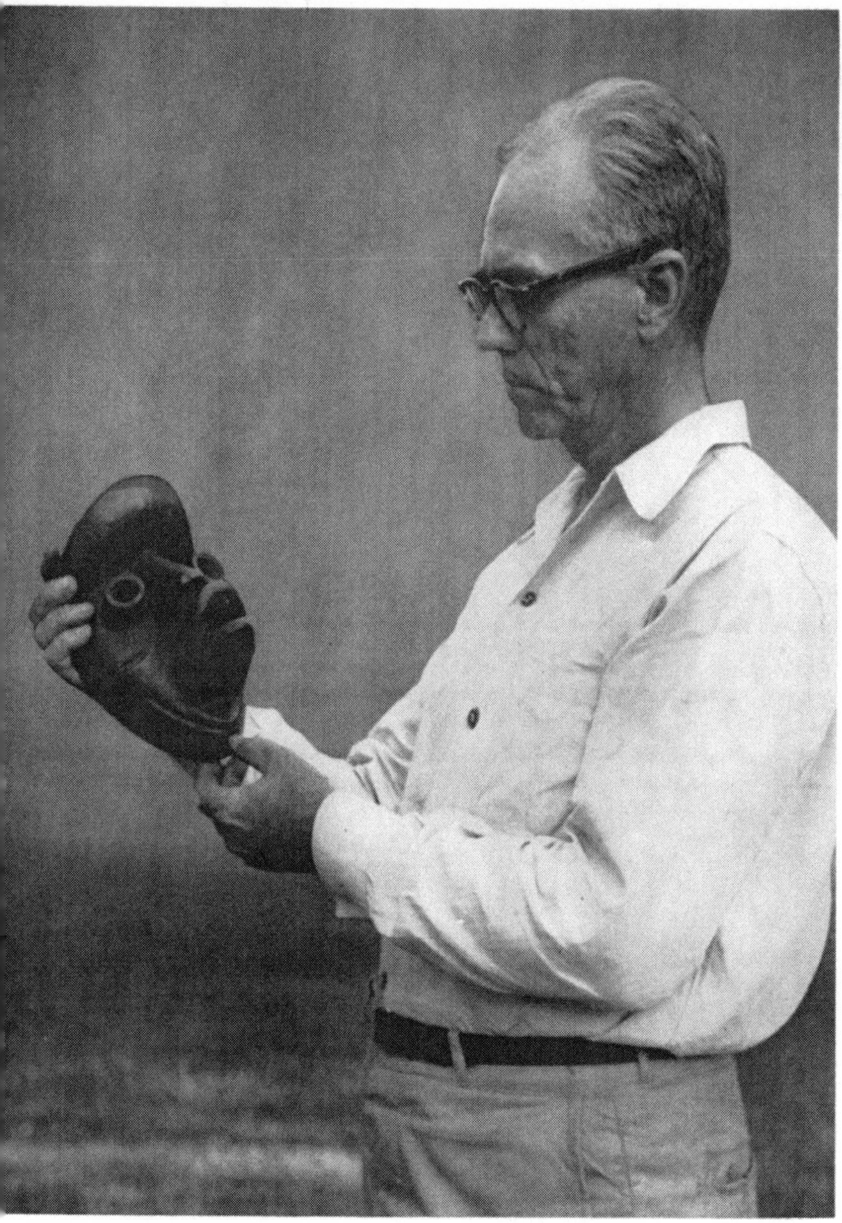

Dr. George W. Harley, head of the Methodist Medical Mission at Ganta, physician, engineer, ethnologist, electrician, blacksmith, cartographer, authority on tropical diseases, consultant to the Firestone Plantations Company and to the U. S. Public Health Mission in Liberia, member of the U. S. Economic Mission, understands the Liberian native better than any other living person. His study of the ceremonial masks gave him the key to native psychology. The mask he is here studying is that of the forest demon—the only one of its kind the Doctor has seen.

Weaving country cloth in a village of the interior, a work done by men. Cloth is woven in strips 4 or 5 inches wide and some 40 feet long. The strips are then sewn together.

Below, Blacksmith shop deep in the interior. Smithing is an ancient and sacred art handed down from father to son. The smithy is sanctuary. Bits of automobile springs now largely take the place of native raw material.

• *Chapter Sixteen* •

THE LIBERIAN GOVERNMENT

POLITICALLY the country we know as Liberia is organized into five counties that comprise the coastal area and three provinces making up the hinterland. Exercise of the governmental function, until quite recently, has been confined to the counties where live the Americo-Liberians, the so-called "ruling class." The provinces of the hinterland, since the time, about forty years ago, when the Liberians actually obtained control of the tribal inhabitants, have been governed as a possession. The pattern is not unlike that of the near-by British Gold Coast and Sierra Leone, where the actual crown colony is in each case a relatively small area near the coast and the hinterland, peopled mainly by native tribes, is governed as a protectorate.

The story of the adoption of Liberia's Constitution has been told in a previous chapter. Officially, and to its citizens, the nation is the Republic of Liberia. This designation, emphasizing the *form* of the government, is as much a matter of pride as of fact, for Liberia is the only republic on the African continent and one of the world's two Negro republics.

The form is modeled after that of the United States, except that there is no counterpart of the federation of states that were welded into the American nation. In a way it is possible to see in the coastal counties and the hinterland some resemblance to the thirteen original states of the Atlantic seaboard and the great American West. But instead of having to subdue a few scattered Indian tribes, the Americo-Liberians have had the task of controlling aborigines who outnumbered them by more than a hundred to one. The administration of the hinterland has thus been a major problem for the Liberians.

For many years the problem was left untouched. Then, when control was established, the isolation of the roadless interior permitted the growth of serious political abuses. Beginning with the administration of President King, the Government at Monrovia has become increasingly concerned with the affairs of the tribal people. But the government of the hinterland still remains one of Liberia's major problems.

Strangely enough, native government among the tribes has always rested in the consent of the governed. Even under the power once wielded by the secret Poro society and enforced by frightfulness, popular favor was necessary for the continuance of any tribal regime. Public opinion was formulated by the elders of the towns and clans, and a chief or even a *ge* who went contrary to such public opinion was soon superseded. Some of the basic elements of democracy were actually indigenous in Liberia. How the native tribal government is being gradually amalgamated with the civilized administration of the Americo-Liberians, and how the process has been hindered by abuses fostered by the lack of roads and other means of communication, would in itself be well worth thorough study.

The general scheme of government established by the Liberian Constitution, and applying in the first instance to the coastal area, comprises the three basic branches, corresponding to those of the United States: legislative, executive, and judicial, with a bi-cameral Legislature, a President, Vice President, and Cabinet, and a Supreme Court, with lesser courts as established from time to time by statute.

The County Jurisdiction embraces the seaboard to a depth of about forty miles. In it are five counties and one territory. Beginning at the northwest end of the coast, they and the people who inhabit them are the following:

1. Grand Cape Mount County; Americo-Liberians, the Vai's and part of the Golas
2. Montserrado County; Americo-Liberians and the De tribe
3. Territory of Marshall; Americo-Liberians and part of the Bassa tribe

4. Grand Bassa County; Americo-Liberians and most of the Bassa tribe
5. Sinoe Sounty; Americo-Liberians and the Kru tribe
6. Maryland County; Americo-Liberians, Krus and Grebos

The counties are governed by local administrative officials termed County Superintendents, who are directly responsible to the President. In the County Jurisdiction the constitutional and statutory laws of the Republic apply, together with the common law of America and England and current administrative regulations in the form of Executive Orders and Administrative Circulars issued from time to time by the President and approved by the legislature. The county officials are appointed by the President with the "advice and consent" of the Liberian Senate, and hold office during good behavior. The County Jurisdictions send senators to the upper house of the Legislature, and on a basis of enfranchised population they elect the House of Representatives.

Political recognition in the Legislature has been gradually extended to the tribes, first by delegates sitting in the House of Representatives with the right to discuss and vote upon matters affecting native interests. During Mr. Tubman's first year in office the Legislature, at his instance, took steps to amend the Constitution so as to admit to full membership in the House of Representatives a representative from each of the three hinterland Provinces and to extend the right of suffrage to tax-paying tribal citizens, a very long move in the direction of eliminating the distinction between the Amerco-Liberians and the aboriginal people. These amendments were adopted by vote of the people in May of the following year, when suffrage was also extended to women.

Commenting on these reforms the President, in his third annual message to the Legislature (November 15, 1946) said, "It is . . . our bounden duty and service to effectuate the aims and purposes for which this nation was instituted, regarding everyone as a Liberian without regard to Clan, Tribe or Ancestry."

Just how this very real attempt to break down the distinction between the aborigines and the civilized people will actually work remains to be seen. Even if it should prove for the time being to be little more than a gesture, it is an important experiment in government.

The Hinterland Jurisdiction is divided into three administrative Provinces and eight Districts, as follows:

The Western Province: Bopulu-Suehn District; Kolahun-Voijama District.
The Central Province: Gbarnga District; Sanniquellie District; Tappita District; Kakata District.
The Eastern Province: Webo District; Tchien District.

The Hinterland Jurisdiction is primarily tribal territory and contains an insignificant number of Americo-Liberians, mainly government officials. Government in an original sense is by Clan and Paramount Chiefs under the direct supervision of District Commissioners. For the supervision of the District administration President Tubman introduced into the public service three Provincial Commissioners, whose duties are primarily inspectorial and advisory. They, in turn, are answerable to the Department of the Interior.

As stated in an earlier chapter, Clan and Paramount Chiefs are elected by the tribesmen of their respective clans and chiefdoms, or derive their authority by operation of tribal custom. District and Provincial Commissioners are appointed by the President with the advice and consent of the Senate, and hold office during good behavior. By his right of appointment and removal in respect of both the Counties and the Provinces, the President has very great power.

The court of a Paramount Chief has jurisdiction within his own tribe in civil cases involving not more than $100, and in criminal cases when the punishment is by fine of not over ten dollars. In a primitive country these sums are relatively high. Clan Chiefs have jurisdiction up to $25 in civil cases and five dollars where a fine is involved. Cases between a tribe member and a civilized person are tried jointly by the District Commissioner and the Paramount Chief.

Administration of the Hinterland Jurisdiction has been most difficult and complex and will continue so until by gradual education and cultural advancement a substantial proportion of the tribal people are prepared for the responsibilities of citizenship. How greatly such progress depends on the improvement of communications has been pointed out. The failure of early Liberian administrations to grapple with this problem was one of the excuses for the British and French boundary encroachments.

The first real attempt at bringing order into the administration of the native tribes was made under President King in 1923. He called a great conference of Chiefs from the hinterland and from Montserrado County. For almost a month this conference held daily sessions at Suehn, with President King presiding. The Chiefs, with their speakers, singers, messengers, and other staff members numbered upwards of five hundred. Complaints were patiently heard, grievances investigated. The Chiefs and the Government officials collaborated in the formulation of rules and regulations, based on native laws and customs, for the government of the native districts. These rules were approved by President King on March 29, 1923.[1] Although they have been modified from time to time, they have formed the basis of the administration of the hinterland.

Pawning was regulated by these rules, thus bringing within the scope of the code a deeply rooted custom. But in 1930, following the report of the Christy Commission, the taking or giving of a pawn was made a penal offense.

In 1936, under President Barclay, there was a general revision of the hinterland regulations, and further revision during the Tubman administration, all with a view to gradually raising the status of the tribal people and improving the government of the Districts.

In the hinterland areas where roads have not yet penetrated, supervision of the District Commissioners is extremely difficult. Isolated as they are, and of necessity clothed officially with considerable authority, District Commissioners have tended to be far more autocratic than the law nominally permits, and have often been accused of exercising their power for personal gain. The opportunities for such irregularities have been great. Unless a Government agent is scrupulously honest and fair in his relations with the tribal people in the collection of taxes, the requisitioning of labor for road work and other public purposes, and the dispensation of justice, there is a natural tendency to build up a personal regime and seriously to abuse power.

It was the existence of conditions of this kind that led President Tubman to institute the office of Provincial Commissioner. This has helped. But it has not yet solved the problem and it will not be fully solved until all parts of the interior have been made accessible and until a new spirit of public service and responsibility is built up; not an easy thing to accomplish, especially as irregularities have in the past not been entirely confined to the inaccessible hinterland.

It was almost inevitable that in a situation where the ruling class has numbered only fifteen thousand or so, and where so large a proportion of this class has looked to the Government for their livelihood, the Government itself should have come to be looked upon as a sort of proprietary estate. Politicians in our own country have often taken a similar attitude, especially in city governments where corrupt rings have been in power. It was such a condition that provided the opportunity for the League of Nations investigations. Its correction, partly a problem of morals, partly of economics, is the key to the introduction of outside capital for the development of the country's resources. It is the task to which much of Mr. Tubman's effort is being directed.

William V. S. Tubman is the eighteenth President of Liberia. Here is the list of those who have held office before him.[2]

1.	Joseph Jenkins Roberts	1848-1856
2.	Stephen Allen Benson	1856-1864
3.	Daniel Bashiel Warner	1864-1868
4.	James Spriggs Payne	1868-1870
5.	Edward James Roye	1870-1871
6.	Joseph Jenkins Roberts	1872-1876
7.	James Spriggs Payne	1876-1878
8.	Anthony William Gardner	1878-1883
9.	Alfred F. Russell	1883-1884
10.	Hilary Richard Wright Johnson	1884-1892
11.	Joseph James Cheeseman	1892-1896
12.	William David Coleman	1896-1900
13.	Garretson Wilmot Gibson	1900-1904
14.	Arthur Barclay	1904-1912
15.	Daniel Edward Howard	1912-1920
16.	Charles Dunbar Burgess King	1920-1930
17.	Edwin James Barclay	1930-1944

Until the time of Mr. Arthur Barclay's administration the term of office of the President was two years, most of the Presidents serving for from two to four such terms. In 1907 the term was increased to four years. Mr. Edwin Barclay, who served longer than any other President, carrying the Republic through the most critical period of its history, brought about the adoption of a constitutional amendment increasing the term of office to eight years with the proviso that a President may not seek re-election. This change was made in 1935, in which year he was returned to office for the eight-year term that expired January 1, 1944. Mr. Tubman, succeeding him, was thus elected to serve for eight years or until 1952, but the limitation to a single term has since been removed.

Although the office of President of Liberia is elective, possession of the election machinery by the political party in power has in the past made success by an opposition candidate virtually impossible. It was this condition, and the failure of his "People's Party" to unseat the "True Whig" administration of President King in successive elections, that led Thomas Faulkner to start the propaganda campaign that resulted in the League of Nations inquiry into alleged slavery in Liberia.

Actually, throughout the political history of the Republic, Liberia has been under one-party domination, and since 1870 this has been the True Whig Party. A "United Whig Party" appeared in 1935, and in 1943 a "Democratic Party" opposed the election of Mr. Tubman. Apparently, however, the True Whig control of the Government is not being seriously challenged.

Nevertheless Mr. Tubman has sought to bring about reform in the conduct of elections. At his instance a statute was enacted early in his administration guaranteeing equal rights and privileges to all organized parties. In accordance with it, an Elections Commission has been constituted with members from each of the two organized parties, the True Whig and the Democratic, with a third member appointed by the President. This Commission is charged with the responsibility of conducting honest elections, and is given the authority to do so. But in declaring that under this plan "all political parties . . . stand on the same footing, enjoy the same privileges and will reap just what they sow," President Tubman issued at the same time a challenge to the opposition. "If any other political party contests the Whig Party at the polls," said he, in his third annual message to the Legislature, "we shall welcome the opposition and the challenge, and the elections shall be conducted fairly and implicitly within the regulations of the statute; but you cannot be indifferent or expect the Whig Party or any other political party that may be in power to donate their powers to you. You will have to fight for and take it."[3]

To a very marked degree the Government of Liberia reflects the personality of President Tubman. So much is this the case that he has sometimes been called, quite erroneously, a benevolent dictator. Actually the unquestionable power he exercises over all the affairs of the Republic stems from the way he has endeared himself to its people, not only by the soundness of his policies, but by his deep understanding of human nature, including especially that of the tribal people, and by his easy approachability.

Mr. Tubman was born in 1895 at Harper, in the Cape Palmas area. He was educated in the mission schools of Liberia and by study under several of the country's leading lawyers. He is a devout churchman and a lay preacher in the Methodist Conference. As a practicing lawyer he attained eminence, served for many years in the Liberian Senate to which he was elected at the age of twenty-five, and in 1937 became an Associate Justice of the Supreme Court. It was from the bench of that tribunal that he was called to the presidency to succeed Mr. Edwin Barclay in January, 1944.

Earlier he had served as Collector of Internal Revenue in Maryland County. As a member of the Liberian Militia he had risen from private to colonel. His military training was not perfunctory; its effects have been reflected in his insistence, as President, that the Liberian Frontier Force be trained in field tactics instead of display parading.

Notable among the accomplishments of his administration have been the reform of the election laws, already referred to, the extension of the right of representation in the Legislature to the hinterland Provinces, the adoption of woman suffrage. Under Mr. Tubman, too, a civil service law was enacted, a rather drastic step in view of the extent to which the Government had been looked upon as the natural support of the influential. The reaction to this reform may be inferred from a paragraph quoted by Mr. Tubman in his fifth annual message and written by the Civil Service Commissioner: "This new and strange policy of drafting the services of the several employees of government subject to a standard test and a system of classification without regard for political affiliation or family connections, has not met with the enthusiasm and cooperation which naturally could not be expected from the old hard-boiled politicians so used to the spoils system. This slow transition should not however be discouraging."

The broad policy of inviting foreign and especially American capital and enterprise, begun by President King, who opened the door, and furthered by President Barclay, who held the door open, has been continued in accelerated tempo by Mr. Tubman. The harbor improvement, negotiated jointly by Mr. Barclay and his successor-elect with President Roosevelt has been brought to completion in the Tubman administration. The motor road across the country to the French Guinea frontier has been completed and extended, opening up the country as far as Sanniquellie and Tappita and a program of further road construction and improvement has been undertaken.

The development of the Bomi Hills iron mine and the building of Liberia's first railroad have been started under Mr. Tubman's policy of cooperation. So have the activities resulting from the plan of Mr. Stettinius, outlined in another chapter. The United States Health and Economic Missions are in Liberia at Mr. Tubman's invitation. Liberia College has been educationally rejuvenated and physically rebuilt. A new interest in such professions as engineering, medicine, and scientific agriculture has been awakened among Liberian youth.

Several hospitals and public clinics, partly Government, partly mission, belong in the Tubman list. An attack on the problem of illiteracy among the natives has been initiated. The efficiency of the Frontier Force has been vastly improved. In the early 1930's an appropriation of $25,000 for publc health was considered a large sum; how this item figures in the budgets of the Tubman administration can be seen in the data appearing later in this chapter.

The fact that foreign ownership of land is prohibited by the Liberian Constitution has stood as a barrier to the needed availability of foreign capital for mortgage loans. This problem has been attacked by President Tubman and a plan worked out whereby the inability of the Bank of Monrovia to acquire title through foreclosure and so to protect a loan is offset by a form of limited Government guarantee. The result has been a stimulation in building construction, for both business and residential purposes, a sorely needed change, especially in the city of Monrovia.

Perhaps the most difficult task and at the same time the most spectacular to which Mr. Tubman has addressed himself has been the reform of the hinterland administration. The organizational steps taken in that connection have already been described. But the President has not left the matter of creating an effective and honest government in the Provinces to the unsupervised authority of subordinates, not even to subordinates of cabinet rank. Instead, he has time and again made extensive trips into the interior, has heard complaints, tried cases, acquainted himself on the spot with local conditions, dispensed summary justice where, as happened in some instances, he found District Commissioners or other officials abusing their power.

In 1945 Mr. Tubman made a comprehensive tour of the Western Province. In March of the following year he covered the Central and Eastern Provinces, passing through Gbarnga on his way to the Tappita District. On April 2 he arrived at Tchien, where, for nineteen days, he held council with the Chiefs and tribesmen. From Tchien he proceeded to Nyaake-Webbo, which he reached on April 27, and there he opened a six-day council. His journey on to Harper completed the circuit of the Eastern Province, during which his Secretary of the Interior journeyed through the Central and Western Provinces.

These tours of the interior were not simple affairs to manage. Books have been written about much less extensive journeys into the bush and forest by daring foreign travellers, who found adventure in the experience. In 1945 and 1946 there were still virtually no roads. The motor road that now crosses the country from Monrovia had been completed only as far as Gbarnga. Almost every mile of the President's tours had to be made afoot or by hammock over the native trails.

Since these two comprehensive and historical journeys, frequent trips have been made by Mr. Tubman into the interior, recently somewhat more easily by reason of the work that has been done on the construction of roads. But even as late as 1950 a presidential journey to Zorzor, which resulted in the dismissal of a District Commissioner, involved many miles of travel by foot-trail.

These visits of the President to the Provinces have much of

the glamour of a triumphal progress. To the natives of the interior, to Paramount, Clan, and village Chiefs, the coming of the President, with his entourage, which often includes cabinet members and other men of prominence, is an event that calls for extensive celebration. Roads and trails, at the approaches to a village, are arched with palm branches, special food is prepared, each village vies with the next in its reception of the Great Chief and in his entertainment.

But for President Tubman such a journey involves a lot of hard work, fortunately lightened by his keen sense of humor and his knowledge and understanding of the customs and psychology of the aborigines. Thus, for example, at Gbarnga, which he visited in March of 1950, following an earlier journey that same year into the hinterland, the President held a general hearing, giving to all comers an opportunity to air their grievances. With Mr. Tubman, who of course presided over the gathering, were the Secretary of the Interior, the Provincial Commissioner, the District Commissioners, and various other officials and assistants. Present were all the Chiefs of the District, thirty or forty of them, Paramount, Clan and town Chiefs, their staffs and village elders.

All were free to bring in their complaints and be heard. The proceedings were conducted in the native tongue, even when a Chief or other witness could speak English. An interpreter was used in every case, so that every word was heard in both the native tongue and in English. Thus the entire gathering got all the testimony and arguments. With respect to one Paramount Chief there was evident a strong current of tribal politics and indications of an attempt to unseat him. The President listened with great patience to all sides and conducted the proceedings in constant good humor, giving full scope to the time-honored customs of the people.

During this council a criminal case came up—five natives accused by a Chief of plotting to bring about the death of one of the lesser chiefs by witchery. Included in the evidence was the "medicine" that had been used. The testimony showed that while no physical attack had been made, the intended victim had been terrorized by the threats of witchcraft. The President's decision of "guilty" was based on the deep belief in tribal life in the efficacy of witchcraft, so that men have been known to die of prolonged fright. This, the President said, was of course nonsense but the effect was nevertheless real, and so was the criminal intent. The guilty ones were sentenced to eight months in prison.

Throughout these proceedings it was evident that the President's decisions were fair, leaning toward leniency. Or perhaps they might be more accurately described as tempered with mercy. It is thus that Mr. Tubman is bringing justice and understanding to the native tribes, learning their problems, correcting abuses, improving the administration of the hinterland by changes of personnel when needed, endearing himself to his people. Politically he has opponents—what two-fisted man in official life has not? But a constitutional amendment that received popular support has permitted his election to the presidency for another term; his second inauguration took place on January 7, 1952.

Liberia has the unique distinction of a balanced budget. This condition is a recent one, made possible by the great changes in the nation's economy that have resulted from the Firestone project, the building and operation of Roberts Field, the work of constructing the Monrovia harbor, and the activities of the Liberia Mining Company. These have built up the national income, have led to a rapid increase in foreign trade, have brought money into the country, and have greatly improved the Government's revenues.

It was not until 1937 that Liberia's total exports reached the two-million mark, a figure that has since risen to over thirteen million dollars and is due for further increases now that the iron ore has begun to move and other projects, such as that having to do with cocoa, come to fruition.

A glance at the accompanying chart will show the very low state of the country's export trade before the rubber plantation came into production. It will show, too, the gradual build-up of exports prior to World War I, and how this trade was cut to half the small volume it had reached when war came. The effect of the great world depression of the 1930's is reflected, too, in a new low point, this time less than a third the previous peak.

The almost negligible export trade during the period up to the beginning of the rubber era gave little sustenance to the Government's treasury and led to a succession of foreign loans and to situations where floating debt and arrears in interest payments had to be refinanced. The problem was aggravated by the fact that a large proportion of the ruling citizens were dependent on Government payrolls.[4] Neither were the money lenders always kind to Liberia, notably the London financiers who made the loan of 1870, when a debt of £100,000 was incurred out of which only 25 per cent was actually received by Liberia.[5]

Mention has already been made of the so-called "International Loan" of 1912. Under its terms a receivership of customs was set

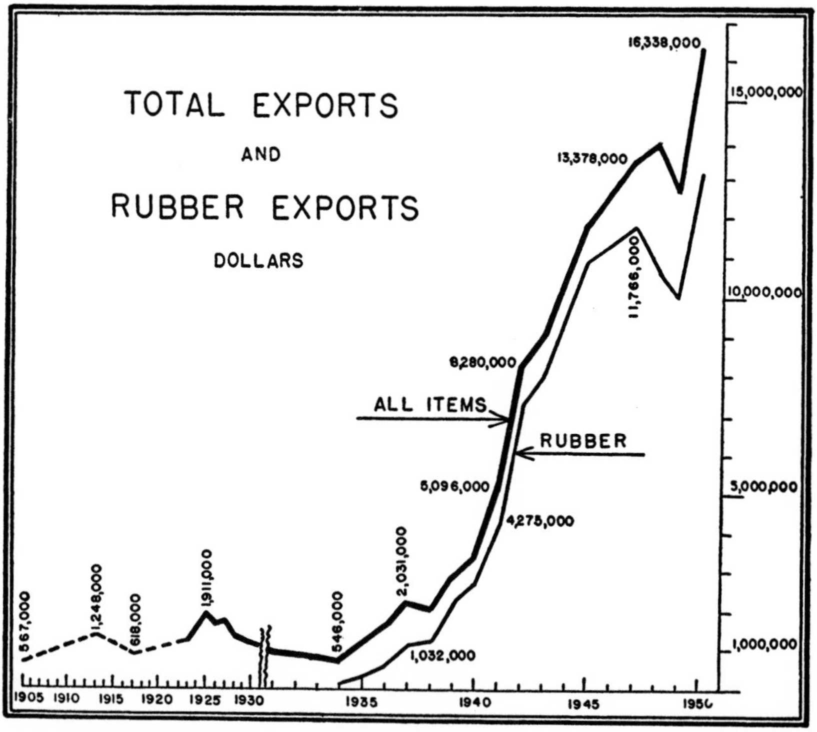

up, and from that time on the Liberian Government has had outside financial advice and to some extent outside control, sometimes onerous, sometimes beneficial. World War I left the customs office in the hands of the American representative of the consortium, and when the International Loan was replaced by that of the Finance Corporation of America, as part of the arrangements that brought Firestone to Liberia, provision was made for a Financial Advisor, who is responsible for the collection of customs and taxes and exercises restraint upon expenditures. From 1935 to 1951 the office of Financial Advisor to the Liberian Government was ably filled by John A. Dunaway under whose guidance the Government's annual budget was prepared for action by the

Legislature. He earned the confidence and respect of the President, and indeed of the whole community, and laid down his duties only when the Finance Corporation loan had been reduced to an insignificant figure.

The crisis in Liberia's finances occurred before Mr. Dunaway's time. It coincided with the attack on the country's inde-

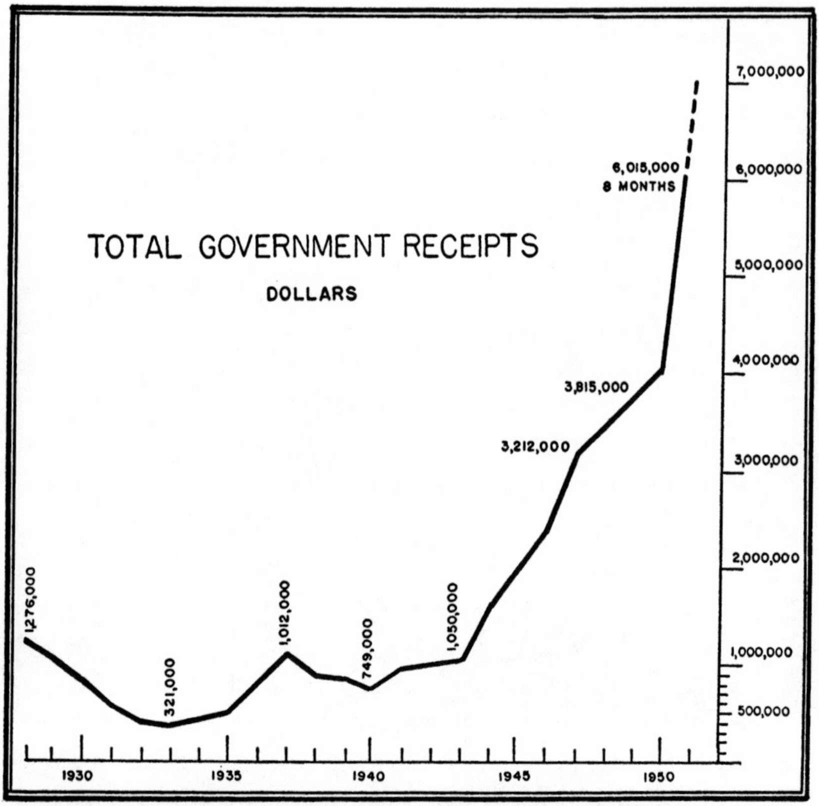

pendence by the League of Nations and provided one of the excuses for that attack. How severe the crisis was can be seen in the accompanying chart of Total Government Revenues, which shows a close correspondence between exports and revenues. The impact of the world depression, which we have seen reflected in Liberia's export trade, cut the Government revenues by 1933 to a quarter of what they were at the time the Firestone loan was made and brought about the very serious debtor-creditor situation with the Firestone interests that has already been referred to.

The chart shows, too, the ultimate wisdom of President

Barclay's policy of staving off the League attack while he waited for the turn of the tide.

The position of the Finance Corporation since the clearing of the atmosphere after the League of Nations episode, and the position of the Firestone Company itself, have been most constructive. An inherently tense condition that obtained while the loan was in default, has developed into a relationship of friendly cooperation. The arrearages in the Finance Corporation loan, which had been so troublesome at the time of the League investigations, were, as we have seen, refunded. The interest rate was drastically reduced. Not only that, but Firestone agreed to the cancellation of $650,000 of the outstanding bonds. Of this cancellation, $400,000 represented an estimate of rents that would become due under the Planting Agreement during the balance of the term of the lease and which were thus, in effect, paid in advance. The remaining $250,000 was nominally in consideration of franchise and tax exemptions, a rather hypothetical item and really a contribution by Firestone to Liberia.

Although Firestone and President Barclay got together shortly after the dropping of the League of Nations' Plan of Assistance, and effected a revison of the loan agreement, it was still some time before the outflow of rubber and the build-up of the country's exports were such as to have a real impact on Government finances. The import-export figures appearing below on page 228, especially the figures of rubber export, will serve to illustrate this fact. As late as 1938, amortization payments on the loan were still in arrears, in the amount of $172,000, but the situation was rapidly improving. In that year interest and amortization payments totaling $258,000 were made, close to 25 per cent of the Government's budget. From that time on, and quite aside from the $650,000 cancellation (which, however, helped), debt reduction has been steady at the contract rate of $35,000 per year.

The bonds issued to the Finance Corporation, including those refunding arrearages, totalled $2,588,000. On November 5, 1951, the figure of outstanding bonds stood at $495,000. Sinking fund payments accounted for $1,443,000 of this reduction. During December, 1951, a final payment was made retiring the loan. Meanwhile the floating debt, which in 1932 was $550,000, and which previously had always had a tendency to rise to a point where refunding became necessary, has been virtually extinguished. By these means interest and amortization charges on the bonds and on the floating debt have been reduced to less than 2 per cent of the annual budget. There would seem to be, therefore, a basis for a good credit standing on the part of the Liberian Government, at least within the scope of its present revenues and so long as expenditures are kept in firm control. A comparison of the 1949 budget with the actual expenditures over a twelve months period from August 31, 1948, to August 31, 1949, is interesting;

BUDGET, 1949		Actual 12 months	
		Aug. 31, '48 to Aug. 31, '49	Aug. 31, '49 to Aug. 31, '50
General Government	$ 340,567	$ 378,606	$ 254,275
Chief Executive office	199,905	183,134	305,839
Dept. of State, foreign service, etc.	321,469	281,738	427,557
War Dept. & Frontier Force	201,183	215,475	208,791
Dept. of Justice & Judiciary	251,111	238,543	282,655
Interior Dept.	96,556	93,228	110,754
Dept. of Agri. & Commerce	90,696	89,645	114,646
Treas. Dept., Bu. Int. Rev., Audits & Financial Adv.	376,346	336,276	417,772
Post Office & Govt. Radio	161,176	149,303	187,456
Legislative	138,430	125,273	131,623
County, Municipalities, Light Houses, etc.	116,072	92,265	100,301
Various other	137,414	131,360	124,876
Public Works	509,049	564,123	636,973
Pub. Health & hospitals	385,181	362,482	405,228
Public instruction	269,829	258,425	330,628
	$3,594,984	$3,499,876	$4,039,374
Debt service (interest & sinking fund)	59,492	59,108	60,181
Floating debt	....	2,452	....
	$3,654,476	$3,561,436	$4,099,555

Revenues for the year ending December 31, 1949 amounted to $3,815,834 against the expenditure budget of $3,654,476 for the corresponding period, and an actual expenditure total for the 12 months fiscal period ending Aug. 31, 1949 of $3,561,436.

For the 12 months ending August 31, 1950 receipts were:

Hut tax	$375,351
Other taxes	659,433
Consular fees	115,012

Profit on raw gold	20,121
License fees	188,330
Vessel registration fees	162,107
Other internal revenue	106,305
Total internal revenue	$1,626,659
Postal and utility revenues	171,988
Customs revenues	2,020,094
Total revenues	3,818,741

During the year 1951 additional corporation income taxes became effective and the Government's budget for that year was based upon an expected total revenue of $5,000,000. Actual revenue for the calendar year 1951 will materially exceed that figure, receipts for the eight months ending August 31 having amounted to $6,015,000, already a million dollars over the budget figure for the entire year and indicating a probable 1951 revenue of more than $7,000,000. The resulting retirement in full of the Finance Corporation loan is an event in the history of Liberia.

Liberia has never had a currency of its own, except for a few minor coins, nor has it needed it. Until the Second World War British currency was used and the pound sterling and shilling were the units of value, with some French money circulating, mainly in the areas near the Guinea border. The Bank of West Africa operated a branch in Monrovia and, until it was closed as part of the attack on Liberia's independence, provided the needed banking services. After the coming of Firestone a department of the United States Trading Company, subsidiary of the Plantations Company, operated as a bank. Later it became the Bank of Monrovia.

When Roberts Field was created and garrisoned by the American Army Air Forces, American dollars were sent over by the United States Government and the British currency was bought up. Since then the dollar has replaced the pound sterling and American currency has become the medium of exchange within Liberia. To some extent this has offered a standing invitation to European trading companies to do business in Liberia and thus obtain the coveted dollar exchange.

There has been some toying with the idea of creating a Liberian National Bank to function as a bank of issue and thus create a purely Liberian currency. Such a bank was included in the original plans of the Stettinius group, to be specially organized for the purpose and possibly take over the assets and business of the Bank of Monrovia. This project has been dropped so far as The Liberia Company, created by Mr. Stettinius, is concerned, but there has been some thought that the Government itself might take over the Bank of Monrovia.

FOREIGN TRADE OF LIBERIA
(000 omitted)

	Calendar year 1937	Calendar year 1939	Calendar year 1941	Calendar year 1943	Calendar year 1945	Calendar year 1947	12 mos. Sept. 1, '49 to Aug. 31, '50
ALL IMPORTS . . .	$1,958	$2,003	$3,408	$3,984	$3,547	$8,763	$10,371
Petroleum, etc. .	90	117	290	234	215	425	....
Metals, except mch'y & vehicles	316	399	451	522	299	462	....
Mch'y & vehicles	225	296	696	633	305	790	....
Other imports* .	1,327	1,191	1,971	2,595	2,728	7,086	....
ALL EXPORTS . . .	$2,031	$2,813	$5,096	$9,107	$11,719	$13,378	$16,338
Cocoa	41	15	8	...	....	23	69
Coffee	149	66	...	...	2	27	18
Gold	65	141	630	815	234	476	339
Palm oil	43	11	...	...	....	195	308
Kernels	473	142	...	...	4	376	1,807
Rubber†	1,032	2,223	4,275	8,059	10,960	11,766	13,181
Piassava . . .	182	99	67	86	128	192	152
Other	46	116	116	147	391	323	464
TRADE WITH UNITED STATES							
To U.S.	$ 976	$2,137	$4,963	$9,021	$11,418	$12,260	$13,921
From U.S. . . .	684	1,000	2,822	3,567	3,275	7,407	7,402

*"Other imports" are of many and various kinds, the individual amounts of each item being without special significance for the purposes of this presentation. The more important classifications from U.S. point of view are, however, shown separately.

†The figures of rubber exports represent mainly the product of the Firestone Plantation, and the impact upon the economy of the country can be judged accordingly.

· *Chapter Seventeen* ·

THE EVERGREEN FORESTS

LIBERIA's forty thousand square miles contain Africa's greatest evergreen forests. What these forests hide in useful woods is one of the Republic's great mysteries. Vast areas lying inland from the coastal fringe are virtually unexplored. No roads penetrate them, and few native foot-trails. Map makers have written across thousands of their acres "uninhabited."

Fed by the tropical rains, the forest giants of the African West Coast never lose their verdure. Hence the term "evergreen," for there are no coniferous trees as in America's evergreen forests, no pines, no hemlocks, firs, or spruces.

Because of the very mystery that enshrouds them, Liberia's forests have an appeal to the imagination. The thought of their possible wealth in mahogany and other tropical hardwoods seems automatically to take first place in the minds of foreigners the moment they become interested in the possibilities that lie in the development of the country's resources.

Disillusionment soon follows. The difficulties involved in any attempt at making the wealth of the forests usable by the civilized world quickly loom up and overshadow the imaginative appeal. The would-be forester in Liberia is faced at once with the problem of transportation. The great variety of woods is itself an obstacle to their availability, the density of their growth another. The great trees of the high forest reach often to a height of 150 feet or more, their tops so intertwined with tangled vines and creepers that the felling of a single tree is impossible.

Yet in the near-by British Gold Coast, where the terrain is not dissimilar to that of Liberia, the forests have yielded to the penetration of the English. Railroads reach deep into the hinterland of the Ashantis from the coastal cities, Takoradi and Accra, and over a network of excellent motor roads a constant stream of trucks hauls the great mahogany logs to the rail-head at Kumasi for transport to the sea and shipment to the United States or to England. Mahogany has become one of the great staple exports of the Gold Coast, sometimes bringing quick wealth to the shrewd buyer who purchases the logs at their source and sells them to their foreign users.

Why should not Liberia's forests undergo a similar development? Perhaps they will. But it will take courage, effort, and capital. It may require also a deal of education of the possible users of cabinet woods in America, and of the users of other types of lumber as well, for the key may lie in popularizing a great variety of woods with which we, in the United States, are unfamiliar.

There have been two really noteworthy surveys of the Liberian forests. The first resulted from the early steps in the establishment of the Firestone Plantation at Harbel. There a large-scale project of land clearing had to be carried out, and the opportunity was presented of treating the area as a sample of the country's forests and of making a comprehensive study of its trees. Curiously, the suggestion that this be done was first made by a man who had a hobby of collecting specimens of rare woods and making them into walking sticks. Rudolph Block, better known under his pen name of Bruno Lessing, had placed some 1400 such sticks on exhibition in the National Museum at Washington. His idea of making the destructive clearing process in Liberia a means of gaining real knowledge of the country's flora appealed to both Mr. Firestone, Sr., and to Harvey Firestone, Jr., who offered the facilities of the Plantation to the Yale School of Forestry.

So under Firestone sponsorship the University undertook the proposed study, sent one of its experts, Mr. G. Proctor Cooper, to Liberia, and obtained the assistance of the Royal Botanical Gardens at Kew, England. The staff at the Kew Gardens contained eminent authorities on tropical, and especially West African flora, and were qualified to give invaluable assistance in identifying the woods collected.

Long before the advent of Firestone and the Yale forestry

reconnaissance, extensive botanical collections had been made in Liberia, some of these dating back nearly a century. Sir Harry Johnston's very basic descriptive work on Liberia includes a report on the flora of the country compiled for him by Dr. Otto Stapf from data determined earlier by Professor A. Harms of Berlin-Dahlem. At the time of the Yale investigation (1928-1929) a German, one Herr M. Dinklage, who had been in business at Grand Bassa and was retired and living at Monrovia, was working on an extensive botanical study, perhaps using it as a smoke-screen for improving the Reich's general information about the country, on which, with their intended war of conquest in mind, they were keeping a close eye.

But these studies gave no more than passing attention to the larger trees and none at all to the woods. The Yale–Firestone investigation, on the other hand, was made from the standpoint of the forester and the wood-technician, with an eye to the possibilities of scientific lumbering operations and the commercial use of the product. The results of their work have been published by the University and are thus available to any who may be interested in Liberia's forests.[1]

Nearly five hundred specimens were obtained, as Firestone cleared the great acreage for its Plantation. The variety of the trees found can be realized from the fact that some three hundred species were represented, over two hundred genera, and nearly seventy families. From trees that seemed to have possible commercial use, over a hundred hewed bolts were obtained and sent to New Haven for test under standard laboratory conditions. Mahogany, of course, was one of the woods catalogued. But there were many others, some with considerable color, many easily worked, many cited as especially durable.

The woods ranged from exceedingly light and soft to heavy and hard, with an equally great range in durability, color, and texture. Some would take a high luster; others had attractive grain. There were a number of species that suggested themselves as a source of wood pulp. Here is a summary of the uses to which Liberian lumber might be put and the various species suitable in varying degree to these uses, as determined by the Yale School of Forestry:

Furniture and interior trim	21	species
General carpentry, boxes, utility veneers	27	"
Heavy and durable construction	20	"
Tool handles, etc.	16	"
Wood pulp	20	"

It might be noted that some of the varieties adapted to use as wood pulp were of quick and second growth. Whether their use would involve special development, such as that which has made possible the craft-paper industry in our southern states, has not, apparently, been determined.

The second important survey of Liberia's forests has quite recently been completed by a forestry expert working for the United States Economic Mission, Mr. Karl Mayer. This survey, amounting almost to an exploration, differed from that made by the Yale School of Forestry in that it was not so much a sampling of varieties of forest trees in a limited area as it was an actual area survey, covering virtually the entire country, and for the first time making possible, in outline at least, a mapping of the forest lands.

Mr. Mayer and his party made the most extensive tour of the Liberian interior that has ever been attempted. They travelled thirty-three hundred miles, two thousand of it over native foot-trails. There were six separate journeys, each devoted to the reconnoitering of a different area; two hundred and sixteen days of travel.

At this writing the results of the Mayer forest survey have not been published. They doubtless will soon be available, however, and will be an important addition to the knowledge of the Liberian hinterland. The accompanying sketch map will give some idea of how extensive the survey was.

It is the abundance of the rainfall that controls the character of Liberia's forests. In the very wet belt along the whole coast the trees are of little or no commercial value. Inland, where the annual rainfall is over 80 inches, the trees of the high forest thrive in the tropical downpours of the rainy season. This forest belt is crossed by rivers that flow in a southwesterly direction at right angles to the coastline, streams that in the main are impassable, even to native canoes, although some might possibly be cleared sufficiently for part of their length to permit their use in logging operations. A few trails might be made more or less passable for motor vehicles with the building of bridges and culverts. Perhaps narrow-gauge railroads could be made to serve. The engineering

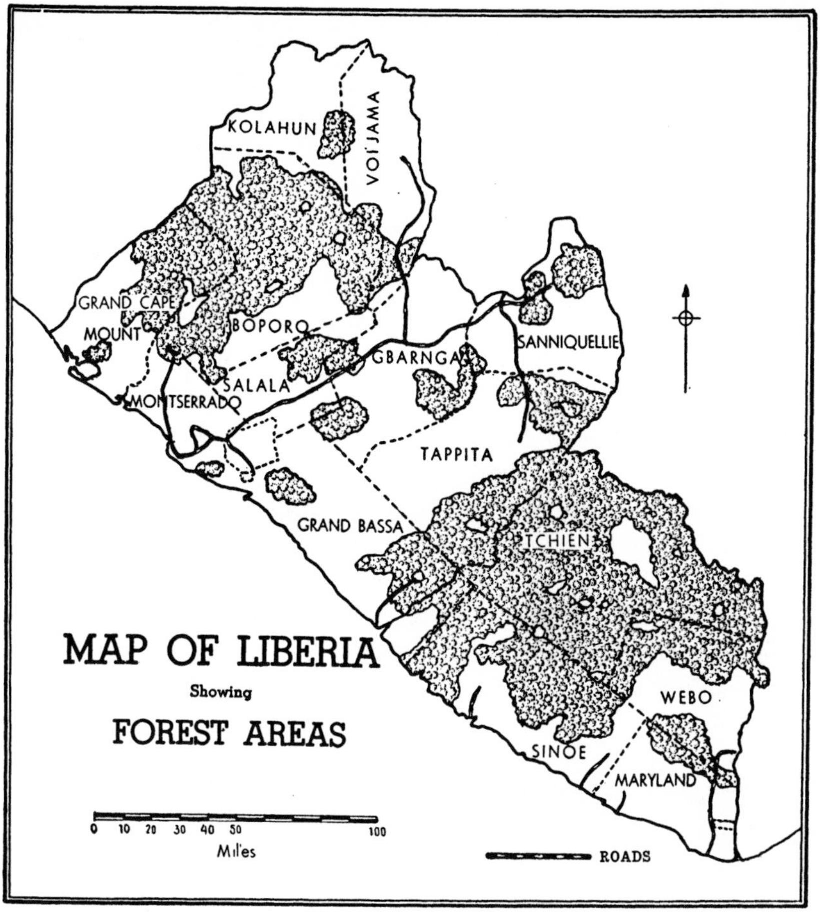

problems of access to this timber area are not great; the economic problems are. The cost of opening up any important area would probably be justified only if the project were fairly extensive, thoroughly organized, and adequately tied in with commercial outlets of an assured nature. But it is in this great belt of high tropical forests that the valuable hardwoods of Liberia are to be found.

Farther inland, on the plateau of the interior, the rainfall is much less, 40 to 80 inches per year. Most of the species of the evergreen forest are to be found, but the growth is not so dense.

The trees are scattered and not so gigantic. Because of the lesser rainfall there is a general shedding of leaves, so that the forests in this area may be considered deciduous.

In the areas near the cities of the coastal plain—Monrovia, Carysburg, Harper—much of the forest is secondary growth, the result of abandoned clearings where at one time or another there have been farms or plantations. The forests that appeal to the imagination, however, are in the vast unexplored tracts, thousands of square miles that probably contain untold billions of feet of hardwood, as yet untouched by man. The great Gola forest back of Cape Mount, in the northwestern part of the country between the Mano and Loffa rivers is believed to be rich in mahogany. Perhaps the lower reaches of the Loffa could be cleared enough to permit rafts to be floated from the interior to the sea.

Practically the entire Tchien District is covered by the great forest which extends into the Webo District and into Sinoe and Grand Bassa counties, covering a large proportion of those areas as well as Tchien, and reported to be the home of mahogany and other hard woods, and oil palms as well. At best, this area is sparsely inhabited, much of it without a single town or village. It is crossed by the Cess or Cestos River, a fairly large stream that might perhaps be made practicable for logging operations, and by the Sanguin, Sino, and Grand Cess rivers, possibly usable to a limited extent if improved. The Ganta road, that now extends to Tappita, is reaching down into this area and may someday contribute to the development of its forests. But the great problem of transportation remains.

Logging operations in a country forested as is Liberia, assuming that a solution to the difficulties of transportation is found, still involve features quite different from those to which foresters in America are accustomed, where great stands of a single variety, spruce, pine, fir, are available. Trees of high individual value, mahogany for example, grow singly. To search them out, fell them under the conditions of dense undergrowth and intertwined canopy, and carry them through the jungle, will involve great difficulties, both mechanical and economical. It seems evident that a successful operation must contemplate the utilization of a considerable variety of timbers, the sorting of them, during or after cutting, into general classes, such as cabinet woods, veneers, construction timbers, and so on. In this way, with proper regard to forestry principles, the bulk of the useful timber of an area might be used, provided, of course, that there are buyers.

This poses the question of whether the American manufacturer will accept the Liberian woods at a price that will pay the costs. Mahogany has a ready market. At the other end of the timber scale, pulpwood would probably be marketable if experimentation with the available varieties showed it to be actually usable. The difficulty with the great variety of other woods is that they are unfamiliar to us. The first step toward making them commercially acceptable would be a much more thorough testing of their utility than has so far been carried out. British experience would help. Not a few of the Liberian varieties, found also elsewhere in West Africa, have been exported from the British colonies for many years.

Before the war, German veneer mills experimented successfully with several woods, notably the Samba, abundant on the West African Coast. A wood known as Okoumé had a similar history. The British and French colonial governments have done important work in conducting laboratory and fabrication tests, placing the results at the disposal of importers and manufacturers, seeking to bring into the market a variety of species that have been commercially unknown and hence unused. These West African timbers, relatively new to commerce, are assuming an increasing importance in Europe, which suggests the possibility of their becoming a significant item in the development of Liberian forest resources.

The United States Economic Mission is continuing the study of Liberia's forests and of improvement in the means of access to them. Should any large-scale development be attempted, advanced methods of forestry will be needed and doubtless will be made a requirement in future Government concessions, so as to avoid danger of denudement and, especially in the case of pulp woods should they come into the picture, to provide for constant reforestation on a crop basis.

The protection of Liberia's forests from improvident lumbering operations involves such matters as the control of cutting so as to leave an adequate residual stand for regeneration, the encouragement of experimental cutting and processing of species having no presently established commercial value, and the current determination by the Government of the quantities of timber taken out for the purpose of assessing proper stumpage charges. The fact that the Government has not yet developed its own personnel qualified to constitute a forestry service for the protection of this most important resource presents a problem. If, however, means should be found for the undertaking of serious lumbering operations, administrative difficulties will have to give way to the obvious need for such a development.

That there is a great potential wealth of useful timber in Liberia's forests seems to be beyond question. So far, however, the appeal has been to the imagination rather than to the pocketbook of possible investors. But with the rapidly increasing scarcity of wood in our own country, and especially if a way is found to duplicate the highly constructive work the British are doing in developing the use of tropical woods, logging operations in the evergreen forests of Liberia may move out of the realm of imagination and become a real industry.

• Chapter Eighteen •

COCOA, KERNELS, AND COFFEE

THE economic future of Liberia may, quite possibly, become as closely related to the production of cocoa as it now is to that of rubber. There was a time when Liberia exported cocoa. Not a very large tonnage of it in comparison with the rest of the world, but large enough to be an important item of income to the country. It was sold mainly to the Dutch for processing in Holland, and it found its way to the European continent in German, Dutch, and English ships.

Liberian cocoa was never of the grades acceptable to the American market; it did not have to be, for the Dutch bought on price and were not over-particular about inspection, which suited conditions as they then were in Liberia, and minimized the care needed in the preparation of the beans. When the Second World War broke out, it put an end to the cocoa trade so far as Liberia was concerned; there were no ships to carry Liberian cocoa to Europe. The British promised shipping space, but their promises were not fulfilled; the pressure of war on the British Merchant Marine was too great.

The soil and climate of Liberia are well suited to the growing of the cocoa bean, or cacao as it is sometimes called. The cacao tree grows only in the tropics, between the latitudes of 20° north and 20° south. Ideally it requires a rainfall of between 50 and 150 inches per year, a temperature of about 80° Fahrenheit, a well drained soil of considerable depth, and protection from drying winds. These conditions obtain in Liberia, especially inland from the coastal plain. The same favorable conditions are found in the

British colony of Gold Coast and in Nigeria. Within a period of less than sixty years the cocoa industry has grown in Gold Coast from zero to where that country is the world's chief supplier.[1]

The annual global production of the cocoa bean is, in round figures, about 600,000 long tons. Nearly half of this, about 285,000 tons, is grown in Gold Coast and Nigeria, mainly in Gold Coast. Brazil produces a little over 100,000 tons, French West Africa about 80,000. The balance comes from Spanish Guinea, Angola, the British West Indies, and a few other favored spots, mainly on the Caribbean. The United States, the greatest consumer of cocoa, uses a quantity about equal to the combined production of Gold Coast and Nigeria, although it buys in the world market and its cocoa therefore comes from all the cocoa-growing lands.

There are three main classes of cocoa, known as Basic, Fine, and Criollo. The first of these, the Basic, is the product of the tree known botanically as *Forastero*, and this is the cocoa grown chiefly in West Africa and Brazil. The Fine cocoa comes from trees classified as *Trinitario*, and is grown in the West Indies and in certain of the Latin American countries. It is used for blending with the Basic to improve the flavor and brings a higher price, but the quantity grown is much less than the Basic. The Criollo is a special type used for a few higher class products only, and is of very limited cultivation.

There are various grades of the Basic cocoa, depending largely on the care used in harvesting the beans and in preparing them for the market. Cocoa is a delicate product to ship and great pains have to be taken to protect it from dampness. The sweating that ordinarily takes place in a vessel's hold as it comes from the humid heat of the tropics into the cold waters of the North Atlantic often causes considerable loss. American-flag vessels within the past few years have made an enviable record in reducing such losses by the superior care taken in handling their cargo and protecting it from damage of this kind.

Cocoa in the Gold Coast is facing calamity. A virus disease, first observed in 1932, and known as "swollen shoot," has been attacking the trees and has already devastated nearly a third of the colony's cocoa producing country. No remedy has been found short of the destruction of the trees and their replacement, a difficult, costly, and time-consuming process, during which the position of the Gold Coast as the world's chief producer of cocoa may be lost. At the time this is written the battle against the swollen shoot is still a losing one. Two and a half million trees are being cut every year, and 50 million trees, out of a total of 400 million are definitely infected. It is even possible that the industry in the Gold Coast will be virtually wiped out; it will be, unless there is a turn for the better in the attempts at its control.[2]

The misfortune of the Gold Coast cocoa growers may be Liberia's opportunity. It is even possible that the phenomenal growth of the cocoa industry in Gold Coast will be repeated in Liberia. If so, the fortune of the Republic will have been made. Cocoa is, in fact, again moving out of Liberia. In 1946, for the first time in five years, Liberia exported cocoa, just a trickle. The following year a few tons more, forty tons or so. In 1949 the figure had risen to about five hundred tons. Still a small quantity, worth a couple of hundred thousand dollars; but look at what happened in Gold Coast!

The first shipment from that British colony, in 1891, was eighty *pounds!* In 1906, nine thousand tons were shipped. Thirty years later the figure was 305,000 tons. That year the world produced over 700,000 tons of cocoa beans and the United States used over 300,000 tons. Although the colony is named for the precious metal gotten from the famous Ashanti mines, its wealth has come mainly from cocoa. Here, for example, are some figures of Gold Coast trade that tell the story of cocoa's place in its economy. In 1946 this British colony imported goods from the United States and Canada, that is to say, from dollar countries, to the value of £3,430,000. Its exports to North America amounted to £10,019,000, and of that total, £6,646,000 was the value of its cocoa, more than £5,500,000 worth sold to the United States. All its exports to America other than cocoa brought it £3,373,000, almost in exact balance with its dollar-area imports. Thus, from a balance-of-trade standpoint the cocoa was all profit. It contributed more than $22,000,000 of dollar exchange to the sterling area. Not at all to be sneezed at! On the contrary, something for the British to worry about. But a remarkable figure for an industry that had been introduced into the country less than six decades ago. Surely there is something here for Liberia to think about. And to do something about.

Actually, cocoa is not indigenous in Africa. It came from South America originally, from Brazil via the Portuguese island of Säo Tomé, just on the equator off the West African coast. From there the industry went to the Spanish island of Fernando Po in the Bight of Biafra, where the African coastline turns from east-and-west to north-and-south.

The British got some beans from Fernando Po, and so did the Liberians, for much of the labor used in the Spanish island came from the Kru Coast, and the Kru boys, returning, brought seed home to Liberia. In 1887 there was an official distribution in Gold Coast of plants bred from seed imported from Säo Tomé. The planting of cocoa trees thereafter spread with a rapidity that has seldom been paralleled elsewhere. It became an industry of small individual farms, generally of only three or four acres, often less, each producing on the average less than a ton of the beans per year. It is estimated that there are about 300,000 cocoa farmers in Gold Coast.

This wide distribution of the industry among the natives might be an advantage to the extent of permitting a large number to be independent small farmers. But it has not worked out quite that way. Like the tenant farmers of our own South, the cocoa farmers live from hand to mouth, have to be financed from crop to crop. The great trading companies that market the crop cannot possibly organize to deal directly with 300,000 individual growers. So the situation produced a class of middlemen or brokers, astute natives, many of them illiterate but none the less shrewd, who borrow from the trading companies on their own credit, which they carefully maintain inviolate. They, in turn, lend to the small farmer, often at exorbitant rates of interest, with the farm and crop as security. Thus they have a hold on the native cocoa grower, as to both the purchase of his cocoa and the sale to him of his supplies.

Attempts have been made to correct the evils of this system, but without great success, for once started, a practice of this kind is difficult or impossible to change. In building a new cocoa industry in Liberia the opportunity exists to profit by the lessons of the Gold Coast and so to organize production as to give the individual native a chance to earn without finding himself in the clutches of unscrupulous brokers.

The plan recommended for Liberia by the United States Economic Mission,[3] and on which a start has already been made, involves the establishment of cocoa farms or plantations of moderate size, perhaps 10,000 acres, large enough to justify one or two skilled resident managers, and to make the undertaking worth while from an investment standpoint. If the plantations are not too large, labor recruited from near-by towns could be used, avoiding the migration of workers, either temporarily or permanently, which is necessary when a force of thousands is required. By reserving areas for food crops, the tribal life would go on without serious disturbance, the men working on the cocoa farm, the women tending the food crop, but with the advantage of guidance from the agriculturists in charge.

Such plantations could also encourage small native production of cocoa, over which skilled supervision would be exercised, the plantation buying the beans, or possibly the cocoa in the pod, and thus controlling the process of fermentation and drying. This would make it possible also to adopt some means for mechanical drying for use when needed, and to use vats for fermentation and concrete drying floors. The plantation staff could transport the crop to the port and arrange for its sale, without the intervention of the more or less rapaceous brokers who have been an unavoidable feature of the Gold Coast set-up.

It cannot be assumed, however, that the cocoa industry can be re-established in Liberia along workable lines without a great deal of skill and a not inconsiderable amount of capital. As with practically every other agricultural product, knowledge and experience are required in cocoa growing and handling on the part of both managers and workers, and anyone planning to enter the business without such knowledge and experience will do well to go into the market for competent help.

It requires about five years of painstaking work before the trees begin to bear. Then the pods, which grow in clusters directly on the trunk and large branches (not from stems, as do other fruits), must be harvested by trained pickers who have learned how to distinguish the ripened pods from those that lack a week or two of being ready, and who know, also, how to remove the ripened pods without injury to the tree. These pods, maybe a dozen from a tree at a picking, must be split open, a trick which itself requires a special skill. The expert breaker will handle perhaps as many as 500 pods per hour; his wrist must be strong and tireless. Stripping the seeds from the placental strings that run lengthwise of the seed-pulp cylinder is a difficult operation, simple as it looks.

These are mechanical operations, requiring no more than manual skill, readily acquired by the natives if they are carefully taught and trained. The next step is chemical, involving the removal of the white pulp that surrounds the beans, by the process of fermentation. The crude way is to gather the beans into heaps, cover them with palm leaves, and allow fermentation for five to seven days. This is the method followed by the small farmer of the Gold Coast, with varying results. A more up-to-date way is by the use of special fermenting boxes or vats. Experience and clear judgment are needed for this process, for it is not amenable to formula; no two batches can be treated quite alike. The smell of the heated pulp, the color of the seeds, their texture as the process of fermentation proceeds, show when the proper stage has been reached, and this can be learned only slowly.

When, over a period of several days, the seeds have been mixed by repeated turnings, to mingle the cooler beans on the outside with those that might be getting too hot near the center, the batch is ready; the beans will be spread out to dry, perhaps on palm mats, perhaps on a drying floor. Drying must be carefully regulated, the beans raked over and turned. Too fast drying will crack them open, expose the seeds within, and affect the flavor and maybe the price of the product. If the weather is cloudy and natural drying is relied on, it may not proceed fast enough; mold may set in and the batch sour. Some form of artificial drying is therefore desirable, especially if the farm or plantation is so located that rain is a possibility during the season of the harvest. In any case, the beans must be under cover at night, for even dew will spoil them.

When after a few days, perhaps a week or more, drying is complete, the beans may be glazed with a very thin coating of clay to protect them from mold while in transit. This is done by making them up into a heap, adding finely powdered red clay with a little water; then barefooted workers tread them.

The cocoa is now ready for shipment in 200-pound sacks. But first it must be inspected and graded. For this purpose random samples are taken and a small inspection board is used, about a foot square, in which are just 100 indentations made with a gouge, each indentation about the size of the ball of one's thumb, so as to accommodate a bean. Into these indentations 100 beans are put, taken from the sample. The inspector then removes all beans that are moldy, unfermented, sprouted, or otherwise faulty. The resulting number of empty indentations then gives the percentage of faulty beans, and, with some other requirements, such as color, taste, and smell, determines the grade.

In the Gold Coast these processes take place partly in the hands of the small cocoa farmer, partly in those of the broker, and partly at the "factories" of the great trading companies through whom the cocoa moves into export.

Before the war, the trading companies, numbering about a dozen, purchased all the cocoa raised in Gold Coast and Nigeria, and sold it, mainly through brokers in London, who in turn dealt on the New York Cocoa Exchange and elsewhere. United Africa Company, or UAC as it is generally called, subsidiary of the British firm of Lever Brothers, did about half the business. The other firms, British, Dutch, Swiss, and French handled the remainder. Competition among them was acute and it is said that at times they operated at a loss. Curiously, one of the results of this set-up was that the American users of cocoa, although taking half the world's supply, kept no buyers in British West Africa, but were content to bid for their requirements on the New York Cocoa Exchange. Another curious fact is that although the annual production of cocoa varied over quite a range, there was no carry-over from year to year; each year's crop was fully marketed, although at a price.

When war came, the British Government moved into the situation. A Gold Coast Marketing Board was set up, acting for the Government, and a similar authority was created in Nigeria. These boards bought and still buy the entire cocoa crop of the two colonies, utilizing the services of UAC and the other trading companies, and selling the product through London, the brokerage houses, and the Cocoa Exchange.

The British Government has thus been able to fix, and still fixes, the price nominally paid the producer for his cocoa, and to a degree the price the American user has to pay. A very substantial profit has resulted, to the discomfiture of the members of the New York Cocoa Exchange, and from this profit a fund of millions of pounds sterling has been set up in the hands of the Marketing Boards, the final disposition of which is one of the problems resulting from the control. The possibility of its being used as a "fighting fund," to control competition cannot be wholly overlooked. (See U. S. imports of cocoa, 1947, 1948, page 153, below.)

The trading companies are licensed by the Marketing Boards to buy the cocoa and to sell it for the Government. The amount of money paid to the brokers who actually sell the cocoa to the trading companies is determined by the price fixed by the Government. But since the producer of the cocoa, the small farmer who raises a ton or less of the beans per year, sells his cocoa and obtains his supplies through the broker and not at the trading company's factory, it is anybody's guess as to what the native producer really receives. The price-stabilizing actions of the British Government thus hardly reach down to the small farmer. Nor do they solve the problem of exorbitant interest, sometimes as much as 50 per cent, exacted by the native brokers for carrying the farmer. There has been some thought of utilizing the fund presently in the hands of the Government to set up a farm bank, or by some other means to use it to help the individual producer. But so far a solution to the problems inherent in the whole system seems not to have been found. One thing is clear; a similar condition must not be permitted to enter into the infant Liberian cocoa industry.

The action of the British Government in taking over all the purchase and sale of Nigerian and Gold Coast cocoa, half the world's supply, led to bitter complaints on the part of the New York Cocoa Exchange. The charge was made that a free market was thus made impossible, that the American user of cocoa was the victim of governmental price-fixing. The situation was reminiscent of the Stevenson Plan of two decades earlier to control the price Americans would have to pay for British-produced rubber, which led directly to the establishment of the Firestone Plantation in Liberia. But long before the cocoa control was set up, the great trading companies, led by Unilever's United Africa Company, were able to exercise an influence over the world's cocoa trade just about as effective, and as inimical to American interests, as that later exerted by the Government-created Marketing Boards. Liberia seems to be in a position possibly to act as a palliative in the cocoa trade, much as it has done in respect to rubber. If it becomes a real factor in the production of cocoa, the grip that the British hold on America's supply may be greatly lessened, to the mutual benefit of Liberia and the users of Hershey Bars.

The first cocoa to come out of Liberia since the war is from the area along the coast, Cape Palmas to Sinoe. It is, in a sense, a hold-over from the days when Kru boys were laborers on the cocoa farms of Fernando Po. The Cape Palmas trees are from seeds brought home from the Spanish island. They have survived the period when Liberian cocoa could not be exported, despite the fact that the coast is much less suitable than the country farther inland, the rainfall being decidedly greater than the optimum, with consequent danger of pod rot and mold.

The Liberian area best adapted to cocoa growing is believed by the United States Economic Mission to be that lying between the St. John and the Cess rivers, to the east and south from Ganta and along the Ganta road. This is the Mano country, well populated, with labor plentiful. Here the rainfall is 80 to 100 inches, the elevation about 2000 feet. In this part of Liberia, and elsewhere on the continental plateau, the soil survey recently completed by the Economic Mission shows that there are as many as two million acres suitable for cocoa farming, an area two and a half times that under cocoa cultivation in the Gold Coast. So far as suitability of the soil is concerned, Liberia could duplicate the output that has brought wealth to the British Colony.

The Liberia Company has undertaken the raising of cocoa as its major project. Two thousand acres have already been planted in trees that will reach bearing age in 1954, and several thousand additional acres are being prepared for the setting out of seedlings that have been started in the Company's nurseries.

This cocoa plantation, which is to serve as a pilot in developing the industry, is located about half-way between Ganta and Sakripi, on the new motor road that now extends to Tapita. In charge is a young American agriculturist, Santiago Porcella III, trained in forestry at Louisiana State University. Some years of employment as a member of the Firestone Plantation staff gave him a thorough knowledge of the ways of the Liberian natives and of the characteristics of the country's soil and climate. In anticipation of his present activity, he became an expert in cocoa growing and in the handling of the product by spending several years on the cocoa plantations of Turrialba, Costa Rica.

By the use of advanced methods of preparation, carefully controlled vat fermentation, proper drying floors, and rigid inspection, Mr. Porcella expects to produce in Liberia cocoa that will grade much higher than the Gold Coast product, and so command a higher price in the American market. The raising of cocoa by native farmers in the vicinity of the plantation is being encouraged; it can be given close supervision by the plantation's agriculturists. Cocoa grown by the natives can be purchased in the pod and processed at the plantation, thus controlling the vital processes that govern its condition as it moves toward export.

While Mr. Porcella has brought to his Liberian task a thorough knowledge of the best practice in cocoa production based on that of the Caribbean area from which come the highest grades of the bean, he has also brought an open mind, listening to the suggestions of experienced native farmers and experimenting with various methods, such as planting seeds directly in a path cut through the bush, the use of nursery-grown stock, and of different degrees of shade in the protection of the young trees, the planting of bananas for shade pending the maturing of the cocoa, seeding in pockets of prepared soil, grafting, and so on.

The workers on the Porcella plantation come from near by, their own farms continuing to provide the native villages with food. A basic force of about 120 is increased to 200 when, in the rainy season, actual planting is done. When the trees reach maturity and harvesting and processing begin a larger temporary force will be required.

A number of independent cocoa farms have recently been started along the Ganta and Bomi Hills roads. These, like the Porcella plantation, are in locations where rainfall conditions are much more favorable than in the Cape Palmas area, and where access to the Port of Monrovia by motor truck is practicable.

To safeguard the quality of cocoa exported from Liberia, the Government, in October, 1947, established by executive order rigid specifications to govern the grading and to set standards for the inspection and export of the cocoa.[4] The highest grade, to be known as "Liberian Cocoa Special Grade," must be packed in new bags sealed with Government seals, accompanied by certificates issued by inspectors of the Bureau of Agriculture. The total of germinated, slaty, weevily, moldy, or unfermented beans, or of beans showing other defects, must not exceed 1 per cent; the color of the meat must be light to chocolate brown; the beans must be uniformly large, plump and smooth; there must be no evidence of smoke taste or smell, and the flavor must be sweet, nutty, and free from bitterness.

The next grades, designated as "Liberian First Grade" and "Liberian Second Grade," respectively, correspond to Gold Coast first and second grades, with germinated, slaty, weevily, or moldy beans not exceeding 5 per cent and 10 per cent. These two grades, more particularly the second grade, are those to which the American market and American taste have become accustomed, so as to accommodate the quantity production of the Gold Coast, in contra-distinction to the higher grade Caribbean cocoa, the standard of which, with its higher market price, Mr. Porcella seeks to equal or surpass. If that is successfully done, it will put Liberian cocoa on the most favorable quality level.

To insure the rigid enforcement of the Government specifications, a rule was promulgated on June 15, 1948, that cocoa not meeting the prescribed grades must be destroyed in the presence of the inspector. Notwithstanding this, one of the Syrian trading companies recently sent a shipment of its own sub-grade cocoa to the United States, only to have it rejected at the American port as unsalable, the violation thus bringing its own punishment.

The experimental work Mr. Porcella is doing is not confined to cocoa, although that is given first place. In the nurseries of his plantation young coffee trees are being started, in the belief that Liberia's once promising coffee trade can also be re-established under conditions that will make it profitable.

Liberia has the distinction of having given its name to one of the five main groups into which the world's coffee is classified, the *Coffea liberica*, the other groups being the *arabica*, *robusta*, *stenophylla*, and the *hybrids*.[5] Both C. liberica and C. robusta grow in Liberia. They have a distinctive flavor, are useful in blending, and ordinarily command a high price. Before the war, Liberian coffee was favorably known the world around, although it never had the benefit of scientific culture; for Liberian coffee farmers knew little or nothing of the art of pruning, and the trees grew to a height making harvesting difficult. The total quantity exported, as compared with Brazil, for example, was not great. But it was an important item among Liberian products. The war killed the business, as it did Liberia's other exports, rubber excepted. The value of Liberia's exported coffee in 1937 was $149,000. It fell in 1938 to $102,000, then to $66,000, to $52,000, and in 1941 to zero. A trifling amount was shipped out in 1945; $37,000 worth in 1946; less than that in the years that followed. The Liberians themselves have great faith in their coffee, and it may be that the trade can be re-established. Like cocoa, it takes special skills in culture and handling. Competition, especially from South and Central America, must be reckoned with. If the marketing problem can be solved, the raising of Liberian coffee should have real possibilities.

In re-establishing these industries in Liberia, it may be found worth while to combine the growing of the oil palm with that of cocoa. Such a combination is included in the plans for the plantation that is being started for The Liberia Company.

There is no such spectacular history back of palm oil and palm kernels as that of the Gold Coast cocoa. Yet the oil palm offers real opportunities for development as an item of Liberian foreign trade. The cocoa and palm nut harvest seasons come one following the other, so that a plantation partly in cocoa, partly in palms, can use the same labor force for both. By utilizing nuts brought in by natives from wild trees in the vicinity, a cash income might be obtained during the period of five years or so required for the seedlings of both trees, palm and cocoa, to reach bearing age.

There are two quite distinct but related products of the oil palm, the red-orange palm oil of commerce, and the palm kernels, from which, in turn, a white edible oil is obtained, known as kernel oil.[6] The first of these is extracted from the fleshy pericarp of the palm nut. Carefully prepared and fresh, it is edible and an important part of the diet of the native African, being rich in vitamins. This oil is the basis of the gravy that enriches and lubricates Liberian "country chop." Commercially, palm oil is an important raw material for the soap manufacturer. In the United States it finds use in the process of the making of tin plate and terne plate, the iron, before being dipped in the molten tin or tin-lead mixture, passing through a bath of palm oil.

The palm kernel is not so well known in the United States as is the palm oil, but quantities of it are used in Europe, where fats are scarce and the edible vegetable oils are consequently in great demand. The oil can be extracted from the kernel locally, and shipped as such from the tropics. Many tons of it are sent that way from Unilever's Belgian Congo company, the "Société Anonyme des Huileries du Congo Belge." But Europe prefers to buy the kernels, partly to process them under favorable conditions, partly because a useful by-product results—an ingredient of cattle fodder.

The palm-kernel oil, white and free from the fatty acids that detract from the value of the pericarp oil, is ideal for the manufacture of margarine. It has the proper melting point, spreads easily, and of all the vegetable fats used for the purpose is the closest to butter. It might find a large market for this use in the United States were it not for the fact that oleo-margarine has long been a political football.

Palm nuts, kernels, and palm oil are produced in the Belgian Congo, Nigeria, French West Africa, Australia, India, Ceylon, Sumatra, and the Dutch East Indies. It is from the group of far-eastern countries that the most severe competition with African oil-palm products comes.

The oil palm grows everywhere throughout West Africa. Every native village is surrounded by an area in which many of the trees are to be found, seeded from discarded nuts. Indeed, although the trees grow wild, it is thought that none exists that has not been seeded by man in some such way.

The trees begin to bear when five or six years old. They are then only a few feet high. At about twelve years they are in full bearing and at fifteen are in their prime. They may continue to bear for as many as forty or fifty years more. The fruit grows at the top of the tree where the palm leaves branch out to form the corm of the palm, and no native likes to climb a trunk that is much over thirty feet tall. When grown in plantations, lower trees are far more economical, especially when, during the rainy season, the trunks are wet and slippery and climbing is more hazardous. Since the trees grow very slowly, the fruit of twenty-year-old plantation trees may still be reached by a small ladder. The tall wild trees are climbed by means of a loop of rope, encircling the tree and the climber's body, a picturesque but slow and uneconomical process.

The fruit forms in clusters or heads that average about eight pounds in weight, although they sometimes run to several times that size. The nuts often reach the native village markets still in the bunch as it was cut from the tree top. The ripe fruit is knocked out of the bunch, or pried out with a stout knife. As processed by the natives, the first step is to put the fruit into kettles with a small amount of water. A half-hour's boiling loosens the pulp or pericarp that surrounds the nut. The fruits are then taken out of the kettle and subjected to pounding in wooden mortars or in troughs, then squeezed in net bags made of strong coarse fiber. The reddish oil, or at least part of it, contained in the pericarp, runs out and is collected, sometimes in a trough, sometimes, perhaps, in a convenient dugout canoe, to be dipped up, strained, and stored away in whatever containers happen to be available—jars, old kerosene tins, gasoline drums. Although the fresh fruit contains over 30 per cent of oil, only about 10 per cent is extracted by the native method.

Much of this oil is consumed by the natives as an important part of their diet. To get it to central points for export shipment often presents a problem, especially where resort must be had to head-loading. At tropical temperatures the oil is liquid, and since containers capable of effective closure are generally lacking, it is far from being an ideal head-load for transport over the foot-trails of the hinterland.

The nuts, once the work of extracting the palm oil from the pericarp has been completed, are given another boiling, then gathered in piles until it is convenient to give them further attention. Then each nut, resembling somewhat a plump peach pit, is cracked open by being placed and held in a slight depression in an anvil of stone or wood and struck with a smaller stone, with just enough force to break the shell without crushing the kernel. This work is done by women and children. The kernels can now be sacked and are thus easily head-loaded to the processing plant, if that be their destination, or to the buyer, who may be a native trader or an agent of one of the great trading companies, and who will move them to export.

Experiments have shown that it is possible to teach the African native to make the edible palm oil well and cheaply by the use of simple machinery, and to keep the fatty acids that result from delayed handling as low as 6 per cent or even better. Processing the pericarp in adequately equipped plants will effect a recovery of two or three times that usually attained by the cruder methods, but there seems to be no settled rule as to what level of operation is necessary to make a central plant economical, much depending on how dense is the growth of oil palms in the area, and how much of a problem is presented by difficulties of transportation. Machines have been devised for separating the pulp from the nuts, for expressing the oil from the pulp, or extracting it by centrifugal action. There are also methods of chemical treatment, whereby the oil is dissolved out of the pulped fruit and then recovered from the solvent. There are nut-cracking machines for freeing the kernels from the shell, and of course the kernels can then be either shipped as such or further processed at the central plant.

The fact that all the natives of the Liberian hinterland know the oil palm and how to extract at least a portion of the available oil and how to separate out the nuts and free the kernels, suggests that this knowledge may well be built upon in starting a new oil-palm plantation. The plantation manager could begin by buying the kernels, and perhaps any of the oil that might be in excess of the food requirements of the natives. Gradually the simpler types of extracting and nut-cracking machines could be put in native hands or be operated under the supervision of the Paramount Chiefs. Experience would be the guide as to further mechanization. Meanwhile the undertaking should carry itself while the trees on the new plantation were coming to maturity. After that, the buying of native-produced oil and kernels could be continued along with the formal operation of the plantation.

It is probable that the planter, whether of oil palms, cocoa, or coffee, would have to go into the business of retailing trade goods to the natives who work on his plantation or from whom he buys oil and kernels, or at least to arrange for such a service by one of the trading companies. Unless trade goods such as textiles, enamelled ware, lanterns and the general run of imported goods are made easily available, and a desire for them created, the native will remain content with his simple tribal life. Money wages will offer him little inducement to become an efficient worker, for there will be no real improvement in his way of living. Firestone had to organize a trading company, not only to supply its managers and their families with their needs, but to give the native workers an opportunity to buy imported articles for everyday use or to take back with them to their tribal villages. The unscrupulous brokers of the Gold Coast provide a similar service, buying from the great trading companies and retailing, at no-one-knows-what profit, to the small cocoa farmer. If the managers of the cocoa, coffee, and oil-palm plantations in Liberia bring to the natives of the hinterland imported factory products, create a demand for such goods, and do it honestly in the interest of their workers, they will contribute importantly to the uplift of the Liberian aborigine.

An actual start has been made in creating a Liberian export business in palm kernels, so far all grown wild. In 1945 the quantity exported was zero. In 1946 something less than 2000 tons left the country. The following year saw the figure more than doubled. In 1948 between 12,000 and 13,000 tons were exported and in 1949 nearly 20,000 tons.[7]

With a view to establishing organized plantations of oil palms, some 700,000 nuts are being gotten from Nigeria from selected stock. From these, seedlings of improved strain will be grown, with the cooperation of the United States Economic Mission. Firestone is also importing seed nuts that have resulted from hand pollination, with which to experiment in the growing of oil palms on the rubber plantation. Liberia's Secretary of State, Gabriel L. Dennis, has a palm-tree nursery on Bushrod Island, not far from Monrovia, where some 500,000 oil palms are being grown, some of them, as this is written, about ready to be set out. On the road between Kakata and Ganta are several oil-palm plantations that are just beginning to yield, with trees five or six feet high.

Oil-palm production per acre of organized plantation is quite high. The Dutch in the East Indies have produced as much as a ton of pericarp oil per acre. In the new Liberian plantations a yield of at least 1250 pounds of pericarp oil per acre is expected, plus about 400 pounds of the valuable kernel oil, or the equivalent in kernels. Cotton seed in the United States yields only about 250 to 300 pounds of oil per acre, although, of course, as a by-product. Peanuts, or ground nuts as they are known in Africa and Europe, yield not over 500 pounds. Comparatively, therefore, the yield of oil palms per acre is quite high.

The market value fluctuates greatly, and competition is severe. Lowering the cost of production and keeping it low by the use of modern methods, and improving the efficiency of transportation, are therefore important. Kernels priced at $90 per ton in Liberia must bring about $140 in Europe before there is a profit to the

UNITED STATES IMPORTS OF COCOA
(In pounds—000 omitted)

	1947	1948
Mexico	9,774	527
Guatemala	103	648
Honduras	4	7
Nicaragua	360	349
Costa Rica	3,144	3,814
Panama	6,215	5,608
Jamaica	100	...
Haiti	4,859	3,410
Dominican Republic	64,151	51,705
Leeward & Windward Islands	4,168	3,681
Barbados	80	19
Trinidad	5,514	9,739
Venezuela	23,999	29,094
Cuba	.....	95
Bermuda	1,404	.....
Total Caribbean, etc.	123,875	108,696
Brazil	130,010	135,882
Ecuador	30,952	22,975
Total Brazil & Ecuador	160,962	158,857
Portuguese possessions	2,529	939
New Zealand	3,282	1,353
Miscl.	10,533	7,408
Total Miscl.	16,344	9,700
Cameroons	2,224	3,314
French W. Africa	9,561	22,178
Gold Coast	166,246	194,164
Nigeria	119,005	61,200
Liberia	23	142
Total West Africa	297,059	280,998
TOTAL U.S. Imports of cocoa	598,240	558,251

—Data from U.S. Department of Commerce

exporter. That is about the figure prevailing as this is written. The market for the kernels in the United States is limited, less than 10 tons per year at the present time. Palm kernel oil shows a somewhat better figure, about 2600 tons, for example, in 1948. Commercial palm oil, however, comes to the United States to a total of over 30,000 tons per year, mainly from the Belgian Congo. It is possible that the use of the edible oil in the United States will increase, especially with the elimination of the discriminatory legislation that has interfered with a natural development of oleo-margarine production.

Some years ago palm oil was used as a source of power in the semi-Diesel engines of Congo River boats. It was also found possible to crack palm oil so as to produce gasoline. The process has not been found economical, but if a permanent world scarcity of gasoline derived from petroleum should develop, the oil palm of the tropics might, conceivably, come to the rescue.

UNITED STATES IMPORTS
PALM NUTS, KERNELS, PALM OIL, AND PALM-KERNEL OIL
(pounds and dollars)

	1947		1948	
	Pounds	Dollars	Pounds	Dollars
Palm Nuts				
Ceylon	11,200	1,318	11,200	1,091
India	.....	.....	11,206	929
Australia	......	.....	12,002	4,010
	11,200	1,318	34,408	6,030
Palm Nut Kernels				
Australia	22,324	7,170	7,560	2,337
Brazil	......	......	435	165
	22,324	7,170	7,995	2,502
Palm Oil				
Neth. Inds.	......	......	397	83
Fr. W. Afr.	3,000	600	......	......
Gold Cst.	420	40	......	......
Nigeria	3,795,517	260,743	3,804,814	599,639
Liberia	342,647	42,042	168,004	35,306
Belg. Congo	59,070,885	9,331,368	59,354,354	10,522,217
	62,212,469	9,634,793	63,327,569	11,157,245
Palm Kernel Oil				
Belg. Congo	2,380,890	427,394	5,360,421	1,023,552

—Data from U.S. Department of Agriculture

Chapter Nineteen

THE STETTINIUS PLAN

In September, 1947, Mr. Edward R. Stettinius, Jr., and others, who had organized the "Stettinius Associates–Liberia Inc.," entered into an agreement, called the "Statement of Understanding," with a group representing the Liberian Government, having for its object "the development of the human and material resources of the Republic of Liberia."

Mr. Stettinius, first as Lend-Lease Administrator, then as the American Secretary of State, had been intimately concerned with the arrangements that resulted in the construction of the harbor at Monrovia. His interest in Liberia had been aroused, stimulated by a visit to the African Republic while he was Secretary of State. The possibilities that lay in the development of that country's natural resources appealed to him.

The Liberian people were eager for assistance but highly suspicious of foreign interests. Their country was in the midst of the great African colonial empires of Britain, France, Belgium, and Portugal. They had seen these colonies bled for the benefit of the European powers, their native inhabitants exploited, their mineral and agricultural resources developed by foreign corporations under governmental protection, the wealth with which nature had endowed the land seemingly drained away to flow toward London, Paris, Brussels.

They knew, of course, that there was another side to the picture; that capital and technical resources from Europe had made possible a great advance in the general level of living in the African colonies, and that, mixed with attendant evils, much real good had been accomplished. But to the Liberians their independence, won with difficulty and for decades maintained under almost constant attack, was a precious possession, not to be bartered for any mess of potage.

From time to time the Liberian Government had been approached by Europeans seeking concessions, sometimes for agricultural developments, sometimes to explore the country's mineral resources and to mine its iron, diamonds, gold. One after another these projects had been abandoned. There had even been an attempt on the part of French interests to obtain a ten-mile-wide corridor directly through Liberia, so as to give to the interior of French Guinea, (the very area the French had grabbed from Liberia), access to the sea at Monrovia.

It was not until the advent of the Firestone Plantations Company that a way had been found for successful use of foreign capital in Liberia, under circumstances that sufficiently protected the nation's independence and the rights of land ownership that resided in the Government of the Republic.

Mr. Stettinius sought to create an organization and to set up a formula under which there would be a general invitation to American capital and enterprise to enter Liberia and be welcomed, a formula that would fully recognize the position of Liberia as the prime owner of its resources, safeguard its treasured independence, and cause the operation of such projects as might be undertaken, if successful, to result in the plowing back of a reasonable share for the advancement of the Liberian people, natives and settler-descendants alike. If that could be done, it would mean a new approach to the problem of making available to the civilized world the hidden resources of undeveloped areas, areas of which Liberia was in many ways typical. Mr. Stettinius believed that, instead of the colonial system of exploitation, a partnership could be established between the inhabitants of such an area and those who could develop its hidden riches.

The Stettinius idea was thus embodied in the Statement of Understanding, which was dated September 3, 1947.[1] Under it The Liberia Company was created to promote the development of Liberian resources; and a philanthropic trust, the Liberian Foundation, Inc., was set up, designed "to accomplish the social aspects of the program for the development of Liberia." Twenty-five per cent of the capital stock of The Liberia Company was issued to the Liberian Government in consideration of rights granted, 10 per cent to the Foundation, the balance to the Stettinius Associates, who undertook to furnish current funds for operating expenses and to seek whatever financing and technological assistance might be required for a variety of commercial and public utility projects.

To The Liberia Company the Liberian Government granted comprehensive rights for a period of eighty years, covering virtually all fields of exploitation except those already granted to others, such as the Firestone concessions and the rights that the Liberia Mining Company had acquired.

With this as a framework, private capital, either Liberian, American, or other, could be invited to undertake the various projects contemplated. Each such project would be handled by a subsidiary of The Liberia Company, from which it would obtain rights in the particular field involved. Such proportion of ownership in the subsidiary as might be appropriate in each case would be retained by The Liberia Company. Thus, if The Liberia Company itself furnished the capital for a given project, it could retain full ownership, and 25 per cent of any profits realized would then inure to the benefit of the Liberian Government, either as dividends or as equity interest in the parent company.

The directorate of The Liberia Company was made up partly of appointees of the Stettinius Associates, partly of Liberians nominated by the President of the Republic. Thus the Government would be kept in intimate touch with whatever was proposed or done under the Stettinius plan, so that, as set forth in the preamble to the Statement of Understanding, "the Liberian Government and the Stettinius Associates–Liberia Inc., will jointly participate in a cooperative effort to bring to bear the advantages and benefits of private resources in capital and specialized knowledge from the United States and the natural resources of Liberia with a view to improving the levels of living of the people of Liberia and to enhance and expand their opportunities for economic and social advancement."

As an additional safeguard of Liberia's rights, it was provided in the agreement that each project undertaken should be subject to "satisfactory conclusion of any appropriate detailed arrangements between The Liberia Company and the Government consistent with this Statement of Understanding." It was further agreed that the priorities accorded to The Liberia Company "must be exercised within a reasonable period of time and that should the Company fail to implement the various projects in an appropriate manner and with reasonable speed others will be free to undertake them."

The Liberian Government, on its part, agreed that it would "for eighty years contribute every governmental facility and the necessary safeguards and privileges lawful and appropriate to the execution of this agreement and subject to the rights of others and the timely implementation of this agreement by The Liberia Company in accordance with its terms." As to taxes, it was provided that, "On all projects under this agreement, in lieu of any special taxes or government charges, other than those of normal and generally applicable character, the Government of Liberia shall receive 25 per cent of the net proceeds of The Liberia Company by virtue of ownership of 25 per cent of its common stock."

The Stettinius Associates had before them the fact that much of Firestone's success in the development of the great Liberian rubber project had been due to the measures taken for health and sanitation on the Plantation and among its employees, and the training and educational facilities it had established for the Liberians working for it. This broad policy was embodied in the Stettinius plan as a contractual obligation. "It shall be a primary concern of The Liberia Company," said the agreement, "to advance the welfare of the people of Liberia, and the inauguration of every project shall be accompanied by provision for health and training of Liberians who are employees or prospective employees of The Liberia Company or any subsidiary thereof." It was also provided that "it shall be the policy of The Liberia Company to employ citizens of Liberia wherever possible."

Ever since the League of Nations episode the Liberian Government had been increasing its appropriations for public health and education, but within the very narrow and wholly inadequate limits of its income. If the Stettinius plan should prove successful the Government income would be increased and its ability to provide funds for health and education enhanced. The Stettinius plan, however, contemplated the channeling of a part of Liberia's share in the proceeds of its undertakings directly into projects for these two objects, and the Liberian Foundation was incorporated and endowed with 10 per cent of the stock of The Liberia Company, so that a total of 35 per cent would thus inure to the benefit of Liberia. The policy of the Foundation was "that health and education are to be aided by the greatest possible emphasis on using experience and institutions already available and by accenting practical application of medical and hygiene principles and the development of vocational training. Facilities of importance already in existence [such as Liberia College, the College of West Africa, the Booker Washington Institute, the mission, public, and Firestone schools] will be assisted and supported rather than establishing new organizations in competition with them."

It was the intention under the Statement of Understanding that the following projects should be inaugurated on or before December 31, 1950:

1. Organization of a national bank.
2. Mining operations (other than the Bomi Hills operation which is not included in the concessions granted The Liberia Company).
3. Organization of machinery for collection, grading, processing, handling and marketing of agricultural products.
4. Organization of a company to import and export commodities and act as the official procurement agency of the Liberian Government and conduct internal trade in consumer goods.
5. Lumbering operations.
6. Fisheries.
7. Transportation and public services, such as roads and bridges; light, power and water for public use; radio, telegraph and telephone.

The agreement provided that all public service type projects inaugurated by or under The Liberia Company should be turned over to the Government of Liberia as rapidly as the Government should be able to assume the financial and managerial responsibilities of them.

This was a very ambitious program, some of it perhaps a bit visionary. Mr. Stettinius died before it could come to fruition, and in his death Liberia lost a very real friend.

Great emphasis had been put upon the items of public works,

such as a water supply and sewerage system for the city of Monrovia, for which there was and is a crying need, a hydroelectric plant, telephones. Just how these projects could be financed in advance of a general improvement in the country's economic condition, and especially in the light of the rather undefined provision looking toward Government ownership, seems never to have been clearly worked out. The hopes of the Liberian people were raised to a high point; their disappointment correspondingly great when, on the passing of the man who had conceived this plan for their good, it seemed that the whole undertaking might fail.

Meanwhile, however, there had been definite progress on some of the features of the Stettinius plan, notably that of cocoa raising. There is good reason to believe that a really important industry in cocoa can be built up in Liberia, which may possibly some day rank with rubber. The possibilities of this project have been discussed in an earlier chapter.

A trading company has been organized pursuant to Item 4 in the list of projects given above and is conducting an active business in Monrovia, importing and distributing consumer goods. This project, the Liberia Trading Company, was formed and is being managed by the Union Trading Company, usually referred to as "UTC," a Swiss concern, the same people who own one of the great trading companies that operate in Gold Coast and Nigeria. They were brought into the picture because of their intimate knowledge of the peculiarities of trade on the African West Coast. Their experience, especially in the handling of cocoa, should be invaluable to Liberia.

At the instance of The Liberia Company a cold-storage plant has been built on Bushrod Island not far from the Port of Monrovia, and in connection with it a small but modern hotel that offers accommodations acceptable to Americans. This cold-storage plant, a project of a Lancaster, Pennsylvania, business man, has made possible the shipment and handling of frozen meats and vegetables. Perhaps its most acceptable activity is the making of ice-cream, a distinct innovation in this tropical city. Even the ice-cream cone has made its appearance, to the great delight of Liberian school children.

Another by-product of The Liberia Company, although not

at present tied in with it through stock ownership, is the International Trust Company, the principal activity of which has been the handling of ship registrations under the Liberian flag. This is not only producing income for itself but has also turned substantial sums into the Liberian treasury.

Two of America's important and successful corporations, Pan American World Airways and the Mississippi Shipping Company, both of which have a stake in Liberia's future, together with some of the former associates of Mr. Stettinius, have undertaken to keep alive and give needed financial strength to the Stettinius plan, albeit on a somewhat less ambitious basis. For this purpose the Liberia Development Company has been organized as a holding company, taking over from the Stettinius Associates–Liberia, Inc., the controlling stock of The Liberia Company.

This has put new life into the Stettinius plan, with powerful interests back of The Liberia Company. A new agreement was entered into with the Liberian Government on December 22, 1949, revising the 1947 Statement of Understanding.[2] It eliminates responsibility of The Liberia Company for projects of the public service type and limits the understanding to the following:

1. Planting, collection, processing and marketing of cocoa, coffee, palm products and incidental agricultural products.
2. Acting as official purchasing agent of the Government.
3. Extraction, processing, purchasing and sale of gold, diamonds, petroleum and other metals and minerals, except iron ore.
4. Such other projects as have already been initiated pursuant to the Statement of Understanding.
5. Such other suitable projects as may be incorporated into the revised Statement of Understanding by further agreement between the parties.

As to cocoa, coffee, and palm products the Government agrees to lease from time to time for a period of forty years from the date of the agreement up to 150,000 acres of land selected, in one or more blocks, by The Liberia Company. Rental is fixed at six cents per acre and the Government agrees to assist the Company should it wish to lease private land.

Item 2, under which the Company is made the official purchasing agent of the Government applies for two years and contemplates that when major purchases are to be made, such as road-building machinery, generating plants, steel bridges, and so forth, The Liberia Company will handle the transactions itself on behalf of the Government. For the run of miscellaneous purchases the facilities of the associated Liberia Trading Company are available, and this company will probably play an important part, also, in the marketing and export of cocoa, coffee, and palm oil and kernels under Item 1.

Under Item 3 the right is given for twelve years to prospect for minerals, but subject to rights granted to others. The Company, subject to such exception, may enter, explore, survey, and prove the extent of mineral deposits and may select up to 150,000 acres as to which the Government agrees to lease the mining rights at $1.00 per acre per year, with a "most-favored-tenant" provision protecting the Company against any lower terms granted to others. The Company agrees to pay to the Government 15 per cent of the sales price of all precious metals, minerals or petroleum, 10 per cent in the case of semi-precious metals or minerals and 5 per cent for all basic metals and minerals, also with the protection of a most favored tenant clause. The right to purchase and sell gold, as well as to mine it, may have important results for the Liberian treasury. During recent years there has been a Government monopoly of gold, all such metal mined in Liberia being required to be sold to the Bank of Monrovia for Government account at $25 per ounce, the idea being that the profit on its export would flow into the Liberian treasury. But the quantity of gold visibly exported fell off one half when the monopoly went into effect, indicating, in all probability, that the rest of it left the country by smuggling. The figures showing this are given in the table on page 228 above.

Item 4 refers to such projects as the Liberia Trading Company, the Liberia Cold Storage Company and the International Trust Company. The cocoa, palm oil, and coffee projects were also well under way when the revision agreement was signed but would come under Item 1 in any case. A lumbering operation had also been started before the new interests took over, and a company had been organized for the purpose; but lumbering as a separate undertaking is in abeyance for the present. It has possibilities, perhaps great possibilities, intimately related, however, to the transportation problem, as already pointed out. The matter of Liberia's timber resources is discussed in another chapter.

The last item of the revised list, number 5, simply leaves the door open to other fields, setting the pattern but otherwise merely being a statement of general intent.

The new agreement provides that each of The Liberia Company's projects shall be tax free for a period of twelve years, except for the specified royalties and rents, and thereafter will be liable only for such taxes as are of general application. The period of tax exemption is shorter than was provided by the original agreement, but otherwise more liberal, for during the twelve-year period it definitely relieves the Company's projects of *all* taxes, other than the specified payments, whereas under the Statement of Understanding, before its modification, the exemptions applied only to "any special taxes or Government charges other than those of normal and generally applicable character."

The eighty-year exclusive rights granted by the 1947 agreement are abrogated, the term being reduced to forty years for the agricultural projects and twelve years for mineral rights, and are now non-exclusive. Rights not exercised within two years from the date of the new agreement lapse. They lapse also in case operations cease over a period of two years, except for reasons of *force majeure*.

The rights according to The Liberia Company accrue, under the revised agreement, to "its affiliated companies designated by it and approved by the President of the Republic of Liberia," provided that the parent company retains not less than 25 per cent ownership of the voting stock, "except with the consent of the President of the Republic of Liberia." The participants other than The Liberia Company "may be Liberian or United States citizens, partnerships consisting of such citizens, or corporations in which a majority of the voting equity stock shall belong to such citizens." Neither The Liberia Company nor any of its affiliates or subsidiaries may assign their rights without the consent of the President of Liberia. The character of The Liberia Company and its sponsored projects as a joint Liberian–American undertaking is thus safeguarded.

In the new agreement The Liberia Company confirms that its primary concern shall be "to advance the welfare of the people of Liberia, and the organization of each project shall be accompanied by appropriate provision for health and training of Liberians who are employees of such project and it shall be the policy of The Liberia Company to give preference of employment to citizens of Liberia." The Liberia Foundation, designed to direct into educational and public health channels the proceeds of its 10 per cent interest in The Liberia Company is not affected by the new agreement, remaining intact and ready to function whenever liquid funds become available to it.

It will be seen that the original conception of Mr. Stettinius of a plan for the development of Liberia's resources in a way that would recognise the inherent rights of the country's inhabitants and operate for their good has been retained and given new life, on a much more workable basis than was at first proposed. Through the medium of The Liberia Company there is today an invitation to American enterprise and venture capital. The continued cooperation of the Liberian Government is assured. The entire plan has been greatly strengthened, its weak spots removed. It may be predicted with some confidence that The Liberia Company will develop into a living monument to Liberia's great friend, Edward R. Stettinius, Jr.

• *Chapter Twenty* •

POINT FOUR

"We must embark on a bold new program for making the benefits of our scientific advances and industrial progress available for the improvement and growth of underdeveloped areas."

In these words President Truman, in his 1949 Inaugural Address, enunciated his "Point Four Program" of American assistance to resource development in the world's less fortunate countries. In his message to Congress of June 24, 1949, he elaborated on this "bold new" idea. "In order to enable the United States to cooperate with other countries," said Mr. Truman, "to assist the peoples of economically underdeveloped areas to raise their standards of living, I recommend the enactment of legislation to authorize an expanded program of technical assistance for such areas, and an experimental program for encouraging the outflow of private investment beneficial to their economic development. These measures are the essential first step in an undertaking which will call upon private enterprise and voluntary organization in the United States, as well as the Government, to take part in a constantly growing effort to improve economic conditions in the less developed regions of the world."

But however *bold* President Truman's expanded program of constantly growing effort embodied in his Point Four proposal may have been, it certainly was not *new,* at least so far as Liberia was concerned. Private enterprise, voluntary organizations, and the American Government have all been at work for years in Liberia in a "constantly growing effort to improve economic conditions."

That is exactly what our effective missionary and philanthropic organizations have been doing for many decades in the African Republic, their enlightened efforts, growing out of religious motives, having been directed in very large part to the improvement of economic conditions as a necessary foundation for the building of a Christian civilization.

That is what Harvey Firestone started out to do when it was decided to create a great rubber plantation in Liberia, and it is what his son Harvey Firestone, Jr., has been carrying out, constantly directing the efforts of his company's organization toward raising the standard of living among the native workers of this underdeveloped country; founding schools and a hospital, improving sanitary conditions, changing the entire economy of the country. The same principles, founded on the solid basis of good business policy, underlie what is being done by the Liberia Mining Company, and by other nascent business projects in Liberia.

That is what was the very foundation of the plan for the development of Liberia's natural resources conceived by Mr. Stettinius and his associates and now being brought toward fulfillment by those who have taken over his ambitious task, as already told.

Nor is the idea a new one from the Government standpoint. The highway built across Liberia with American funds, while it was undertaken as compensation for rights granted to the United States, was a major contribution to the economic development of Liberia. The investment of eighteen million dollars of Lend-Lease funds with which the epoch-making harbor at Monrovia was built certainly falls within the scope of Mr. Truman's Point Four, although it was begun long before he came into office.

For the past six years the United States Public Health Service has been doing highly effective work in Liberia, while an Economic Mission, sent out by the American Department of State, has been studying Liberia's economic resources, making extensive surveys of its soils and forests, guiding the development of such agricultural products as cocoa and palm oil, conducting demonstration farms and gardens, and formulating, in close cooperation with the Government and people of Liberia, "an expanded program of technical assistance," and plans for the creation of sorely needed public services.

Indeed, since 1942, when Roberts Field became an American

Army Air Base, the United States Department of State has devoted much more than a modicum of attention to Liberia. Its Division of African Affairs has been a constructive force in cooperating with the Liberian Government, and such men as Henry S. Villard, Claire H. Timberlake, Andrew G. Lynch, and Harold Sims have extended their efforts in behalf of Liberia far beyond the ordinary call of duty.

This is an impressive recital of what has been going on in Liberia for a long time. It must not be inferred, however, that the objectives of Point Four have been achieved in Liberia or that further assistance is not a pressing need, especially technical assistance. Quite the contrary. In some important respects only the spade work has been done; in others the present accomplishments are outstanding. Yet there is a continuing and a very real obligation on the part of the American people, entirely aside from Point Four, to render to this Republic that America helped to create all the assistance reasonably possible in the efforts being made by the Liberians to realize their ambitions.

In a tropical country the problem of public health takes first place in any development program. When, in 1942, American troops came to Liberia to build and then to operate the great air base at Roberts Field, health conditions in the Republic, and especially in Monrovia, became of vital importance to the United States. Colonel Leon Fox, Medical Corps, U. S. Army, made a rapid survey of the situation. He reported highly unsatisfactory conditions. Flies and mosquitoes were abundant, malaria was rampant, enteric diseases were presenting a serious problem. There were only half a dozen doctors in all of Liberia, hardly any trained nurses. There was no general vaccination program. The water and sewage disposal arrangements in Monrovia were primitive. "The financing of health service for Liberia," said Colonel Fox, "probably offers as great an opportunity to do good as remains in the world."

The efforts of the Army medical staff were of necessity directed mainly toward the establishment of acceptable sanitary conditions at and around Roberts Field and toward mosquito riddance in that area, but with the cooperation of the Liberian Government considerable improvement was effected in Monrovia.

Prior to the coming of the United States Army Air Forces

Liberia had made little progress in public health matters. The country was being bullied by the League of Nations, and torrid speeches were being made in the British Parliament alleging that Monrovia was a menace to the health of the world, a breeding place for yellow fever and other diseases. Nonsense, of course, but part of the British attack on Liberia's independence and not at all conducive to an attitude on the part of the maligned Liberians that would lead them to seek real assistance from Europe or America. That had to wait for the coming of the Army Air Forces to Roberts Field.

When Mr. Tubman took office as President in January, 1944, he was already committed to the constructive policy inaugurated during Mr. Barclay's administration of seeking assistance from the United States in the development of Liberia. He appealed to President Roosevelt for help with the public health problem. The result was that the United States Public Health Service again sent a medical mission to Liberia, this time headed by Dr. John B. West, with Dr. Hildrus A. Poindexter to administer the laboratory work. These were highly qualified medical men of the Negro race, experienced in the problems peculiar to tropical areas. This mission was officially termed the United States Public Health Mission in Liberia, or USPHMIL.

Dr. West, when he arrived in November, 1944, found but six physicians in the whole of Liberia, and two dentists. Nurses were few, only about half of those in nursing service being graduates of qualified schools. Hospital facilities were scarce and, except at the Firestone Hospital, the equipment was poor and the staffs inadequate. There were some ten general clinics scattered through the country, only three of them with a graduate physician in attendance. Of pharmacies or supply houses for the procurement of pharmaceuticals there were none.

But there was an open mind and a genuine resolve on the part of the Liberians to make the most of the help offered and to establish an adequate health service that would ultimately be fully staffed by Liberians with the necessary medical education.[1]

The first activity of the Medical Mission was an attack on the mosquito. A DDT spraying campaign was undertaken, carried on by crews formed around a nucleus of Liberians who had been trained in malaria control at Roberts Field. There followed drainage ditches, fills, and the pumping of casual waters, removing, in the first year of operation, 480 acres of breeding area. This work, at first confined to the city itself, was soon extended to include Bushrod Island, adjacent to Monrovia, where operations were about to begin in the building of Monrovia's new harbor.

While the elimination of malaria takes first place in any health program in the tropics, that disease was only one of the many medical problems in Liberia. Tropical medicine is a highly special science, much better understood than it was a few decades ago, but still in its infancy. The work of the American Medical Mission in Liberia is directed toward the prevention of disease by the removal of causes rather than toward its cure. Hence laboratory work has been of prime importance, and the study of the causes of various tropical diseases by USPHMIL is constantly exploratory and is destined to be of use in a much wider field than Liberia.

Education and training of Liberian personnel to carry on after the withdrawal of the Mission has played a prominent part in its activities. A school of nursing was established and later expanded to provide sub-professional medical and dental training and courses for laboratory and malaria-control technicians. This, now occupying a new and specially equipped building, has become the Tubman National Institute of Medical and Allied Arts at Monrovia. It has had to begin in a small way, but is an important move in the direction of self-sufficiency in medical education, at least up to the actual professional level. Meanwhile the Liberian Government is sending a number of young men to the United States, who, no longer spurning professional life, are studying medicine and dentistry, and will soon be building a real medical group among the Americo-Liberians.

Dr. West decided to make his permanent home in Liberia, resigning from the American Public Health Service and establishing himself in the pharmacy business in Monrovia. Dr. Poindexter now heads the Health Mission.

The Public Health Center over which Dr. Poindexter presides was built by an appropriation made by the United States Congress and is supported partly by American funds, partly by the Liberian Government. It has a free public clinic with special days for children, well babies and sick babies coming on different days. There is X-ray equipment and a laboratory that serves both for routine blood and urine analysis and for special studies. There are two American Public Health Service doctors, two doctors (one Haitian, one Syrian) paid by the Liberian Government, a consulting dentist who is a captain in the U. S. Army Dental Corps, and three American registered nurses, one of whom is Director of the nurses training school. There are also seven or eight Liberian nurses, paid by the Liberian Government, who, while they as yet would rate only as practical nurses, do excellent work. A laboratorian, a full-time X-ray technician, an engineer in charge of the plant, and an administrative officer complete the staff. About 2400 patients a month avail themselves of the public clinic.

The coming to Liberia of the American Public Health Mission was followed by the adoption of a plan formulated by Dr. George W. Harley in consultation with the Public Health Service physicians, for the gradual establishment throughout Liberia of a system of central hospitals and outlying clinics.[2] Progress in this undertaking has necessarily been slow, being governed by the availability of funds and personnel. The several missionary organizations, supported mainly from the United States, figure importantly in this medical work, as outlined elsewhere in this book. Equipment for a 200-bed hospital was obtained by the Liberian Government from American war surplus, and with it the establishment of a general hospital, now functioning in Monrovia, became possible. At Cape Palmas the Tubman Hospital is now in operation. At Sanniquellie a small hospital is under construction, named for Dr. Harley. In one way or another these beginnings of a medical service in Liberia are based on technical assistance stemming from the United States, anticipating the idea embodied in President Truman's Point Four, possibly having suggested it.

At the request of President Tubman, the United States Department of Agriculture sent one of its experts, Mr. Charles E. Trout, to Liberia "to assist and advise the Government in the promulgation of a program of improved agricultural methods, better land utilization, and the introduction of new subsistence crops for local consumption." Mr. Trout arrived in Liberia in September, 1944, and did much to awaken an interest on the part of Liberian farmers in such things as the use of fertilizers and insecticides, modern agricultural implements, the importing of improved seeds, the raising of garden truck.

Working in the broader field of economic development is the U. S. Economic Mission to Liberia, now part of what has become the Technical Cooperative Assistance Mission. Like the Medical Mission it too came to Liberia at the urgent invitation of President Tubman. To a very large extent its efforts have been directed toward the improvement of the country's food supply by the introduction of improved agricultural methods, and toward the development of such agricultural products as cocoa, palm oil, and palm kernels, on which an export trade could be built.

The assignment of duties to the Economic Mission by the American Department of State can be summarized under three heads:

1. To survey the economic resources of Liberia.

2. To make recommendations to the Governments of the Republic and of the United States for the practical development of Liberia's resources.

3. To give continuous technical advice and assistance to the Liberian Government, to Liberian citizens, and to foreign enterprises on projects contributing to the economic development of the country.

Several basic surveys have been made, including a general agricultural survey, a soils survey and a forest survey. An aerial-photo map has been partly completed, a very basic undertaking, for the only existing maps of Liberia are those made by compass traverses over the network of native trails, tied in as best they could be with the not too accurate boundary surveys. Two other basic surveys are contemplated by the Economic Mission, a fisheries survey and a general geological survey.

Several experimental agricultural stations are being operated by the Mission, including one on farm land owned by Secretary of State Gabriel Dennis, where garden crops are being grown under irrigation and several breeds of chickens, raised from chicks flown in by air from the United States are thriving, the development of suitable locally-produced feed being an important part of the experiment. Chickens are common throughout the Liberian hinterland, but they are scrawny fowl, fit for little but the sacrificial use that is their lot. No attempt is made by the natives to utilize hen's eggs as a staple article of food; so egg production is one of the objectives of this hennery.

The work of the Economic Mission was started in Liberia late in 1944 by Mr. Earl Parker Hanson. Mr. Oscar Meier, who until very recently headed the Mission in Liberia, is an experienced American agriculturist who has very effectively directed the work toward practical and realizable objectives. He has been ably assisted by Mr. Frank Pinder, also an agriculturist, and by a small but efficient staff that includes a civil engineer. Dr. George W. Harley, of the Methodist Mission at Ganta, is associated with the American Economic Mission as a member and consultant, making his wide experience in the ways of the Liberian natives, and his own experiments in improving agricultural methods directly available.

The Economic Mission has worked very closely with the Liberian Government, especially with the Departments of Agriculture and of Public Works and Utilities, and is in constant consultation with the American Ambassador, the Honorable Edward R. Dudley, who is functioning not only as an able formal diplomat but as a leader in all that is being done to further the development of the Republic to which he is accredited.

Much of the effort of the Economic Mission has been devoted to the formulation of plans for Point Four assistance to Liberia. The task is not an easy one. The needs of the country are so many and so various that any program for meeting them quickly outruns the possibilities of funds that are likely to become available. This of necessity forces a serious consideration of priorities in determining how assistance can most effectively be applied, with each separate category of need seemingly deserving first place. There are projects such as road construction that would have an almost immediate effect on the country's economy; others, such as public health and education, that certainly are pressingly needed and will pay dividends in the long run, but the economic effect of which cannot be felt for many years, perhaps generations.

A glance at the various fields in which both technical and financial assistance are needed will give some idea of the complexities involved. The entire problem of transportation and the development of a logical system of roads calls for expert study. Much more than the mere mapping out of a network of highways is involved. There are problems of determining how much can economically be spent on any given piece of road in surfacing, grade reduction, and so on, having in mind the probable density of traffic and the relation between the character of the roadway and wear and tear on vehicles. And there will be bridges to be built, some under very difficult conditions.

Monrovia sorely needs a water supply and a sewerage system, both of which are intimately bound up with the constant problem of public health as well as with the question of ability of the population to pay the resultant charges. Monrovia also needs a new electric power plant; the present one, left over from the harbor construction project, is inadequate and nearing the point of break-down. By harnessing the St. Paul River, or perhaps the St. John, it might be possible to supply the capital city with both water and power, but the outlay would be considerable and only the most preliminary kind of engineering survey in this field has as yet been made.

The water problem is serious, especially in the dry season. Open wells supplemented by rain-water cisterns have to be relied upon. The boiling of all water for drinking purposes is, of course, a necessity, as indeed it is throughout the tropics, even where there is an adequate municipal water system.

So pressing has been the need for water and sewer service in the capital city that arrangements have been made for a loan from the Export-Import Bank for this purpose, $1,300,000, which will be used for the sewerage system and for a water supply from wells on Bushrod Island, where a sufficient supply of fresh water at least for immediate needs can be obtained.

Improvement in Liberia's agricultural methods is a crying need. How difficult this problem is can best be judged, if an understanding is had of the primitive ways of the native tribes. It is easy for a theory-bound agronomist to visualize the introduction of American methods of farming, of plows, harrows, tractors. The British tried to mechanize the growing of peanuts on a large scale in Kenya and failed utterly. Only the very slow process of education, of precept and example, such as is now being undertaken by the practical agriculturists of the Economic Mission can possibly be effective.

A strong case can be made for assistance to Liberia in the field of education. If there is to be any uplift in the life of the great native population, a comprehensive educational program must soon be gotten under way. That means school buildings throughout the country, and school equipment, teachers and still more teachers, who themselves must first be taught. To accomplish results commensurate with the need would call for a greater outlay than any Point Four program within the limits of possibility can contemplate. As with agriculture, improvement in human culture, among the tribal people, will have to come slowly. But assistance to the Liberians in building up such institutions as the College of West Africa, Liberia College, Cuttington, the Booker Washington Institute, will help the people of the country to develop their own educational system and will greatly expedite its spread.

Hospitals and clinics are needed, nurses and doctors. Monrovia, it is true, is relatively free of malaria, but that is not true of great areas of the hinterland. Debilitating disease is a terribly serious drain on the vitality of almost the entire population. If, throughout the interior, a really effective attack could be made on malaria, sleeping sickness, and enteric disease, the energy that would be released would be almost beyond calculation. The United States Public Health Mission in Liberia, USPHMIL, has laid some of the foundation for such a work. Firestone has accomplished much on its plantations. Other projects, such as that of the Liberia Mining Company, will contribute to the effort. The Liberian Government is building a small but efficient Public Health Service that soon should be competent to take over the work of the American Medical Mission. Here and there a Government hospital is being started; here and there a clinic. But the problem is much too great for solution by the present available means. In the long run, an investment in public health will pay dividends, but only in the long run.

Any program of development in Liberia based on the Point Four conception will have to look to some or all of three sources for financial support. These are: (1) Grants-in-aid from the American Government; (2) Loans—possibly authorized specially by Act of Congress, or from the Export-Import Bank or the International Bank for Reconstruction and Development; (3) Current Liberian Government revenues.

Some Point Four Projects will be supplemented by private funds, either philanthropic or growing out of industrial activities in the country.

There have been suggestions of a bold approach to the whole

problem, involving total expenditures that, measured by the Liberian yardstick, would be enormous and would saddle the Republic with a debt under which it would stagger for many decades, if indeed it did not bring about quite promptly a hopeless economic situation instead of the freedom from want and from other ills of underdevelopment for which it was supposed to be the cure.

President Tubman has expressed himself as definitely committed to keeping within the scope of what can be carried by the revenues of the Liberian Government, with only such loans as can readily be serviced, and supplemented by technical aid from the United States rather than by largess.

Fortunately a marked improvement in Liberian revenues that began in 1951 and promises to continue, has justified the granting of two important credits by the Export-Import Bank, one of $5,000,000 for roads and the other of $1,300,000 for a water supply and sewerage system for Monrovia.

Chapter Twenty-one

LOOKING AHEAD

In the foregoing pages I have tried to outline, and to some extent to emphasize, the facts which it has seemed to me one would need to understand for a realistic appraisal of Liberia, its people, its resources, its opportunities, and its problems.

There is something very intriguing about this bit of West Africa, this handful of people who, although they failed for so long to develop the resources of their rich tropical land, have nevertheless resolutely withstood an almost constant pressure from the surrounding colonial empires of great European powers, and have maintained their independence, until today they need no longer fear encroachments and can confidently look to the outside world, and especially to the United States, for technical and financial assistance, without fear of any attempt at exploitation.

Clearly whatever assistance is given to Liberia from American sources, governmental or private, must rest, except in the case of missionary efforts, on sound economic ground. The outstanding example of a mutually advantageous relationship is, of course, that of the Firestone Plantations Company. The impact of this great project on every phase of Liberian life has been so great that it can hardly be overstated. It has demonstrated the soundness from a purely business standpoint of a constructive policy that has sought to bring about a constant and basic improvement in the well-being of the entire population of the country. The policies being followed by Mr. Christie and his associates in developing the Bomi Hills iron mine and in building Liberia's first railroad parallel those of the rubber company.

Does Liberia actually offer opportunities for further ventures in the development of its resources? I think the answer to that question is definitely in the affirmative, *provided* the problems involved are clearly understood and the difficulties accepted. There is no reason, for example, why the cocoa farm started by Mr. Porcella under the aegis of the Liberia Company should not be duplicated, even on a smaller scale, by some enterprising young agriculturist if he is willing to take the trouble to acquire the technical skill and experience needed, as did Porcella, and to put in years of very hard work under primitive living conditions. I strongly suspect that the extent to which a modest beginning in the raising of cocoa might grow would be limited in the long run (though perhaps in the *very* long run) only by the initiative and perseverance of the planter.

The possible opportunities in Liberia for Americans of the Negro race should not be overlooked. I do not mean to suggest any mass movement of the race toward Africa; that is neither desirable nor possible, and it would not be welcomed by the Liberians. But there are individuals among the Liberians today, born in the United States, who have found in the African Republic a life free of the embarrassments that unfortunately mar the happiness of colored people in America. They have preferred to accept the absence of some of the amenities of modern life in order to live under the Liberian flag. The skill and courage needed for individual undertakings in Liberia in agriculture, engineering, medicine, or other fields are the same, whether exercised by whites or by Negroes. The white entrepreneur in Liberia, moreover, although welcomed, has the disadvantage that he can neither attain citizenship nor own land; if he develops a plantation he must look to his lease for his rights and contemplate the possibility of their lapsing when the lease expires. The Negro who comes to Liberia with a similar objective has no such limitations; he can become a citizen, can acquire land, can create a plantation that will be his own estate.

What political risks must be taken by an investor in Liberia? The Liberian Government has, through over a century, demonstrated its stability. There has never been a revolution. There has never been even a threat of expropriation of foreign property, except for the seizure of German assets when Liberia became a member of the Allies in World War I. The risks that seem to be always present in American undertakings in some of the Latin American countries are definitely not present in Liberia. Moreover the economic tie, as well as the political, between the United States and Liberia is such that the development of any relationship other than one of stable friendship and mutual reliance seems inconceivable. There are, to be sure, mutterings now and then in Liberian political circles, based sometimes on an imaginary fear of American imperialism, but more often simply reflecting the need of an opposition party for an issue. But these mutterings are *sotto voce;* self-interest would cause them to be quickly dampened in the face of responsibility should such an issue ever come to test.

If projects are undertaken comparable, either individually or in the aggregate, to that of Firestone, the matter of the adequacy of the labor supply will intrude itself. How serious the labor problem can become will depend largely on the extent to which interference with the native food supply is involved. Firestone, despite all the care it has used in this respect, has had to import considerable quantities of rice to offset the withdrawal of laborers from their normal farm activities. Interference by profiteering District Commissioners has at times been partly responsible for restricting the movement of domestic rice, and so have well-intentioned but mistaken measures directed by the Government toward price control. Lack of roads has contributed to the difficulty. These conditions are subject to correction; are in fact being corrected. The primitive nature of farming among the natives is a more serious matter.

It is believed that some decades ago, when conditions within the tribal areas were at their worst, there was a considerable loss of native population by movements over the borders and up and down the coast. Numbers of the Kru tribe certainly worked in other parts of West Africa. Already there are indications of a reversal of this movement. It is significant that in the vicinity of the Bomi Hills, where there were very few villages before the building of the railroad began, there is now plenty of labor.

Any important improvement in health conditions among the natives will be reflected both in the numbers of workers available for industrial projects and in their efficiency. Dr. Harley made the comment to me that a reduction in infant mortality could easily double the population in a generation. If that, or anything like it, should occur, the problem of food supply would become acute—it would have to be met by improved agricultural methods, a slow process, or by importation of food stuffs to be paid for by outward-moving products, just as rubber has paid for rice at the Plantation. These are all closely related problems, not essentially different from those that have to be faced in any underdeveloped area. They can be approached with pessimism or with courage. But they are problems that cannot be avoided.

The fact remains, I firmly believe, that Liberia's greatest resource is to be found in the tribal people. It is for that reason that the early chapters of this book were devoted to an account of the people of Liberia's great hinterland, for it is on them that those who would come to help in the development of Liberia must build their hopes and plans.

How can the doctrine of President Truman's Point Four be best applied in Liberia? I shall not attempt to answer that question categorically; it can be answered only by those who are living with the problems involved. What I have to say is therefore only by way of suggestion.

It seems clear that the work of the Economic Mission and of the Public Health Mission should be continued for an indefinite period. The importance of the health work is obvious. Very wisely, more and more of the responsibility for it is being borne by the Liberians themselves. Meanwhile the expense to the United States is trifling, especially in comparison with the results.

The Economic Mission is concerning itself very largely with the attempt to improve the food supply. Its work in this field is basic, and guidance from the outside is, and for some time will be, essential.

Clearly the various religious missions must and will continue their excellent work. They are the backbone of the present educational system, such as it is, and are carrying much of the burden of health work, especially in the interior. The Liberian Government should itself constantly increase its own efforts in both the educational and the public health fields, and indeed is doing so within the limits of its revenues. It is highly desirable that Liberia become self-reliant in these matters. The attainment of such self-reliance is an important part of President Tubman's long-range policies.

My personal reaction to what I was able to observe as I travelled about Liberia and talked with its people leads me to believe that no one thing will contribute so much to an early meeting of the country's needs in health and education as will the opening up of more main arterial highways. The rapid change wrought in the economic life of the people when a motor road is put through is astonishing. I travelled over the Ganta road early in 1948, only a few weeks after it had been open for through traffic. Already travel over it was relatively heavy. Two years later I again went over the same route, from Monrovia to Ganta, and then on to Sanniquellie. Ganta, when I had first visited it, before there had been time for the new road to change it, was still the strictly aboriginal settlement it had been for many decades, a bit larger than the general run of hinterland villages because the weekly market was held there, but otherwise not to be distinguished from other towns in that area. Within two and a half years after the opening of the road the entire complexion of the place had been changed. The native market was still held there, but it had become mainly a social event among the natives. There now were stores where the business of the town was carried on, run by the trading companies from Monrovia. More stores were soon to be opened. Imported goods were everywhere on display. Huts, mainly new and large ones, were being used as warehouses for rice and palm kernels. Sewing machines were busy, making shorts and other articles of apparel from trade cloth. The women were wearing elaborate foreign prints as their wrap-arounds, much better cloth than had been in evidence when the foot-trails had to serve the town. Gasoline was on sale, heralded by the enamelled emblems of Texaco. More striking still were the flaming red signs on shop after shop urging the natives to "Drink Coca-Cola."

I saw other towns where similar changes were taking place. Sanniquellie, larger than Ganta and deeper in the interior, was going through the same metamorphosis. I journeyed by hammock over native foot-trails, far from the road, deep into the forest, passed through truly aboriginal villages, Gipu for example, where life was just about as it had been for centuries; then came abruptly, only a few miles farther on, to the motor road at Flumpa, where the highway that now runs from Ganta to Tappita had been opened a short time before. Again, the same unmistakable evidence of change—trade goods on display, the red Texaco and Coca-Cola signs, motor trucks roaring through, all in marked contrast to Gipu, deep in the bush, through which I had passed only a short time before. But even in Gipu the men were wearing shorts, the women displaying their imported finery, though life in the town seemed otherwise untouched.

The President was expected soon to pass through Flumpa on one of his frequent trips into the interior; the road over which he would travel was being decorated with arched palm branches.

It is on this same road, a little beyond Flumpa, that the cocoa plantation of the Liberia Company is being developed by my friend Santiago Porcella. Without the road the plantation could hardly have been undertaken.

When the road from Gbarnga to Zorzor is opened, the Western Province will begin to feel some of the same stimulus that is so evident along the Ganta-Sanniquellie-Tappita highway. If the Zorzor road is pushed on past the topographical obstacle of the Wanigisi hills where it now stops, into the Voinjama-Kolahun area, some of the potentially richest territory of all Liberia will become capable of relatively quick development. Its products now go into Sierra Leone, first by trail, then road, then the railroad that runs to Freetown, without benefit, other than local, to Liberian economy.

It seems to me, therefore, that nothing would contribute so surely or so promptly to the national income of Liberia, and to the revenue of the Government, as an extension of the country's highways. Even a few miles of road, built where most needed, might so stimulate the development of the interior as to have a material effect on exports and on local taxes as well, and thus make possible increased expenditures for education and public health, perhaps even for the much-desired and badly needed water and sewerage systems for Monrovia. Indeed it is only by such internal changes that self-reliance in these respects can be achieved.

Should the Liberian Government borrow money for an extensive program of public improvements? Or, put it another way. Should the United States Government, as part of the Point Four program, make further loans to Liberia, directly, or through the Export-Import Bank?

Liberia, before it applied to the Export-Import Bank for the $5 million credit for road building and the smaller sewerage and water supply loan, had gotten itself nearly out of debt. Its past experience with foreign loans was not a happy one. Ever since the refinancing of the International Loan by the Finance Corporation of America, incident to the coming of Firestone to Liberia, there has been praiseworthy resistance by the Liberians to further Government borrowing. The friendly control that has been exercised through the office of the Financial Advisor under the present Loan Agreement has been altogether salutary. The new loan for road construction, and any further credits for other purposes, will of necessity carry dispersement safeguards. Yet if such loans are kept well within the ability of the Liberian Government to service them, with suitable interest rates and sound provisions for amortization, they can conceivably be highly constructive.

I venture the suggestion that any steps that would tend to change materially the present fiscal situation of the Government should be taken only with the greatest caution. The Liberians are earnestly tackling the problems of financial management, but they are hardly yet ready to handle these very vital matters unaided. Take, for example, the plans that have been under consideration for the creation of a national bank and a national currency. The wisdom of such a move at the present time would seem to be open to question. So long as Liberia has a balanced budget and a favorable balance of international trade there is little reason why the use of American currency should be objectionable to the United States, and it certainly is highly advantageous to Liberia. Should the Republic's financial affairs for any reason take a turn for the worse, an operating deficit be incurred, exports fall off seriously, or the Government gets itself into an unmanageable debt, a purely Liberian currency would quickly reflect such conditions. The results might be sudden and calamitous.

Banking, and the control of the currency of a nation, are highly technical arts. Especially is this so when foreign exchange is involved. If, in the working out of plans under Point Four, further substantial credits should be extended to Liberia, the financial controls will obviously have to be adjusted accordingly, so as to conform to whatever special requirements might be necessary. The advisability of creating a Liberian bank of issue might well rest for determination until it is seen whether it would help or interfere with the credit of the Government.

How far is the United States justified, from the viewpoint of its own self-interest, in meeting Liberia's needs for financial and technical assistance? To answer this question in dollars and cents is beyond the scope of what I have attempted in this book. In fact, the answer cannot be entirely a matter of dollars and cents. We have, to be sure, a considerable financial investment in Liberia, both governmental and private. The rubber, cocoa, iron, shipping and other commercial activities can be counted upon to achieve their own successes, and in so doing to make a major contribution to Liberian welfare. The highly constructive operations of the two great shipping companies, the Farrell Lines and the Delta Line, with their vessels under the American flag, are strengthening our commercial relations with the entire West African Coast. They are developing a constantly increasing volume of trade with that important area and in so doing are making a major contribution to the growth of Liberia. This is especially true because of the use to which the Free Port of Monrovia is being put, not only for Liberian exports and imports but as a key point in operations that extend far beyond Liberia, both up and down the coast and into the interior of French West Africa. This in turn is serving to develop, much more rapidly than had even been hoped for, an income from the port itself, from which repayments are already being made to the United States of Lend-Lease funds that built the harbor.

As to technical assistance, it has seemed to me that in addition to the work the Economic Mission has done so well, a major contribution to Liberian development could be made if some outstanding American engineer from civil life, with both a technical and a business experience as a background, and with a small but competent staff, could be found, who would be willing to devote two to three years to the country as a public service, finding his chief compensation in the opportunity offered to be of vital service to the people of Liberia while doing a noteworthy piece of professional work. Such a man, obtainable perhaps from one of our great engineering firms, would be able not only to envision the over-all problems of road construction, bridge building, water supply, hydroelectric power and the many other purely engineering projects that are crying for realization, but would grasp also, and help to solve the underlying economic and fiscal problems with which, in a country like Liberia, the engineering needs are so closely interwoven.

But it is the strategic situation of Liberia that, from the viewpoint of American self-interest, may well outweigh all other considerations and justify in the future, as it has in the past, our active interest in the well-being of the Republic.

Liberia is the eastern gate-post guarding the "Narrows of the Atlantic." Roberts Field is only sixteen hundred and twenty nautical miles from Natal on the Brazilian bulge of South America, practically the same distance as from Natal to Dakar in French West Africa. Through this Narrows of the Atlantic pass some of the most important sea lanes of the world. Ships plying between the British Isles or the countries of Continental Europe and the River Plate must traverse it. So must vessels carrying to the United States the increasingly important strategic materials of the Belgian Congo, including uranium. When, in World War II, the United States became the arsenal of the United Nations, the supply lines from the American continent to the Red Sea and the Persian Gulf passed through the Narrows of the Atlantic. Over these supply lines vast quantities of military matériel were carried. From Monrovia harbor, where the United States has a continuing right to establish a naval base, and from Roberts Field, whence an effective air cover could quickly be made operative, these vital sea routes could again be protected from hostile attack by planes or submarines.

The whole continent of Africa looms large in any concept of war with a European or an Asiatic power. Especially is this true of the area comprised within the West Coast. Here a chain of air bases, with Liberia as its western bastion, easily supplied by sea, would be invaluable. Linked with a friendly Ethiopia, it would give command, by air, of the Red Sea, and would facilitate control of the vital oil fields of the Near East; might make possible an attack behind the Iron Curtain by methods similar to those of our island-hopping campaign in the Pacific.

If the U.S.S.R. develops overwhelming numbers of submarines, as it is apparently seeking to do, the possibility must not be lost sight of that the Mediterranean would be denied to American and allied war and merchant shipping. Were this to happen, the entire northern coast of Africa would be highly vulnerable. But between the Mediterranean Sea and the strategic West Coast of Africa lies the Great Desert, the Sahara. It gives to the area, including the British and French colonies as well as Liberia, protection on their north like that of a coastline, but the coastline of a sea of sand, which cannot be traversed by submarines, nor does it provide a path for conquering armies or even an easy route for airplanes.

As this is being written, the American War Department is sending to Liberia a military mission, its objective, to give to the already able Frontier Force special training directed toward strengthening the internal security of the Republic, and, especially, to assist the Liberian Government in guarding against subversive influences such as have recently troubled the British in Gold Coast and Nigeria.

In two world conflicts Liberia has elected to ally itself with the United States. Neither the risk it took in so doing, nor the importance of its contribution to the Allied cause should be underestimated. Nor can we afford to underestimate the part that Liberia may be called upon to play again in world affairs should our hopes of peace be once more shattered. We can, without question, count on the friendship of Liberia. But a friendly ally needs to be a strong ally, strong not only in its purposes but in its economy as well. That is the fundamental consideration that should be our guide in determining what assistance we should extend to the people of Liberia, as they seek to strengthen themselves and to develop the resources that nature has placed in their keeping.

As the sun of a new day rises over Liberia, its people look with confidence and determination toward the future. Their problems are great. But they have won the respect and the friendship, not only of America, but of the very European Colonial Powers that so long sought their downfall.

Most important of all, the barrier between the Americo-Liberians and the tribal people, which for so many years stood in the way of real progress, has been broken down. Today, all are Liberians.

America has at times fallen somewhat short of what may have been its full duty toward the African Republic. Yet, over a period of more than a century, the ties between the two countries have grown constantly stronger. Today the United States is doing much to strengthen the economic life of Liberia, doing it on a business basis. The resources of the country are being developed to the mutual advantage of the people of the Republic and of those who are bringing to it the needed capital and technical skill. The contrast between this interested partnership and the sometimes ruthless exploitation that unhappily has marred much of the development of Africa by the European colonial powers is striking. Liberia is entering upon a new era, born of its stubborn resistance to pressures that once threatened to overwhelm it. The Negro Republic, proud of its growing strength, has well vindicated the refusal of the United States, in the 1930's, to be a party to the scheme that would have set up a protectorate over it and thus have ended self-rule in Africa. Now, free of the shadow of unrest that darkens so much of Africa from Cairo to Capetown, and in a world torn by mistrust and hatred, Liberia stands out as America's friend.

NOTES

CHAPTER TWO

THE TRIBAL PEOPLE

1. For the facts and theories respecting tribal life as outlined in this and succeeding chapters, I have relied largely on Dr. Charles Schwab's *Tribes of the Liberian Hinterland,* edited by Dr. George W. Harley, with valuable additions from his own experience (Papers of the Peabody Museum of American Archeology and Ethnology, Vol. XXXI, Cambridge, Mass., 1947), and on information given me by Dr. Harley during my stay with him at the Ganta Mission in Liberia, supplemented by personal observation. The *Tribes* volume of 536 pages is an invaluable detailed study of Liberian native life.

2. This matter is discussed more fully in Chapter VII.

3. See Chapter VI.

CHAPTER THREE

LIFE IN THE HINTERLAND

1. This chapter is based largely on Schwab, *op. cit.*

2. Unpublished report on soil survey by U.S. Economic Mission to Liberia.

CHAPTER FOUR

MEDICINES AND DEVILS

1. Much of the material for this chapter was given me by Dr. George W. Harley in conversations at the Ganta Mission. Reliance has also been had on Dr. Harley's *Native African Medicine* (Cambridge, Mass., 1941), and on two important papers by Dr. Harley published by the Peabody Museum: *Notes on the Poro in Liberia* (Peabody Papers, Vol. XIX, No. 2) and *Masks as Agents of Social Control in Northeast Liberia* (Peabody Papers, Vol. XXXII, No. 2).

CHAPTER FIVE

THE AMERICO-LIBERIANS

1. Pamphlet by J. Emery Knight, *Liberia's Eighteenth President* (Monrovia, 1946), p. 24.

2. Historical data covering the organization and operations of the American Colonization Society, the emigration of American free Negroes, their subsequent struggles, etc., are voluminous. The records of the American Colonization Society, *The African Repository*, published by the Society, and records of the various State Colonization Societies are the principal sources. The best digested accounts are to be found in Sir Harry Johnston's comprehensive treatise, *Liberia* (London, Hutchinson & Co., 1906); Prof. Frederick Starr's *Liberia* (Chicago, 1913—privately printed), *Liberia—Old and New*, by J. L. Sibley (London, 1928), and especially Dr. Charles H. Huberich's scholarly work *The Political and Legislative History of Liberia* (New York, 1943). I have relied on Dr. Huberich's book for much of the background of this chapter.

3. Letter of instruction to Samuel Bacon from Secretary of the Navy Thompson, Jan. 17, 1820.

4. The original of this document is missing, but its text is given in 5th Annual Report, American Colonization Society.

5. Huberich, *op. cit.*, p. 249.

6. *Ibid.*

7. *Ibid.*, p. 274.

8. *Ibid.*, p. 329.

9. *Ibid.*, p. 738.

10. 28th Cong., 1st Sess., House Ex. Doc. 162, 8-10.

11. *African Repository*, XXI. See also Huberich, *op. cit.*, p. 774.

12. Huberich, *op. cit.*, p. 788. See also Sir Harry Johnston, *op. cit.*, pp. 192 *et seq.*

13. *African Repository*, XXII.

14. Huberich, *op. cit.*, p. 94.

15. *Ibid.*, p. 265.

16. *African Repository*, XXII.

17. Huberich, *op. cit.*, p. 832.

CHAPTER SIX

BOUNDARY ENCROACHMENTS

1. The boundary questions are discussed at length and authoritatively in Chapter XIV of Sir Harry Johnston's *Liberia*, which has been my principal reliance for the present account. The matter is also gone into in the Report of the U.S. Commission to Liberia, transmitted to Congress by President Taft, March 25, 1910. I had the advantage of discussions with ex-Presidents King and Barclay, both of whom gave me valuable information from their personal knowledge of various phases of the boundary matters.

2. Sir Harry Johnston says, in error, that Shufeldt was chosen as arbitrator. The naval officer, however, had no authority so to act.

3. The story of the seizure of the northwest territory and of the Liberian

protest was outlined to me orally by Mr. Charles D. B. King. He became President of Liberia in 1920 and is now (1950) Liberia's Ambassador to the United States.

4. The Liberians had earlier created a record as to which was the right and which the left bank of a river. The Anglo-Liberian treaty of 1885, in Article II, says: "The line marking the northwest boundary of the Republic of Liberia shall commence at the point of the sea coast at which at low water the line of the southeastern or *left* bank of the Mannah River intersects the general line of the sea coast . . ." (italics mine).

5. An account of the first of the Benjamin Anderson explorations was published in 1870 (New York, S. W. Green, Printer) under the title, *Narrative of a Journey to Musardu, the Capital of the Western Mandingoes.* It is a vivid description of conditions in the hinterland before any governmental control had been attempted. Long out of print, copies are rare. I had the advantage of discussing with ex-President Barclay the Anderson explorations and their failure to gain for Liberia the territory they actually covered.

CHAPTER SEVEN

THE ATTACK

1. *Slavery*, by Kathleen Simon, with preface by The Rt. Hon. Sir John Simon, London, 1929.

2. Sir John Allsebrook Simon—called to Bar 1899; K.C., 1908; M.P., 1906-18, 1922-31; Solicitor General, 1910-13; Attorney General with Cabinet Seat, 1913-15; Secretary of State for Home Affairs, 1915-16; Secretary of State for Foreign Affairs, 1931-35; Secretary of State for Home Affairs and Leader House of Commons, 1935-37; Chancellor of Exchequer, 1937-40; 1st Viscount, created 1940, of Stackpole Elidor.

3. *New York Times*, Jan. 19, 1930, Sec. V, p. 10. A second article by Caroline Singer (Mrs. C. LeRoy Baldridge) appeared in the Jan. 18, 1931, issue of the *New York Times.*

4. *The Black Republic of Liberia*, by Henry Fenwick Reeve (Late Colonial Secretary, Gambia), London, 1923. Reeve spent some time in Liberia prospecting for gold and diamonds. His book results from pre-World War I notes. In an introduction by Sir Alfred Sharpe, the taking over of every branch of administration in Liberia by "some civilized power or powers" is urged.

5. The inadequacy of Buell's work and the untrustworthiness of his conclusions are commented upon in the report of the Harvard Expedition to Liberia, *The African Republic of Liberia* (Cambridge, Mass., 1930), I, 208.

6. There are numerous sources for the official record of Mr. Stimson's communication and of what followed. I have relied, in this narrative, principally on the *Report of the International Enquiry into the existence of Slavery and Forced Labor in the Republic of Liberia*, dated Monrovia, Liberia, August, 1930, League of Nations Publ. 1930, ser. 6B, No. 6, and on the pamphlet *The Suppression of Slavery—Geneva Special Studies*—Vol. II, No. 4, April, 1931, published by the Geneva Research Information Committee.

7. The phrase seems to have been picked up by Lady Simon from Reeves, *The Black Republic.* "A transaction of another nature, only differ-

ing slightly from the worst form of slavery may be noted here . . ." says Mr. Reeves (p. 121), who then quotes a plantation manager who quotes a chief concerning Fernando Po.

8. For some interesting, though not disinterested, comments on the investigation, see *Historical Lights on Liberia's Yesterday and Today*, by Ernest Jerome Yancy (son of Vice President Yancy), Aldine Publishing Co., Aldine, Ohio, 1934.

9. Simon, *op. cit.*, p. 84.

10. *New York Times*, Oct. 16, 1930, p. 9.

11. *British Blue Book*, "Liberia No. 1 (1934)," p. 7. (See note 1, Chapter 8, immediately below.)

CHAPTER EIGHT

THE PLAN OF ASSISTANCE

1. *British Blue Book, Papers Concerning Affairs in Liberia—December, 1930–May, 1934, Liberia, No. 1.* "Presented by the Secretary of State for Foreign Affairs to Parliament by Command of His Majesty," (London—H. M. Stationery Office). In outlining the history of the "Plan of Assistance" I have relied principally on this *Blue Book* because of its British source and its authenticity. Hereafter cited as *British Blue Book.*

2. *Ibid.*, p. 8.

3. Telegram of Jan. 27, 1932, Mr. Graham to Sir John Simon, *British Blue Book*, p. 11.

4. Telegram of Feb. 18, 1932, Sir John Simon to Mr. Graham, Monrovia, *British Blue Book*, p. 11.

5. Mr. Rydings' report, transmitted by Mr. Graham to Sir John Simon under date of April 21, 1932 (received in London May 9) is a factual and highly interesting account of the Kru disturbance, and of the decidedly blameworthy actions of the Frontier Force. It is illustrative of the difficulties with which the Monrovia Government was faced, including incompetent officials, and of the inadequacy of the steps actually taken. The report, given in full on pp. 14-36 of the *Blue Book*, deserves reading. It has been necessary here to confine reference to that part of it that was used as a weapon of attack on the Liberian Government, and to do that briefly. Mr. Graham's letter of transmittal very adroitly laid the groundwork for misinterpretation of the Rydings report.

6. The full report is contained in the League of Nations document *Request for Assistance submitted by the Liberian Government* (Official No. C 469.M.238-1932 VII). The report, without certain appendices, is also contained in the *British Blue Book*, pp. 57 *et seq.*

7. The final report of the Liberia Committee was dated Oct. 13, 1933 (League of Nations document C 595.M.277—1933 VII, Geneva, Oct. 14, 1933) and is also in the *British Blue Book*, p. 54 *et seq.*

8. This is the estimated cost of administering the Plan of Assistance as first estimated. Mr. Ligthart later produced a lower figure, $202,000. The Commission estimated that revenues would quite promptly increase to $650,000, plus $300,000 to be added to the then-existing loan (*Blue Book*, pp.

79-80). In this connection, the chart showing actual Government revenues over this period, page 224 herein, is of interest.

9. See the charts of rubber exports and Government receipts, pp. 223 and 224 herein.

10. *British Blue Book*, p. 54.

11. On May 19, 1932, while the Plan of Assistance was still in embryonic form, the Committee on Liberia adopted a tentative program that included a radical revision of the Firestone Planting Agreement, increasing the rental figure from 6 cents to 50 cents per acre per annum and reducing the total area under option. See *British Blue Book*, p. 56. See also *Liberia, the League and the United States, Foreign Policy Association Reports*, Vol. X, No. 19, p. 241, and an article by W. E. B. DuBois in *Foreign Affairs*, Vol. 11, No. 4, July 1933, pp. 682 *et seq.*

12. *British Blue Book*, p. 54.

13. *Ibid.*, p. 66.

14. *Foreign Policy Reports*, Vol. X, No. 19, p. 241.

15. So stated to me by ex-President Barclay.

16. See U.S. Dept. of State Press Release, Feb. 4, 1933, p. 80, and March 4, 1933, pp. 150-51.

17. *British Blue Book*, p. 5.

18. *Ibid.*, p. 5.

19. Telegram, Sir John Simon to Mr. Routh (Monrovia) Aug. 23, 1933. *British Blue Book*, p. 37.

20. Telegram, Mr. Routh to Sir John Simon, Sept. 9, 1933, *British Blue Book*, p. 37.

21. Telegram, Consul Patterson (Geneva) to Sir John Simon, Oct. 14, 1933. *British Blue Book*, pp. 37-38.

22. Minutes of 4th Meeting, 78th Session, Council of the League of Nations, held Jan. 19, 1934. See *British Blue Book*, p. 39.

23. Telegram, Mr. A. Henderson to Sir R. Lindsay (Washington), Jan. 13, 1931, *British Blue Book*, p. 8.

24. See *British Blue Book*, p. 40.

25. Extract from Final Minutes of the 4th Meeting, 79th Session, Council of the League of Nations. See *British Blue Book*, p. 42 *et seq.*

26. League of Nations Document C 202/1934/VII, Geneva, May 17, 1934. See *British Blue Book*, p. 41.

27. Dispatch from Sir John Simon to Sir Ronald Lindsay (Washington), dated May 29, 1934, and quoted in full in the *British Blue Book*, p. 49 *et seq.*

CHAPTER NINE

FIRESTONE

1. See *Liberia Rediscovered*, by James C. Young (New York, Doubleday Doran & Co., 1934), p. 19 *et seq.* One of the more recent books on Liberia, this was written when the League of Nations investigations of Liberian affairs had barely been completed and before the findings and reports could be digested. It therefore ends in something of a fog. If this fact is realized, the book has value, particularly its reprints of various documents elsewhere obtainable but here presented in convenient form.

2. *Liberia*, by Charles Morrow Wilson (New York, William Sloan Associates, 1947), p. 84. This is an excellent sketch of the country and its people, coupled with a careful and authentic description of the Firestone Plantation and of rubber production. It avoids most of the country's political and economic problems, antedates some of the recent developments of major importance, but gives a broad and sympathetic picture of Liberia.

3. *Ibid.*, p. 89.

4. Young, *op. cit.*, p. 32.

5. *Ibid.*, p. 170.

6. For the story of the building of this road see Chapter XI.

7. Young, *op. cit.*, p. 71.

CHAPTER TEN

ROBERTS FIELD

1. The material for this chapter was largely obtained from official sources through the courtesy of the Historical Divisions of the Army Special Staff and the Army Air Forces.

2. The facts with respect to the McBride-Barclay negotiation were given me personally by Colonel Harry A. McBride.

3. Executive Agreement Series 275, Department of State Publication No. 1859.

CHAPTER ELEVEN

THE ROAD TO GANTA

1. The outline of this episode was given me personally by Colonel Harry A. McBride. He is now Director of the National (Mellon) Art Gallery in Washington.

2. As related to me personally by ex-President Barclay.

3. From official reports in Army and Air Force Historical Divisions.

4. As related to me by Firestone engineer Joseph Waller.

5. As related to me by Firestone engineer.

CHAPTER TWELVE

THE FREE PORT OF MONROVIA

1. The account of what occurred at the luncheon at Roberts Field and at the subsequent visit of the Liberian President and President-elect at the White House is as given me personally by Mr. Barclay.

2. This, and the later quotations of official correspondence relating to the harbor, including the various cost estimates, are from the files of the State Department.

3. Mr. Hull's letter of June 16, 1943.

4. Mr. Hull's letter to the President, dated Sept. 4, 1943.

5. Cordell Hull to E. R. Stettinius, Jr., Sept. 24, 1943.

6. Executive Agreement Series 411, Department of State Publication 2186. The agreement was transmitted to the State Department by Mr. Walton by letter dated Monrovia, Liberia, Jan. 6, 1944.

7. The harbor agreement was accompanied by a qualifying letter, dated Dec. 31, 1943, signed by C. L. Simpson, Secretary of State (Liberia) stating that Liberia accepts the agreement on understanding that "the contract to be entered into between the Government of the Republic of Liberia and an American Company shall provide for adequate and equitable representation by the Liberian Government on any Board of Directors of the Port Authority which may be set up for the operation of the Port. . . ."

8. Memorandum, Mr. Stettinius to the President, Nov. 28, 1944.

9. Personal interview with ex-President Barclay.

10. Letter, Secretary of Navy to Secretary of State, May 7, 1946.

11. The background of the State Department request to Congress for additional authorization is contained in a letter of Feb. 16, 1948, Secretary of Navy to Secretary of State.

12. From information given me by the Port Management Company.

CHAPTER THIRTEEN

THE BOMI HILLS

1. The material for this chapter was obtained by personal observation of the operations at the Bomi Hills, from information given me by Mine Superintendent Beuken, Mr. Christie, and, especially as to the geology of the Bomi Hills, by Dr. T. P. Thayer of the U.S. Geological Survey, who himself furnished me the greater part of the geological description.

2. *Steel Facts*, publication of American Iron and Steel Institute, Issue No. 101, April, 1950.

3. *Ibid.*

CHAPTER SIXTEEN

THE LIBERIAN GOVERNMENT

1. Huberich, *op. cit.*, p. 1234.
2. Knight, *op. cit.*, p. 16.
3. *Ibid.*, p. 12.
4. *Ibid.*, p. 24.
5. Huberich, *op. cit.*, p. 1134.

CHAPTER SEVENTEEN

THE EVERGREEN FORESTS

1. *The Evergreen Forests of Liberia*, Yale School of Forestry Bulletin No. 31, 1931.

CHAPTER EIGHTEEN

COCOA, KERNELS, AND COFFEE

1. For the facts with respect to the cocoa industry I have relied partly on *Statistical and Economic Review*, No. 2, Sept., 1948, published by United Africa Co. (Lever Bros. Subsidiary) and on data from the U.S. Department of Commerce.

2. The general facts with respect to the swollen shoot were obtained by personal visit at the government agricultural laboratory at Kumasi, Gold Coast. See also *N. Y. Journal of Commerce*, May 22, 1950 (dispatch from Accra dated May 21).

3. As stated to me orally by Mr. Oscar Meier, Chief of the Economic Mission in Monrovia.

4. Executive Circular *Establishment of Cocoa Grades and Standards and Providing for the Inspection of Cocoa for Export.* Issued October 29, 1947.

5. *The Tropical Crops*, by Otis Warren Barrett (New York, the Macmillan Co., 1928), pp. 78-81.

6. For the facts with respect to the oil-palm products, more particularly as related to the industry in Gold Coast and Nigeria, I have relied largely on United Africa's *Statistical and Economic Review No. 3*, March, 1949; and on the *Report of the Mission appointed to enquire into the production and transport of vegetable oils and oil seeds produced in the West African Colonies*, London, H.M. Stationery Office, Colonial No. 211, 1947. See also Barrett, *op. cit.*, and *Oil Palms and Their Fruits*, by Dr. A. A. L. Rutgers (and others), London, 1922. The last-mentioned book contains much information relative to the Lever Bros. undertakings in the Belgian Congo.

7. Data from office of Financial Advisor to the Liberian Government.

CHAPTER NINETEEN

THE STETTINIUS PLAN

1. The original "Statement of Understanding" was signed on behalf of the "Liberian Government Mission" by Gabriel L. Dennis, William E. Dennis and A. Dash Wilson, Jr., and on behalf of Stettinius Associates–Liberia, Inc., by Edward R. Stettinius, Jr., and Blackwell Smith.

2. The "Revised Statement of Understanding" was signed on behalf of the Government of the Republic of Liberia by Gabriel L. Dennis, Secretary of State, and on behalf of The Liberia Company by Allen W. Morton, President, The Liberia Company. The revised agreement bears date December 17, 1949, and became effective December 22.

CHAPTER TWENTY

POINT FOUR

1. An account of the work of the U.S. Health Mission will be found in the Public Health Reports, Vol. 63, No. 42, Oct. 1948, pp. 1351-1364.

2. See Knight, *op. cit.*, pp. 62-63, for an outline of Dr. Harley's plan.

INDEX

CPSIA information can be obtained at www.ICGtesting.com
Printed in the USA
267038BV00002B/15/P